HANDBOOK
FOR BOYS

1993 Printing
Copyright 1976
Boy Scouts of America
Irving, Texas
ISBN 0-8395-3100-1
No. 33100

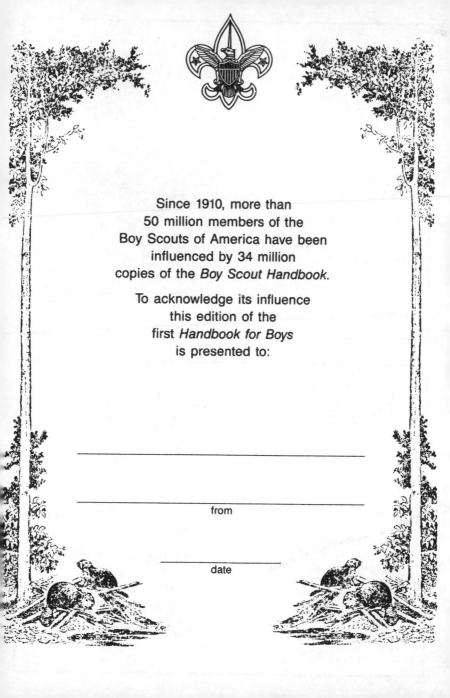

Since 1910, more than
50 million members of the
Boy Scouts of America have been
influenced by 34 million
copies of the *Boy Scout Handbook*.

To acknowledge its influence
this edition of the
first *Handbook for Boys*
is presented to:

_____

_____
from

_____
date

1911

First edition
300,000 copies

The invitation to join shouted by the Scout camper on the cover of the first handbook was accepted by thousands of youngsters. They wore that cover thin duplicating the handbook's frontier skills in countless city vacant lots and on hikes into the country.

1914

Second edition
3,000,000 copies

From 1914 to 1927 the cover of the *Handbook for Boys* featured a semaphore signaling team. The Scouts who patterned their signaling stance from the cover and their behavior and development from the book itself created a great record of service to the nation in World War I.

1927

**Third edition
4,000,000 copies**

From 1927 to 1940 the cover told a story of youth facing in the same direction as Benjamin Franklin, George Washington, Abraham Lincoln, Theodore Roosevelt, and Charles Lindbergh. The boys who used this book found in it purpose and direction to meet the depression and grow with confidence.

1940

**Fourth edition
3,000,000 copies**

From 1940 to 1948 the cover portrayed a Cub Scout, Boy Scout, and Sea Scout. Wartime Scouts read this book between scrap drives, wastepaper collections, messenger service, and a thousand special jobs the country asked of them in World War II.

1948

**Fifth edition
840,000 copies**

1949

**Fifth edition
5,160,000 copies**

Scout spirit, Scout participation, and Scoutcraft helped train boys for good citizenship in the early years of the cold war with Russia and through the hot war in Korea as America sought to stop the spread of communism.

1959

**Sixth edition
4,000,000 copies**

This cover was the third that was painted by Norman Rockwell, who began his career with *Boys' Life*. This was a tense period of the arms race and Cuban missile crisis. Some Americans built bomb shelters; others said "Better dead than Red." Scouting was a stabilizing influence.

1965

**Seventh edition
4,375,000 copies**

In spite of turmoil at home and abroad, millions of American boys identified themselves with this book. In it they found permanent values. Those boys are now grown men who are beginning to exercise leadership roles throughout America.

1972

**Eighth edition
First three
printings
2,750,000 copies**

1976

**Eighth edition
Fourth and fifth
printings
950,000 copies**

The improved Scout program broadened its appeal. Twelve skill awards were added along with new merit badge subjects, and all of the merit badge requirements were added to the book. The slogan was "Scouting today's a lot more than you think."

1979

**Ninth edition
First seven printings
2,750,000 copies**

This edition of the handbook with its Rockwell cover is based firmly upon the fundamentals. It is the complete book containing all of the skills and ideals of Boy Scouting. In it Scouts follow a Trail to Eagle marked out in the pages of this book.

1990

**Tenth edition
First two printings
1,000,000 copies**

Opportunities for Scouts to take real action and make a real difference in the outdoors and in their communities are presented in this edition of the handbook. The cover shows real Scouts sharing in the excitement of outdoor adventures.

The Best Food for

**The
Boy Scouts**

is

Shredded Wheat

because it has all the muscle-building, bone-making material in the whole wheat grain prepared in a digestible form, supplying all the strength needed for work or play.

It is ready-cooked and ready-to-eat. It has the greatest amount of body-building nutriment in smallest bulk. Its crispness compels thorough mastication, and the more you chew it the better you like it.

Shredded Wheat is the favorite food of athletes. It is on the training table of nearly every college and university in this country. The records show that the winners of many brilliant rowing and track events have been trained on Shredded Wheat.

The BISCUIT is in little loaf form. It is baked a crisp, golden brown. It is eaten with milk or cream, or fruit, or is delicious when eaten as a toast with butter. TRISCUIT is the Shredded Wheat wafer — the ideal food for the camp or the long tramp.

Building buster boys is bully business — that's the reason we want to help the Boy Scout movement.

The Shredded Wheat Company
Niagara Falls, N. Y.

Getting the final word before hiking

BOY SCOUTS *of* AMERICA

THE OFFICIAL HANDBOOK
FOR BOYS

Published for
THE BOY SCOUTS OF AMERICA
200 FIFTH AVENUE
NEW YORK

GARDEN CITY   NEW YORK
DOUBLEDAY, PAGE & COMPANY
1911

BOY SCOUT CERTIFICATE

This is to certify that . . . .

of . . . . State of . . . .
Street and City or Town address

Age . . . . Height . . . . Weight . . . .

is a member of . . . . Patrol, of Troop No . . . .

. . . .
Scout Master

SCOUT HISTORY

Qualified as Tenderfoot . . . . 191 . .

Second Class Scout . . . . . . 191 . . First Class Scout . . . . . . 191 . .

QUALIFIED FOR MERIT BADGES

SUBJECT	DATE
1.	. . . .
2.	. . . .
3.	. . . .
4.	. . . .
5.	. . . .

Qualified as Life Scout . . . .

Qualified as Star Scout . . . .

Qualified as Eagle Scout . . . .

Awarded Honor Medal . . . .

PREFACE

The Boy Scout Movement has become almost universal, and wherever organized its leaders are glad, as we are, to acknowledge the debt we all owe to Lieut.-Gen. Sir Robert S. S. Baden-Powell, who has done so much to make the movement of interest to boys of all nations.

The BOY SCOUTS OF AMERICA is a corporation formed by a group of men who are anxious that the boys of America should come under the influence of this movement and be built up in all that goes to make character and good citizenship. The affairs of the organization are managed by a National Council, composed of some of the most prominent men of our country, who gladly and freely give their time and money that this purpose may be accomplished.

In the various cities, towns, and villages, the welfare of the boy scouts is cared for by local councils, and these councils, like the National Council are composed of men who are seeking for the boys of the community the very best things.

In order that the work of the boy scouts throughout America may be uniform and intelligent, the National Council has prepared its "Official Handbook," the purpose of which is to furnish to the patrols of the boy scouts advice in practical methods, as well as inspiring information.

The work of preparing this handbook has enlisted the services of men eminently fitted for such work, for each is an expert in his own department, and the Editorial Board feels that the organization is to be congratulated in that such men have been found willing to give their time and ripe experience to this movement. It would be impossible adequately to thank all who by advice and friendly criticism have helped in the preparation of the book, or even to mention their names, but to the authors whose names are attached to the various chapters, we acknowledge an especial obligation. Without their friendly help this book could not be. We wish especially to express our appreciation of the helpful suggestions made by Daniel Carter Beard.

We have carefully examined and approved all the material which goes to make up the manual, and have tried to make it as complete as possible; nevertheless, no one can be more conscious than we are of the difficulty of providing a book which will meet all the demands of such widely scattered patrols with such varied interests. We have constantly kept in mind the evils that confront the boys of our country and have struck at them by fostering better things. Our hope is that the information needed for successful work with boy scouts will be found within the pages of this book.

In these pages and throughout our organization we have made it obligatory upon our scouts that they cultivate courage, loyalty, patriotism, brotherliness, self-control, courtesy, kindness to animals, usefulness, cheerfulness, cleanliness, thrift, purity and honor. No one can doubt that with such training added to his native gifts, the American boy will in the near future, as a man, be an efficient leader in the paths of civilization and peace.

It has been deemed wise to publish all material especially for the aid of scout masters in a separate volume to be known as "The Scout Masters' Manual."

We send out our "Official Handbook," therefore, with the earnest wish that many boys may find in it new methods for the proper use of their leisure time and fresh inspiration in their efforts to make their hours of recreation contribute to strong, noble manhood in the days to come.

THE BOY SCOUTS OF AMERICA

WILLIAM D. MURRAY }
GEORGE D. PRATT, } Editorial Board.
A. A. JAMESON, }

OFFICERS AND MEMBERS OF THE NATIONAL COUNCIL

BOY SCOUTS OF AMERICA

THE FIFTH AVENUE BUILDING, 200 FIFTH AVENUE

NEW YORK CITY

Honorary President . . . THE HON. WILLIAM H. TAFT
Honorary Vice-President . Colonel THEODORE ROOSEVELT
President . . . . . . COLIN H. LIVINGSTONE, Washington, D. C.
1st Vice-President . . . B. L. DULANEY, Bristol, Tenn.
2d Vice-President . . . . MILTON A. McRAE, Detroit, Mich.
3d Vice-President . . . DAVID STARR JORDAN, Stanford, Cal.
Chief Scout . . . . . ERNEST THOMPSON SETON, Cos Cob, Conn.
National Scout Commissioner, DANIEL CARTER BEARD, Flushing, L. I., N.Y.
National Scout Commissioner, Adj.-Gen. WILLIAM VERBECK, Albany, N. Y.
National Scout Commissioner, Colonel PETER S. BOMUS, New York City
Treasurer . . . . . . GEORGE D. PRATT, Brooklyn, N. Y.

MEMBERS OF THE EXECUTIVE BOARD

COLIN H. LIVINGSTONE, Chairman

Daniel Carter Beard	Milton A. McRae	Mortimer L. Schiff
Col. Peter S. Bomus	William D. Murray	Ernest Thompson Seton
B. L. Dulaney	George D. Pratt	Seth Sprague Terry
Lee F. Hanmer	Frank Presbrey	Adj.-Gen. William Verbeck
George W. Hinckley	Edgar M. Robinson	

JAMES E. WEST, Executive Secretary

MEMBERS OF NATIONAL COUNCIL

Charles Conrad Abbott,
Arthur Adams,
Dr. Felix Adler,
Harry A. Allison,
Henry Morrell Atkinson,
B. N. Baker,
Ray Stannard Baker,

Evelyn Briggs Baldwin,
Clifford W. Barnes,
Daniel Carter Beard,
Henry M. Beardsley,
Martin Behrman,
August Belmont,
Ernest P. Bicknell,

vii

Edward Bok,
Colonel Peter S. Bomus,
Hon. Charles J. Bonaparte,
William D. Boyce,
H. S. Braucher,
Roeliff Brinkerhoff,
Dr. Elmer E. Brown,
Luther Burbank,
Dr. Richard C. Cabot,
Rev. S. Parkes Cadman,
Arthur A. Carey,
E. C. Carter,
Richard B. Carter,
W. D. Champlin,
Thomas Chew,
Winston Churchill,
G. A. Clark,
P. P. Claxton,
Randall J. Condon,
C. M. Connolly,
Ernest K. Coulter,
Dr. C. Ward Crampton,
George H. Dalrymple,
Dr. George S. Davis,
E. B. DeGroot,
Judge William H. De Lacy,
William C. Demorest,
Dr. Edward T. Devine,
Admiral George Dewey,
Gov. John A. Dix,
Myron E. Douglas,
Benjamin L. Dulaney,
Hon. T. C. Du Pont,
Dr. George W. Ehler,
Griffith Ogden Ellis,
Robert Erskine Ely,
Henry P. Emerson,
Hon. John J. Esch,
J. W. Everman,
Eberhard Faber,
Dr. George J. Fisher,
Horace Fletcher,
Homer Folks,
Dr. William Byron Forbush,

Dr. Lee K. Frankel,
Robert Ives Gammell,
Hon. James R. Garfield,
Hamlin Garland,
Robert Garrett,
William H. Gay,
Bishop David H. Greer,
Jesse A. Gregg,
George B. Grinnell,
S. R. Guggenheim,
Luther Halsey Gulick, M. D.,
Dr. G. Stanley Hall,
Dr. Winfield Scott Hall,
Lee F. Hanmer,
Dr. Hastings H. Hart,
Hon. W. M. Hays,
Prof. C. R. Henderson,
Clark W. Hetherington,
George W. Hinckley,
Allen Hoben,
Hon. R. P. Hobson,
Rev. R. W. Hogue,
John Sherman Hoyt,
C. R. H. Jackson,
Prof. Jeremiah W. Jenks,
G. E. Johnson,
Dr. David Starr Jordan,
Mayor William S. Jordan,
Otto Herman Kahn,
Dr. William J. Kerby,
Charles H. Kip,
Dr. J. H. Kirkland,
Judge Henry E. Klamroth,
Rev. Walter Laidlow,
Charles R. Lamb,
Joseph Lee,
Samuel McC. Lindsay,
Judge Ben B. Lindsey,
Colin H. Livingstone,
Col. Frank L. Locke,
Hon. Nicholas Longworth,
Hon. Frank O. Lowden,
Hon. Lee McClung,
William McCormick,

A MESSAGE FROM THE CHIEF SCOUT

To THE BOY SCOUTS OF AMERICA:
There was once a boy who lived in a region of rough farms. He was wild with the love of the green outdoors — the trees, the tree-top singers, the wood-herbs and the live things that left their nightly tracks in the mud by his spring well. He wished so much to know them and learn about them, he would have given almost any price in his gift to know the name of this or that wonderful bird, or brilliant flower; he used to tremble with excitement and intensity of interest when some new bird was seen, or when some strange song came from the trees to thrill him with its power or vex him with its mystery, and he had a sad sense of lost opportunity when it flew away leaving him dark as ever. But he was alone and helpless, he had neither book nor friend to guide him, and he grew up with a kind of knowledge hunger in his heart that gnawed without ceasing. But this also it did: It inspired him with the hope that some day he might be the means of saving others from this sort of torment — he would aim to furnish to them what had been denied to himself.

There were other things in the green and living world that had a binding charm for him. He wanted to learn to camp out, to live again the life of his hunter grandfather who knew all the tricks of winning comfort from the relentless wilderness — the foster-mother so rude to those who fear her, so kind to the stout of heart.

And he had yet another hankering — he loved the touch of romance. When he first found Fenimore Cooper's books, he drank them in as one parched might drink at a spring. He reveled in the tales of courage and heroic deeds, he gloated over records of their trailing and scouting by red man and white; he gloried in their woodcraft, and lived it all in imagination, secretly blaming the writer, a little, for praising without describing it so it could be followed. "Some day," he said, "I shall put it all down for other boys to learn."

As years went by he found that there were books about most of the things he wished to know, the stars, the birds, the quadrupeds, the fish, the insects, the plants, telling their names; their hidden power or curious ways, about the camper's life the language of signs and even some of the secrets of the trail.   But they were very expensive and a whole library would be needed to cover the ground.   What he wanted — what every boy wants — is a handbook giving the broad facts as one sees them in the week-end hike, the open-air life.   He did not want to know the trees as a botanist, but as a forester; nor the stars as an astronomer, but as a traveler.   His interest in the animals was less that of anantomist than of a hunter and camper, and his craving for light on the insects was one to be met by a popular book on bugs, rather than by a learned treatise on entomology.

So knowing the want he made many attempts to gather the simple facts together exactly to meet the need of other boys of like ideas, and finding it a mighty task he gladly enlisted the help of men who had lived and felt as he did.

Young Scouts of America that boy is writing to you now.   He thought himself peculiar in those days.   He knows now he was simply a   normal boy with the interests and desires of all normal boys, some of them a little deeper rooted and more lasting perhaps — and all the things that he loved and wished to learn have now part in the big broad work we call *Scouting*.

"Scout" used to mean the one on watch for the rest.   We have widened the word a little.   We have made it fit the town as well as the wilderness and suited it to peace time instead of war.   We have made the scout an expert in Life-craft as well as Wood-craft, for he is trained in the things of the heart as well as head and hand.   Scouting we have made to cover riding, swimming, tramping, trailing, photography, first aid, camping, handicraft, loyalty, obedience, courtesy, thrift, courage, and kindness.

Do these things appeal to you?   Do you love the woods? Do *you* wish to learn the trees as the forester knows them?   And the stars not as an astronomer, but as a traveler?

Do you wish to have all-round, well-developed muscles, not those of a great athlete, but those of a sound body that will not fail you?   Would you like to be an expert camper who can always make himself comfortable out of doors, and a swimmer that fears no waters?   Do you desire the knowledge to help the wounded quickly, and to make yourself cool and self-reliant in an emergency?

Do you believe in loyalty, courage, and kindness?   Would

you like to form habits that will surely make your success in life?

Then, whether you be farm boy or shoe clerk, newsboy or millionaire's son, your place is in our ranks, for these are the thoughts in scouting; it will help you to do better work with your pigs, your shoes, your papers, or your dollars; it will give you new pleasures in life; it will teach you so much of the outdoor world that you wish to know; and this Handbook, the work of many men, each a leader in his field, is their best effort to show you the way. This is, indeed, the book that I so longed for, in those far-off days when I wandered, heart hungry in the woods.

ERNEST THOMPSON SETON,
Chief Scout.

Headquarters Boy Scouts of America,
    200 Fifth Avenue, New York City.
June 1, 1911.

CONTENTS

HANDBOOK FOR BOYS

CHAPTER I

SCOUTCRAFT

This chapter is the result of the work of the Committee on Scout Oath, Scout Law, Tenderfoot, Second-class and First-class Requirements; the Committee on Badges, Awards, and Equipment; the Committee on Permanent Organization and Field Supervision, and John L. Alexander and Samuel A. Moffat.

Aim of the Scout Movement

By John L. Alexander, Boy Scouts of America

The aim of the Boy Scouts is to supplement the various existing educational agencies, and to promote the ability in boys to do things for themselves and others. It is not the aim to set up a new organization to parallel in its purposes others already established. The opportunity is afforded these organizations, however, to introduce into their programs unique features appealing to interests which are universal among boys. The method is summed up in the term Scoutcraft, and is a combination of observation, deduction, and handiness, or the ability to do things. Scoutcraft includes instruction in First Aid, Life Saving, Tracking, Signaling, Cycling, Nature Study, Seamanship, Campcraft, Woodcraft, Chivalry, Patriotism, and other subjects. This is accomplished in games and team play, and is pleasure, not work, for the boy. All that is needed is the out-of-doors, a group of boys, and a competent leader.

What Scouting Means

In all ages there have been scouts, the place of the scout being on the danger line of the army or at the outposts, protecting those of his company who confide in his care.

The army scout was the soldier who was chosen out of all the army to go out on the skirmish line.

The pioneer, who was out on the edge of the wilderness,

guarding the men, women, and children in the stockade, was also a scout. Should he fall asleep, or lose control of his faculties, or fail on his watch, then the lives of the men, women, and children paid the forfeit, and the scout lost his honor.

But there have been other kinds of scouts besides war scouts and frontier scouts. They have been the men of all ages, who have gone out on new and strange adventures, and through their work have benefited the people of the earth. Thus, Columbus discovered America, the Pilgrim Fathers founded New England, the early English settlers colonized Jamestown, and the Dutch built up New York. In the same way the hardy Scotch-Irish pushed west and made a new home for the American people beyond the Alleghanies and the Rockies.

These peace scouts had to be as well prepared as any war scouts. They had to know scoutcraft. They had to know how to live in the woods, and be able to find their way anywhere, without other chart or compass than the sun and stars, besides being able to interpret the meaning of the slightest signs of the forest and the foot tracks of animals and men.

They had to know how to live so as to keep healthy and strong, to face any danger that came their way, and to help one another. These scouts of old were accustomed to take chances with death and they did not hesitate to give up their lives in helping their comrades or country. In fact, they left everything behind them, comfort and peace, in order to push forward into the wilderness beyond. And much of this they did because they felt it to be their duty.

These little-known scouts could be multiplied indefinitely by going back into the past ages and reading the histories and stories of the knights of King Arthur, of the Crusaders, and of the great explorers and navigators of the world.

Wherever there have been heroes, there have been scouts, and to be a scout means to be prepared to do the right thing at the right moment, no matter what the consequences may be.

The way for achievement in big things is the preparing of one's self for doing the big things — by going into training and doing the little things well. It was this characteristic of Livingstone, the great explorer, that made him what he was, and that has marked the career of all good scouts.

To be a good scout one should know something about the woods and the animals that inhabit them, and how to care for one's self when camping.

The habits of animals can be studied by stalking them and watching them in their native haunts.

The scout should never kill an animal or other living creature needlessly. There is more sport in stalking animals to photograph them, and in coming to know their habits than in hunting to kill.

But woodcraft means more than this. It means not only the following of tracks and other signs, but it means to be able to read them. To tell how fast the animal which made the tracks was going; to tell whether he was frightened, suspicious, or otherwise.

Woodcraft also enables the scout to find his way, no matter where he is. It teaches him the various kinds of wild fruit,

Scout Stalking

roots, nuts, etc., which are good for food, or are the favorite food of animals.

By woodcraft a scout may learn a great number of things. He may be able to tell whether the tracks were made by an animal or by man, bicycle, automobile or other vehicle.

By having his power of observation trained he can tell by very slight signs, such as the sudden flying of birds, that someone is moving very near him though he may not be able to see the person.

Through woodcraft then, a boy may train his eye, and be able to observe things that otherwise would pass unnoticed. In this way he may be able to save animals from pain, as a horse from an ill-fitting harness. He may also be able to see little things which may give him the clew to great things and so be able to prevent harm and crime.

Torture (*Note the check or bearing-rein*)   Comfort

Besides woodcraft one must know something of camp life. One of the chief characteristics of the scout is to be able to live in the open, know how to put up tents, build huts, throw up a lean-to for shelter, or make a dugout in the ground, how to build a fire, how to procure and cook food, how to bind logs together so as to construct bridges and rafts, and how to find his way by night as well as by day in a strange country.

Living in the open in this way, and making friends of the trees, the streams, the mountains, and the stars, gives a scout a great

Camp loom, for making mats and mattresses

deal of confidence and makes him love the natural life around him.

To be able to tell the difference between the trees by their bark and leaves is a source of pleasure; to be able to make a bed out of rough timber, or weave a mattress or mat out of grass to sleep on is a joy. And all of these things a good scout should know.

Then too, a good scout must be chivalrous. That is, he should be as manly as the knights or pioneers of old. He should be unselfish. He should show courage. He must do his duty. He should show benevolence and thrift. He should be loyal to his country. He should be obedient to his parents, and show respect to those who are his superiors. He should be very courteous to women. One of his obligations is to do a good turn every day to some one. He should be cheerful and seek self-improvement, and should make a career for himself.

All these things were characteristics of the old-time American scouts and of the King Arthur knights. Their honor was sacred. They were courteous and polite to women and children, especially to the aged, protected the weak, and helped others to live better. They taught themselves to be strong, so as to be able to protect their country against enemies. They kept themselves strong and healthy, so that they might be prepared to do all of these things at a moment's notice, and do them well.

So the boy scout of to-day must be chivalrous, manly, and gentlemanly.

When he gets up in the morning he may tie a knot in his necktie, and leave the necktie outside his vest until he has done a good turn. Another way to remind himself is to wear his scout badge reversed until he has done his good turn. The good turn may not be a very big thing—help an old lady across the street; remove a banana skin from the pavement so that people may not fall; remove from streets or roads broken glass, dangerous to automobile or bicycle tires; give water to a thirsty horse; or deeds similar to these.

The scout also ought to know how to save life. He ought to be able to make a stretcher; to throw a rope to a drowning person; to drag an unconscious person from a burning building, and to resuscitate a person overcome by gas fumes. He ought also to know the method of stopping runaway horses, and he should have the presence of mind and the skill to calm a panic and deal with street and other accidents.

This means also that a boy scout must always be in the pink of condition. A boy cannot do things like these unless he is healthy and strong. Therefore, he must be systematically taking exercise, playing games, running, and walking. It means that he must sleep enough hours to give him the necessary strength, and if possible to sleep very much in the open, or at least with the windows of his bedroom open both summer and winter.

It means also that he should take a cold bath often, rubbing dry with a rough towel. He should breathe through the nose and not through the mouth. He should at all times train himself to endure hardships.

In addition to these the scout should be a lover of his country. He should know his country. How many states there are in it, what are its natural resources, scope, and boundaries. He ought to know something of its history, its early settlers, and of the great deeds that won his land. How they settled along the banks of the James River. How Philadelphia, New York, and other great cities were founded. How the Pilgrim Fathers established New England and laid the foundation for our national life. How the scouts of the Middle West saved all that great section of the country for the Republic. He ought to know how Texas became part of the United States, and how our national heroes stretched out their hands, north and south, east and west, to make one great united country.

He ought to know the history of the important wars. He ought to know about our army and navy flags and the insignia of rank of our officers. He ought to know the kind of government he lives under, and what it means to live in a republic. He ought to know what is expected of him as a citizen of his state and nation, and what to do to help the people among whom he lives.

In short, to be a good scout is to be a well-developed, well-informed boy.

Scout Virtues

There are other things which a scout ought to know and which should be characteristic of him, if he is going to be the kind of scout for which the Boy Scouts of America stand. One of these is obedience. To be a good scout a boy must learn to obey the orders of his patrol leader, scout master, and scout commissioner. He must learn to obey, before he is able to command. He should so learn to discipline and control himself that he will have no thought but to obey the orders of his officers. He should keep such a strong grip on his own life that he will not allow himself to do anything which is ignoble, or which will harm his life or weaken his powers of endurance.

Another virtue of a scout is that of courtesy. A boy scout

ought to have a command of polite language. He ought to show that he is a true gentleman by doing little things for others.

Loyalty is also a scout virtue. A scout ought to be loyal to all to whom he has obligations. He ought to stand up courageously for the truth, for his parents and friends.

Another scout virtue is self-respect. He ought to refuse to accept gratuities from any one, unless absolutely necessary. He ought to work for the money he gets.

For this same reason he should never look down upon any one who may be poorer than himself, or envy any one richer than himself. A scout's self-respect will cause him to value his own standing and make him sympathetic toward others who may be, on the one hand, worse off, or, on the other hand, better off as far as wealth is concerned. Scouts know neither a lower nor a higher class, for a scout is one who is a comrade to all and who is ready to share that which he has with others.

The most important scout virtue is that of honor. Indeed, this is the basis of all scout virtues and is closely allied to that of self-respect. When a scout promises to do a thing on his honor, he is bound to do it. The honor of a scout will not permit of anything but the highest and the best and the manliest. The honor of a scout is a sacred thing, and cannot be lightly set aside or trampled on.

Faithfulness to duty is another one of the scout virtues. When it is a scout's duty to do something, he dare not shirk. A scout is faithful to his own interest and the interests of others. He is true to his country and his God.

Another scout virtue is cheerfulness. As the scout law intimates, he must never go about with a sulky air. He must always be bright and smiling, and as the humorist says, "Must always see the doughnut and not the hole." A bright face and a cheery word spread like sunshine from one to another. It is the scout's duty to be a sunshine-maker in the world.

Another scout virtue is that of thoughtfulness, especially to animals; not merely the thoughtfulness that eases a horse from the pain of a badly fitting harness or gives food and drink to an animal that is in need, but also that which keeps a boy from throwing a stone at a cat or tying a tin can on a dog's tail. If a boy scout does not prove his thoughtfulness and friendship for animals, it is quite certain that he never will be really helpful to his comrades or to the men, women, and children who may need his care.

And then the final and chief test of the scout is the doing of a good turn to somebody every day, quietly and without boasting. This is the proof of the scout. It is practical religion, and a boy honors God best when he helps others most. A boy may wear all the scout uniforms made, all the scout badges ever manufactured, know all the woodcraft, campcraft, scoutcraft and other activities of boy scouts, and yet never be a real boy scout. To be a real boy scout means the doing of a good turn every day with the proper motive and if this be done, the boy has a right to be classed with the great scouts that have been of such service to their country. To accomplish this a scout should observe the scout law.

Every boy ought to commit to memory the following abbreviated form of the scout law.

The Twelve Points of the Scout Law

1. A scout is trustworthy.
2. A scout is loyal.
3. A scout is helpful.
4. A scout is friendly.
5. A scout is courteous.
6. A scout is kind.
7. A scout is obedient.
8. A scout is cheerful.
9. A scout is thrifty.
10. A scout is brave.
11. A scout is clean.
12. A scout is reverent.

The Boy Scout Organization*

To do good scouting a boy must understand the organization of which he is a part. The Boy Scouts of America is promoted and governed by a group of men called the National Council. This National Council is made up of leading men of the country and it is their desire that every American boy shall have the opportunity of becoming a good scout.

The National Council holds one meeting annually at which it elects the officers and the members of the Executive Board. It copyrights badges and other scout designs, arranges for their manufacture and distribution, selects designs for uniforms and scout equipment, issues scout commissioners' and scout masters' certificates, and grants charters for local councils.

* Result of work of Committee on Permanent Organization and Field Supervision:—H. S. Braucher, Chairman, Lorillard Spencer, Jr., Colin H. Livingstone, Richard C. Morse, Mortimer L. Schiff, Dr. George W. Ehler, C. M. Connolly, E. B. DeGroot, Lee F. Hanmer.

A local council through its officers — president, vice-president, secretary, treasurer, and scout commissioner, its executive committee, court of honor, and other committees — deals with all local matters that relate to scouting.

The scout commissioner is the ranking scout master of the local council and presides at all scout masters' meetings as well as at all scout field meets. It is also the duty of the scout commissioner to report to and advise with the Chief Scout through the Executive Secretary concerning the scouts in his district. The scout commissioner's certificate is issued from National Headquarters upon the recommendation of a local council after this council has been granted a charter.

The scout master is the adult leader of a troop, and must be at least twenty-one years of age. He should have a deep interest in boys, be genuine in his own life, have the ability to lead, and command the boys' respect and obedience. He need not be an expert at scoutcraft; a good scout master will discover experts for the various activities. His certificate is granted upon the recommendation of the local council.

An assistant scout master should be eighteen years of age or over. His certificate is granted by the National Council upon the recommendation of the scout master of his troop and the local council.

Chief Scout and Staff

The Chief Scout is elected annually by the National Council and has a staff of deputies each of whom is chairman of a committee of scoutcraft. These deputies are as follows:

Chief Scout Surgeon.
Chief Scout Woodsman.
Chief Scout Stalker.
Chief Scout Master.
Chief Scout Camp Master.

Chief Scout Director of Health.
Chief Scout Athletic Director.
Chief Scout Citizen.
Chief Scout Director of Chivalry.

Scouts are graded as follows:

Chief Scout and Staff.
Scout Commissioner.
Scout Master.
Assistant Scout Master.
Patrol Leader.
Assistant Patrol Leader.

Eagle Scout.
Star Scout.
Life Scout.
First-class Scout.
Second-class Scout.
Tenderfoot.

How to Become a Boy Scout

The easiest way to become a boy scout is to join a patrol that has already been started. This patrol may be in a

Sunday School, Boys' Brigade, Boys' Club, Young Men's Christian Association, Young Men's Hebrew Association, Young Men's Catholic Association, or any other organization to which you may belong. If there is no patrol near you, get some man interested enough to start one by giving him all the information.

A patrol consists of eight boys, one of whom becomes the patrol leader and another the assistant patrol leader.

A troop consists of three or more patrols, and the leader of the troop is called a scout master. There can be no patrols or troops of boy scouts without this scout master.

The Scout Motto

The motto of the boy scouts is *Be Prepared*, and the badge of the boy scouts is a copyrighted design with this motto, "Be Prepared," on a scroll at its base.

The motto, "Be Prepared," means that the scout is always in a state of readiness in mind and body to do his duty. To be prepared in mind, by having disciplined himself to be obedient, and also by having thought out beforehand any accident or situation that may occur, so that he may know the right thing to do at the right moment, and be willing to do it. To be prepared in body, by making himself strong and active and able to do the right thing at the right moment, and then to do it.

The Scout Badge

The scout badge is not intended to represent the fleur-de-lis, or an arrowhead. It is a modified form of the sign of the north on the mariner's compass, which is as old as the history of navigation. The Chinese claim its use among them as early as 2634 B. C., and we have definite information that it was used at sea by them as early as 300 A. D. Marco Polo brought the compass to Europe on his return from Cathay. The sign of the north on the compass gradually came to represent the north, and pioneers, trappers, woodsmen, and scouts, because of this, adopted it as their emblem. Through centuries of use it has undergone modification until it has now assumed the shape of our badge.

This trefoil badge of the scouts is now used, with slight local variations, in almost every civilized country as the mark of brotherhood, for good citizenship, and friendliness.

Its scroll is turned up at the ends like a scout's mouth, because he does his duty with a smile and willingly.

The knot is to remind the scout to do a good turn to someone daily.

The arrowhead part is worn by the tenderfoot. The scroll part only is worn by the second-class scout. The badge worn by the first-class scout is the whole badge.

The official badges of the Boy Scouts of America are issued by the National Council and may be secured only from the National Headquarters. These badges are protected by the U. S. Patent Laws (letters of patent numbers 41412 and 41532) and any one infringing these patents is liable to prosecution at law.

In order to protect the Boy Scout Movement and those who have qualified to receive badges designating the various degrees in scoutcraft, it is desired that all interested coöperate with the National Headquarters in safeguarding the sale and distribution of these badges. This may be done by observing the following rules:

1. Badges should not be ordered until after boys have actually complied with the requirements prescribed by the National Council and are entitled to receive them.

2. All orders for badges should be sent in by the scout master with a certificate from the local council that these requirements have been complied with. Blanks for this purpose may be secured on application to the National Headquarters.

Where no local council has been formed, application for badges should be sent direct to Headquarters, signed by the registered scout master of the troop, giving his official number.

Scout commissioners', scout masters', and assistant scout masters' badges can be issued only to those who are registered as such at National Headquarters.

Tenderfoot Badge — Gilt metal.

Patrol Leader's Tenderfoot Badge —Oxidized silver finish.

These badges are seven eighths of an inch wide and are made either for the button-hole or with safety-pin clasp. Price 5 cents.

Second-Class Scout Badge — Gilt metal.

Patrol Leader's Second-Class Scout Badge — Oxidized silver.

These badges — safety-pin style — to be worn upon the sleeve. Price 10 cents.

First-Class Scout Badge — Gilt metal.

Patrol Leader's First-Class Scout Badge — Oxidized silver.

Both badges safety-pin style — to be worn upon the sleeve. Price 15 cents.

Scout Commissioner's, Scout Master's, and *Assistant Scout Master's Arm Badges.*

These badges are woven in blue, green, and red silk, and are to be worn on the sleeve of coat or shirt. Price 25 cents.

Buttons — The official buttons worn on the scout uniforms sell for 10 cents per set for shirt and 15 cents per set for coat.

Merit Badges — Price 25 cents each.

Boy Scout Certificates — A handsome certificate in two colors, 6 x 8 inches, has been prepared for boy scouts who wish to have a record of their enrolment. The certificate has the Scout Oath and Law and the official Seal upon it, with place for the signature of the scout master. The price is 5 cents.

Directions For Ordering

Important ! When ordering supplies send exact remittance with order. If check is used add New York exchange. Make checks and money orders payable to Boy Scouts of America. All orders received without the proper remittance will be shipped C. O. D., or held until remittance arrives.

The Scout Oath

Before he becomes a scout a boy must promise:

On my honor I will do my best:

1. To do my duty to God and my country, and to obey the scout law;

2. To help other people at all times;

3. To keep myself physically strong, mentally awake, and morally straight.

When taking this oath the scout will stand, holding up his right hand, palm to the front, thumb resting on the nail of the little finger and the other three fingers upright and together.

The Scout Sign

This is the scout sign. The three fingers held up remind him of his three promises in the scout oath.

The Scout Salute

When the three fingers thus held are raised to the forehead, it is the scout salute.

The scout always salutes an officer.

The Scout Law*

There have always been certain written and unwritten laws regulating the conduct and directing the activities of men.

---

*Result of work of Committee on Scout Oath, Scout Law, Tenderfoot, Second-class and First-class Scout Requirements:—

Prof. Jeremiah W. Jenks, Chairman. Dr. Lee K. Frankel, George D. Porter, E. M. Robinson, G. W. Hinckley, B. E. Johnson, Clark W. Hetherington, Arthur A. Carey.

We have such unwritten laws coming down from past ages. In Japan, the Japanese have their Bushido or laws of the old Samurai warriors. During the Middle Ages, the chivalry and rules of the Knights of King Arthur, the Knights Templar and the Crusaders were in force. In aboriginal America, the Red Indians had their laws of honor: likewise the Zulus, Hindus, and the later European nations have their ancient codes.

The following laws which relate to the Boy Scouts of America, are the latest and most up to date. These laws a boy promises to obey when he takes his scout oath.

1. A scout is trustworthy.

A scout's honor is to be trusted. If he were to violate his honor by telling a lie, or by cheating, or by not doing exactly a given task, when trusted on his honor, he may be directed to hand over his scout badge.

2. A scout is loyal.

He is loyal to all to whom loyalty is due: his scout leader, his home, and parents and country.

3. A scout is helpful.

He must be prepared at any time to save life, help injured persons, and share the home duties. He must *do at least one good turn to somebody every day.*

4. A scout is friendly.

He is a friend to all and a brother to every other scout.

5. A scout is courteous.

He is polite to all, especially to women, children, old people, and the weak and helpless. *He must not take pay for being helpful or courteous.*

6. A scout is kind.

He is a friend to animals. He will not kill nor hurt any living creature needlessly, but will strive to save and protect all harmless life.

7. A scout is obedient.

He obeys his parents, scout master, patrol leader, and all other duly constituted authorities.

8. A scout is cheerful.

He smiles whenever he can. His obedience to orders is prompt and cheery. He never shirks nor grumbles at hardships.

9. A scout is thrifty.

He does not wantonly destroy property. He works faithfully, wastes nothing, and makes the best use of his opportunities. He saves his money so that he may pay his own way, be generous to those in need, and helpful to worthy objects.

He may work for pay but must not receive tips for courtesies or good turns.

10. A scout is brave.

He has the courage to face danger in spite of fear and has to stand up for the right against the coaxings of friends or the jeers or threats of enemies, and defeat does not down him.

11. A scout is clean.

He keeps clean in body and thought, stands for clean speech, clean sport, clean habits, and travels with a clean crowd.

12. A scout is reverent.

He is reverent toward God. He is faithful in his religious duties and respects the convictions of others in matters of custom and religion.

The Three Classes of Scouts

There are three classes of scouts among the Boy Scouts of America, the tenderfoot, second-class scout, and first-class scout. Before a boy can become a tenderfoot he must qualify for same. A tenderfoot, therefore, is superior to the ordinary boy because of his training. To be a tenderfoot means to occupy the lowest grade in scouting. A tenderfoot on meeting certain requirements may become a second-class scout, and a second-class scout upon meeting another set of requirements may become a first-class scout. The first-class scout may then qualify for the various merit badges which are offered in another part of this chapter for proficiency in scouting. The requirements of the tenderfoot, second-class scout, and first-class scout, are as follows:

Tenderfoot

To become a scout a boy must be at least twelve years of age and must pass a test in the following:

Tenderfoot

1. Know the scout law, sign, salute, and significance of the badge.

2. Know the composition and history of the national flag and the customary forms of respect due to it.

3. Tie four out of the following knots: square or reef, sheet-bend, bowline, fisherman's, sheepshank, halter, clove hitch, timber hitch, or two half hitches.

He then takes the scout oath, is enrolled as a tenderfoot, and is entitled to wear the tenderfoot badge.

Second-class Scout

To become a second-class scout, a tenderfoot must pass, to the satisfaction of the recognized local scout authorities, the following tests:

1.   At least one month's service as a tenderfoot.

2.   Elementary first aid and bandaging; know the general directions for first aid for injuries; know treatment for fainting, shock, fractures, bruises, sprains, injuries in which the skin is broken, burns, and scalds; demonstrate how to carry injured, and the use of the triangular and roller bandages and tourniquet.

Second-class Scout

3.   Elementary signaling: Know the semaphore, or American Morse, or Myer alphabet.

4.   Track half a mile in twenty-five minutes; or, if in town, describe satisfactorily the contents of one store window out of four observed for one minute each.

5.   Go a mile in twelve minutes at scout's pace — about fifty steps running and fifty walking, alternately.

6.   Use properly knife or hatchet.

7.   Prove ability to build a fire in the open, using not more than two matches.

8.   Cook a quarter of a pound of meat and two potatoes in the open without the ordinary kitchen cooking utensils.

9.   Earn and deposit at least one dollar in a public bank.

10.   Know the sixteen principal points of the compass.

First-class Scout

To become a first-class scout, the second-class scout must pass the following tests:

1.   Swim fifty yards.

2.   Earn and deposit at least two dollars in a public bank.

3.   Send and receive a message by semaphore, or American Morse, or Myer alphabet, sixteen letters per minute.

4.   Make a round trip alone (or with another scout) to a point

at least seven miles away, going on foot or rowing boat, and write a satisfactory account of the trip and things observed.

First-class Scout

5. Advanced first aid: Know the methods for panic prevention; what to do in case of fire and ice, electric and gas accidents; how to help in case of runaway horse, mad dog, or snake bite; treatment for dislocations, unconsciousness, poisoning, fainting, apoplexy, sunstroke, heat exhaustion, and freezing; know treatment for sunburn, ivy poisoning, bites and stings, nosebleed, earache, toothache, inflammation or grit in eye, cramp or stomach ache and chills; demonstrate artificial respiration.

6. Prepare and cook satisfactorily, in the open, without regular kitchen utensils, two of the following articles as may be directed. Eggs, bacon, hunter's stew, fish, fowl, game, pancakes, hoe-cake, biscuit, hardtack or a "twist," baked on a stick; explain to another boy the methods followed.

7. Read a map correctly, and draw, from field notes made on the spot, an intelligible rough sketch map, indicating by their proper marks important buildings, roads, trolley lines, main landmarks, principal elevations, etc. Point out a compass direction without the help of the compass.

8. Use properly an axe for felling or trimming light timber; or produce an article of carpentry or cabinet-making or metal work made by himself. Explain the method followed.

9. Judge distance, size, number, height and weight within 25 per cent.

10. Describe fully from observation ten species of trees or plants, including poison ivy, by their bark, leaves, flowers, fruit, or scent; or six species of wild birds by their plumage, notes, tracks, or habits; or six species of native wild animals by their form, color, call, tracks, or habits; find the North Star, and name and describe at least three constellations of stars.

11. Furnish satisfactory evidence that he has put into practice in his daily life the principles of the scout oath and law.

12. Enlist a boy trained by himself in the requirements of a tenderfoot.

NOTE. — No deviation from above requirements will be permitted unless in extraordinary cases, such as physical inability, and the written consent of the National Headquarters has been obtained by the recognized local scout authority.

Patrol Signs

Each troop of boy scouts is named after the place to which it belongs. For example, it is Troop No. 1, 2, 3, 4, etc., of New York or Chicago. Each patrol of the troop is named after an animal or bird, but may be given another kind of name if

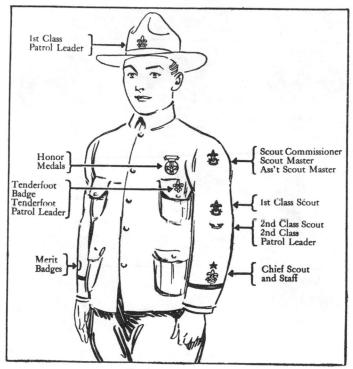

1st Class
Patrol Leader

Honor
Medals

Tenderfoot
Badge
Tenderfoot
Patrol Leader

Merit
Badges

Scout Commissioner
Scout Master
Ass't Scout Master

1st Class Scout

2nd Class Scout
2nd Class
Patrol Leader

Chief Scout
and Staff

Positions of Various Badges

there is a valid reason. In this way, the Twenty-seventh New York Troop, for instance, may have several patrols, which may be respectively the Ox, Wolf, Jackal, Raven, Buffalo, Fox, Panther, and Rattlesnake.

Each scout in a patrol has a number, the patrol leader being No. 1, the assistant patrol leader No. 2, and the other scouts the remaining consecutive numbers. Scouts in this way should

MONGOOSE
Squeak—"Cheep"
BROWN AND ORANGE

HAWK
Cry (same as Eagle)
—"Kreeee" PINK

WOLF
Howl—"How-oooo"
YELLOW AND BLACK

PEEWIT
Whistle—"Tewitt"
GREEN AND WHITE

HOUND
Bark—"Bawow-wow"
ORANGE

CAT
Cry—"Meeaow"
GRAY AND BROWN

JACKAL
Laughing Cry—"Wah-
wah-wah-wah-wah."
GRAY AND BLACK

RAVEN
Cry—"Kar-kaw"
BLACK

BUFFALO
Lowing (same as Bull)
"Um-maouw"
RED AND WHITE

PEACOCK
Cry—"Bee-oik"
GREEN AND BLUE

BULL
Lowing—"Um-maouw"
RED

SEAL
Call—"Hark"
RED AND BLACK

OWL
Whistle "Koot-koot-koo"
BLUE

TIGER
Purr—"Grrrao"
VIOLET

LION
Roar—"Eu-ugh"
YELLOW AND RED

KANGAROO
Call—"Coo-ee"
RED AND GRAY

HORSE
Whinney—"Hee-e-e-e"
BLACK AND WHITE

FOX
Bark —"Ha-ha"
YELLOW AND GREEN

BEAR
Growl —"Boorrr"
BROWN AND RED

STAG
Call —"Baow"
VIOLET AND BLACK

STORK
Cry —"Korrr"
BLUE AND WHITE

PANTHER
Tongue in side of mouth —
"Keeook"
YELLOW

CURLEW
Whistle —"Curley"
GREEN

HYENA
Laughing Cry —
"Ooowah-oowah-wah"
YELLOW AND BROWN

RAM
Bleat —"Ba-a-a"
BROWN

WOOD PIGEON
Call —"Book-hooroo"
BLUE AND GRAY

EAGLE
Very shrill cry —"Kreeee"
GREEN AND BLACK

HIPPO
Hiss —"Brrussssh"
PINK AND BLACK

RATTLESNAKE
Rattle a pebble in a small
potted meat tin

WILD BOAR
Grunt —"Broof-broof"
GRAY AND PINK

COBRA
Hiss —"Pssst"
ORANGE AND BLACK

CUCKOO
Call —"Cook-koo"
GRAY

OTTER
Cry —"Hoi-oi-oick"
BROWN AND WHITE

BEAVER
Slap made by clapping
hands
BLUE AND YELLOW

work in pairs, Nos. 3 and 4 together; 5 and 6 together; 7 and 8 together.

Each scout in a patrol should be able to imitate the call of his patrol animal. That is, the scouts of the Wolf patrol should be able to imitate a wolf. In this way scouts of the same patrol can communicate with each other when in hiding, or in the dark of night. It is not honorable for a scout to use the call of any other patrol except his own.

The patrol leader calls up his patrol at will by sounding his whistle and by giving the call of the patrol.

When the scout makes signs anywhere for others to read he also draws the head of his animal. That is to say, if he were out scouting and wanted to show that a certain road should not be followed by others, he would draw the sign, "not to be followed," across it and add the name of his patrol animal, in order to show which patrol discovered that the road was bad, and by adding his own number at the left of the head to show which scout had discovered it.

Each patrol leader carries a small flag on the end of his staff

BLUE BUFFALO
on white ground

FLYING EAGLES
"Yeh-yeh-yeh"
Black and white on red

BLUE HERONS
"Hrrrr"
Blue and green

**HORNED
KINGBIRDS**

SINAWA
Black on red

BLACKBEARS
Black on red

AHMEEKS

SILVER FOXES

RED TRAILERS

MOON BAND
Yellow on blue

OWNEOKES

BLAZING ARROW

or stave with the head of his patrol animal shown on both sides. Thus the Tigers of the Twenty-seventh New York Troop should have the flag shown below.

The Merit Badges*

When a boy has become a first-class scout he may qualify for the merit badges.

The examination for these badges should be given by the Court of Honor of the local council. This examination must not be given any boy who is not qualified as a first-class scout. After the boy has passed the examination, the local council may secure the merit badge for him by presenting the facts to the National Council. These badges are intended to stimulate the boy's interest in the life about him and are given for general knowledge. The wearing of these badges does not signify that a scout is qualified to make his living by the knowledge gained in securing the award.

Scouts winning any of the following badges are entitled to place after their names the insignia of the badges won. For instance, if he has successfully passed the signaling and seamanship tests, he signs his name in this manner —

James E. Ward ⚜ ✕ ⚓

---

* Result of work of Committee on Badges, Awards and Equipment: Dr. George J. Fisher, Chairman, Gen. George W. Wingate, Dr. C. Ward Crampton, Daniel Carter Beard. C. M. Connolly, A. A. Jameson, Ernest Thompson Seton.

Agriculture

To obtain a merit badge for Agriculture a scout must

1. State different tests with grains.
2. Grow at least an acre of corn which produces 25 per cent. better than the general average.
3. Be able to identify and describe common weeds of the community, and tell how best to eliminate them.
4. Be able to identify the common insects and tell how best to handle them.
5. Have a practical knowledge of plowing, cultivating, drilling, hedging, and draining.
6. Have a working knowledge of farm machinery, haymaking, reaping, loading, and stacking.
7. Have a general acquaintance of the routine seasonal work on the farm, including the care of cattle, horses, sheep, and pigs.
8. Have a knowledge of Campbell's Soil Culture principle, and a knowledge of dry farming and of irrigation farming.

Angling

To obtain a merit badge for Angling a scout must

1. Catch and name ten different species of fish: salmon or trout to be taken with flies; bass, pickerel, or pike to be caught with rod or reel, muskallonge to be caught by trolling.
2. Make a bait rod of three joints, straight and sound, 14 oz. or less in weight, 10 feet or less in length, to stand a strain of 1½ lbs. at the tip, 13 lbs. at the grip.
3. Make a jointed fly-rod 8–10 feet long, 4–8 ozs. in weight, capable of casting a fly sixty feet.
4. Name and describe twenty-five different species of fish found in North American waters and give a complete list of the fishes ascertained by himself to inhabit a given body of water.
5. Give the history of the young of any species of wild fish from the time of hatching until the adult stage is reached.

Archery

To obtain a merit badge for Archery a scout must

1. Make a bow and arrow which will shoot a distance of one hundred feet with fair precision.
2. Make a total score of 350 with 60 shots in one or

two meets, using standard four-foot target at forty yards or three-foot target at thirty yards.

3. Make a total score of 300 with 72 arrows, using standard target at a distance of fifty yards.

4. Shoot so far and fast as to have six arrows in the air at once.

Architecture

To obtain a merit badge for Architecture a scout must

1. Present a satisfactory free-hand drawing.

2. Write an essay on the history of Architecture and describe the five orders.

3. Submit an original design for a two-story house and tell what material is necessary for its construction, giving detailed specifications.

Art

To obtain a merit badge for Art a scout must

1. Draw in outline two simple objects, one composed of straight lines, and one of curved lines, the two subjects to be grouped together a little below the eye.

2. Draw in outline two books a little below the eye, one book to be open; also a table or chair.

3. Make in outline an Egyptian ornament.

4. Make in outline a Greek or Renaissance ornament from a cast or copy.

5. Make an original arrangement or design using some detail of ornament.

6. Make a drawing from a group of two objects placed a little below the eye and show light and shade.

7. Draw a cylindrical object and a rectangular object, grouped together a little below the eye, and show light and shade.

8. Present a camp scene in color.

Astronomy

To obtain a merit badge for Astronomy a scout must

1. Have a general knowledge of the nature and movements of stars.

2. Point out and name six principal constellations; find the North by means of other stars than the Pole-star in case of that star being obscured by clouds, and tell the hour of the night by the stars and moon.

3. Have a general knowledge of the positions and movements of the earth, sun, and moon, and of tides, eclipses, meteors, comets, sun-spots, and planets.

Athletics

To obtain a merit badge for Athletics a scout must

1. Write an acceptable article of not less than five hundred words on how to train for an athletic event.

2. Give the rules for one track and one field event.

3. Make the required athletic standard according to his weight, classifications and conditions as stated in chapter eight.

Automobiling

To obtain a merit badge for Automobiling a scout must

1. Demonstrate how to start a motor, explaining what precautions should be taken.

2. Take off and put on pneumatic tires.

3. Know the functions of the clutch, carburetor, valves, magneto, spark plug, differential cam shaft, and different speed gears, and be able to explain difference between a two and four-cycle motor.

4. Know how to put out burning gasoline or oil.

5. Have satisfactorily passed the requirements to receive a license to operate an automobile in the community in which he lives.

Aviation

To obtain a merit badge for Aviation a scout must

1. Have a knowledge of the theory of aeroplanes, balloons, and dirigibles.

2. Have made a working model of an

aeroplane or dirigible that will fly at least twenty-five yards; and have built a box kite that will fly.

3. Have a knowledge of the engines used for aeroplanes and dirigibles, and be able to describe the various types of aeroplanes and their records.

Bee Farming

To obtain a merit badge for Bee Farming a scout must

1. Have a practical knowledge of swarming, hiving, hives and general apiculture, including a knowledge of the use of artificial combs.

2. Describe different kinds of honey and tell from what sources gathered.

Blacksmithing

To obtain a merit badge for Blacksmithing a scout must

1. Upset and weld a one-inch iron rod.
2. Make a horseshoe.
3. Know how to tire a wheel, use a sledge-hammer and forge, shoe a horse correctly and roughshoe a horse.
4. Be able to temper iron and steel.

Bugling

To obtain a merit badge for Bugling a scout must

1. Be able to sound properly on the Bugle the customary United States Army calls.

Business

To obtain a merit badge for Business a scout must

1. Write a satisfactory business, and a personal letter.
2. State fundamental principles of buying and selling.
3. Know simple bookkeeping.
4. Keep a complete and actual account of personal receipts and expenditures for six months.

5. State how much money would need to be invested at 5 per cent. to earn his weekly allowance of spending money for a year.

Camping

To obtain a merit badge for Camping a scout must

1. Have slept in the open or under canvas at different times fifty nights.

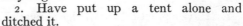

2. Have put up a tent alone and ditched it.

3. Have made a bed of wild material and a fire without matches.

4. State how to choose a camp site and how to prepare for rain; how to build a latrine (toilet) and how to dispose of the camp garbage and refuse.

5. Know how to construct a raft.

Carpentry

To obtain a merit badge for Carpentry a scout must

1. Know the proper way to drive, set and clinch a nail.

2. Know the different kinds of chisels, planes and saws, and how to sharpen and use them.

3. Know the use of the rule, square, level, plumb-line and mitre.

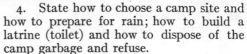

4. Know how to use compasses for scribing both regular and irregular lines.

5. Make an article of furniture with three different standard joints or splices, with at least one surface of highly polished hard or decorative wood. All work to be done without assistance.

Chemistry

To obtain a merit badge for Chemistry a scout must be able to pass the following test:

1. Define physical and chemical change. Which occurs when salt is dissolved in water, milk sours, iron rusts, water boils, iron is magnetized and mercuric oxide is heated above the boiling point of mercury?

2. Give correct tests for oxygen, hydrogen, nitrogen, chlorine, and carbon dioxide gases.

3. Could you use the above gases to extinguish fire? How?

4. Why can baking soda be used to put out a small fire?

5. Give tests for a chloride, sulphide, sulphate, nitrate, and carbonate.

6. Give the names of three commercial forms of carbon. Tell how each is made and the purpose for which it is used.

7. What compound is formed when carbon is burned in air?

8. Tell process of making lime and mortar from limestone.

9. Why will fresh plaster harden quicker by burning charcoal in an open vessel near it?

Civics

To obtain a merit badge for Civics a scout must

1. State the principal citizenship requirements of an elector in his state.

2. Know the principal features of the naturalization laws of the United States.

3. Know how President, Vice-President, senators, and congressmen of the United States are elected and their terms of office.

4. Know the number of judges of the Supreme Court of the United States, how appointed, and their term of office.

5. Know the various administrative departments of government, as represented in the President's Cabinet.

6. Know how the governor, lieutenant-governor, senators, representatives, or assemblymen of his state are elected, and their terms of office.

7. Know whether the judges of the principal courts in his state are appointed or elected, and the length of their terms.

8. Know how the principal officers in his town or city are elected and for what terms.

9. Know the duties of the various city departments, such as fire, police, board of health, etc.

10. Draw a map of the town or city in which he lives, giving location of the principal public buildings and points of special interest.

11. Give satisfactory evidence that he is familiar with the

provisions and history of the Declaration of Independence, and the Constitution of the United States.

Conservation

To obtain a merit badge for Conservation a scout must

1. Be able to recognize in the forest all important commercial trees in his neighborhood; distinguish the lumber from each and tell for what purpose each is best suited; tell the age of old blazes on trees which mark a boundary or trail; recognize the difference in the forest between good and bad logging, giving reasons why one is good and another bad; tell whether a tree is dying from injury by fire, by insects, by disease or by a combination of these causes; know what tools to use, and how to fight fires in hilly or in flat country. 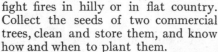 Collect the seeds of two commercial trees, clean and store them, and know how and when to plant them.

2. Know the effect upon streamflow of the destruction of forests at head waters; know what are the four great uses of water in streams; what causes the pollution of streams, and how it can best be stopped; and how, in general, water power is developed.

3. Be able to tell, for a given piece of farm land, whether it is best suited for use as farm or forest, and why; point out examples of erosion, and tell how to stop it; give the reasons why a growing crop pointed out to him is successful or why not; and tell what crops should be grown in his neighborhood and why.

4. Know where the great coal fields are situated and whether the use of coal is increasing, and if so at what rate. Tell what are the great sources of waste of coal, in the mines, and in its use, and how they can be reduced.

5. Know the principal game birds and animals in his neighborhood, the seasons during which they are protected, the methods of protection, and the results. Recognize the track of any two of the following: rabbit, fox, deer, squirrel, wild turkey, ruffed grouse and quail.

Cooking

To obtain a merit badge for Cooking a scout must

1. Prove his ability to build a fireplace out of stone or sod

or logs, light a fire, and cook in the open the following dishes in addition to those required for a first-class scout: Camp stew, two vegetables, omelet, rice pudding; know how to mix dough, and bake bread in an oven; be able to make tea, coffee, and cocoa, carve properly and serve correctly to people at the table.

Craftsmanship

To obtain a merit badge for Craftsmanship a scout must

1. Build and finish unassisted one of the following articles: a round, square or octagonal tabouret; round or square den or library table; hall or piano bench; rustic arm chair or swing to be hung with chains; or rustic table.

2. He must also make plans or intelligent rough sketch drawing of the piece selected.

Cycling

To obtain a merit badge for Cycling a scout must

1. Be able to ride a bicycle fifty miles in ten hours.

2. Repair a puncture.

3. Take apart and clean bicycle and put together again properly.

4. Know how to make reports if sent out scouting on a road.

5. Be able to read a map and report correctly verbal messages.

Dairying

To obtain a merit badge for Dairying a scout must

1. Understand the management of dairy cattle.

2. Be able to milk.

3. Understand the sterilization of milk, and care of dairy utensils and appliances.

4. Test at least five cows for ten days each, with the Babcock test, and make proper reports.

Electricity

To obtain a merit badge for Electricity a scout must

1. Illustrate the experiment by which the laws of electrical attraction and repulsion are shown.

2. Name three uses of the direct current, and tell how it differs from the alternating current.

3. Make a simple elctro-magnet.

4. Have an elementary knowledge of the action of simple battery cells and of the working of electric bells and telephones.

5. Be able to remedy fused wire, and to repair broken electric connections.

6. Construct a machine to make static electricity or a wireless apparatus.

7. Have a knowledge of the method of resuscitation and rescue of a person insensible from shock.

Firemanship

To obtain a merit badge for Firemanship, a scout must

1. Know how to turn in an alarm for fire.

2. Know how to enter burning buildings.

3. Know how to prevent panics and the spread of fire.

4. Understand the use of hose; unrolling, joining up, connecting two hydrants, use of nozzle, etc.

5. Understand the use of escapes, ladders, and chutes, and know the location of exits in buildings which he frequents.

6. Know how to improvise ropes and nets.

7. Know what to do in case of panic, understand the fireman's lift and drag, and how to work in fumes.

8. Understand the use of fire extinguishers; how to rescue animals; how to save property; how to organize a bucket brigade, and how to aid the police in keeping back crowds.

First Aid

To obtain a merit badge for First Aid a scout must

1. Be able to demonstrate the Sylvester and Schaefer methods of resuscitation.

2. Carry a person down a ladder.
3. Bandage head and ankle.
4. Demonstrate treatment of wound of the neck with severe arterial hemorrhage.

5. Treat mangling injury of the leg without severe hemorrhage.
6. Demonstrate treatment for rupture of varicose veins of the leg with severe hemorrhage.
7. Show treatment for bite of finger by mad dog.
8. Demonstrate rescue of person in contact with electric wire.
9. Apply tourniquet to a principal artery.
10. State chief differences between carbolic poisoning and intoxication.
11. Explain what to do for snake bite.
12. Pass first aid test of American Red Cross Society.

First Aid to Animals

To obtain a merit badge for First Aid to Animals a scout must
1. Have a general knowledge of domestic and farm animals.
2. Be able to treat a horse for colic.
3. Describe symptoms and give treatment for the following: wounds, fractures and sprains, exhaustion, choking, lameness.
4. Understand horseshoeing.

Forestry

To obtain a merit badge for Forestry a scout must
1. Be able to identify twenty-five kinds of trees when in leaf, or fifteen kinds of deciduous (broad leaf) trees in winter, and tell some of the uses of each.
2. Identify twelve kinds of shrubs.
3. Collect and identify samples of ten kinds of wood and be able to tell some of their uses.
4. Determine the height, and estimate the amount of timber, approximately, in five trees of different sizes.

5. State laws for transplanting, grafting, spraying, and protecting trees.

Gardening

To obtain a merit badge for Gardening, a scout must

1. Dig and care for during the season a piece of ground containing not less than 144 square feet.

2. Know the names of a dozen plants pointed out in an ordinary garden.

3. Understand what is meant by pruning, grafting, and manuring.

4. Plant and grow successfully six kinds of vegetables or flowers from seeds or cuttings.

5. Cut grass with scythe under supervision.

Handicraft

To obtain a merit badge for Handicraft a scout must

1. Be able to paint a door.
2. Whitewash a ceiling.
3. Repair gas fittings, sash lines, window and door fastenings.
4. Replace gas mantles, washers, and electric light bulbs.

5. Solder.
6. Hang pictures and curtains.
7. Repair blinds.
8. Fix curtains, portière rods, blind fixtures.
9. Lay carpets and mend clothing and upholstery.
10. Repair furniture and china.
11. Sharpen knives.
12. Repair gates.
13. Fix screens on windows and doors.

Horsemanship

To obtain a merit badge for Horsemanship a scout must

1. Demonstrate riding at a walk, trot, and gallop.
2. Know how to saddle and bridle a horse correctly.
3. Know how to water and feed and to what amount, and how to groom a horse properly.

4. Know how to harness a horse correctly in single or double harness and to drive.

5. Have a knowledge of the power of endurance of horses at work and know the local regulations concerning driving.

6. Know the management and care of horses.

7. Be able to identify unsoundness and blemishes.

8. Know the evils of bearing or check reins and of ill-fitting harness or saddlery.

9. Know two common causes of, and proper remedies for, lameness, and know to whom he should refer cases of cruelty and abuse.

10. Be able to judge as to the weight, height, and age of horses; know three breeds and their general characteristics.

Interpreting

To obtain a merit badge for Interpreting, a scout must

1. Be able to carry on a simple conversation.

2. Write a simple letter on subject given by examiners.

3. Read and translate a passage from a book or newspaper, in French, German, English, Italian, or any language that is not of his own country.

Invention

To obtain a merit badge for Invention a scout must

1. Invent and patent some useful article.

2. Show a working drawing or model of the same.

Leather Working

To obtain a merit badge for Leather Working a scout must

1. Have a knowledge of tanning and curing.

2. Be able to sole and heel a pair of boots, sewed or nailed, and generally repair boots and shoes.

3. Be able to dress a saddle, repair traces, stirrup leathers, etc., and know the various parts of harness.

Life Saving

To obtain a merit badge for Life Saving a scout must

1. Be able to dive into from seven to ten feet of water and bring from bottom to surface a loose bag of sand weighing five pounds.

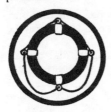

2. Be able to swim two hundred yards, one hundred yards on back without using the hands, and one hundred yards any other stroke.

3. Swim fifty yards with clothes on (shirt, long trousers, and shoes as minimum).

4. Demonstrate (a) on land — five methods of release; (b) in the water — two methods of release; (c) the Schaefer method of resuscitation (prone pressure).

Machinery

To obtain a merit badge for Machinery a scout must

1. State the principles underlying the use and construction of the lathe, steam boiler and engine, drill press and planer.

2. Make a small wood or metal model illustrating the principles of either levers, gears, belted pulleys, or block and fall.

Marksmanship

To obtain a merit badge for Marksmanship a scout must

1. Qualify as a marksman in accordance with the regulations of the National Rifle Association.

Masonry

To obtain a merit badge for Masonry a scout must
1. Lay a straight wall with a corner.

2. Make mortar and describe process.

3. Use intelligently a plumb-line, level, and trowel.

4. Build a stone oven.

5. Demonstrate a knowledge of various uses for cement.

6. Build a dry wall.

Mining

To obtain a merit badge for Mining a scout must

1. Know and name fifty minerals.

2. Know, name and describe the fourteen great divisions of the earth's crust (according to Geikie).

3. Define watershed, delta, drift, fault, glacier, terrace, stratum, dip; and identify ten different kinds of rock.

4. Describe methods for mine ventilation and safety devices.

Music

To obtain a merit badge for Music a scout must

1. Be able to play a standard musical instrument satisfactorily.

2. Read simple music.

3. Write a satisfactory essay of not less than five hundred words on the history of American music.

Ornithology

To obtain a merit badge for Ornithology a scout must

1. Have a list of one hundred different kinds of birds personally observed on exploration in the field.

2. Have identified beyond question, by appearance or by note, forty-five different kinds of birds in one day.

3. Have made a good clear photograph of some wild bird, the bird image to be over one half inch in length on the negative.

4. Have secured at least two tenants in bird boxes erected by himself.

5. Have daily notes on the nesting of a pair of wild birds from the time the first egg is laid until the young have left the nest.

6. Have attracted at least three kinds of birds, exclusive of the English sparrow, to a "lunch counter" which he has supplied.

Painting

To obtain a merit badge for Painting a scout must

1. Have knowledge of how to combine pigments in order to produce paints in shades and tints of color.

2. Know how to add positive colors to a base of white lead or of white zinc.

3. Understand the mixing of oils, turpentine, etc., to the proper consistency.

4. Paint a porch floor or other surface evenly and without laps.

5. Know how and when to putty up nail holes and uneven surfaces.

6. Present for inspection a panel covered with three coats of paint, which panel must contain a border of molding, the body of the panel to be painted in one color and the molding in another.

Pathfinding

To obtain a merit badge for Pathfinding a scout must

1. Know every lane, by-path, and short cut for a distance of at least two miles in every direction around the local scouts' headquarters in the country.

2. Have a general knowledge of the district within a five-mile radius of his local headquarters, so as to be able to guide people at any time, by day or night.

3. Know the general direction and population of the five principal neighboring towns and be able to give strangers correct directions how to reach them.

4. Know in the country in the two-mile radius, approximately, the number of horses, cattle, sheep, and pigs owned on the five neighboring farms: or in a town must know in a half-mile radius what livery stables, garages and blacksmiths there are.

5. Know the location of the nearest meat markets, bakeries, groceries, and drug stores.

6. Know where the nearest police station, hospital, doctor, fire alarm, fire hydrant, telegraph and telephone offices, and railroad stations are.

7. Know something of the history of the place, its principal public buildings, such as town or city hall, post-office, schools, and churches.

8. As much as possible of the above information should be entered on a large scale map.

Personal Health

To obtain a merit badge for Personal Health a scout must

1. Write a statement on the care of the teeth.

2. State a principle to govern in eating, and state in the order of their importance, five rules to govern the care of his health.

3. Be able to tell the difference in effect of a cold and hot bath.

4. Describe the effect of alcohol and tobacco on the growing boy.

5. Tell how to care for the feet on a march.

6. Describe a good healthful game and state its merit.

7. Describe the effects of walking as an exercise.

8. Tell how athletics may be overdone.

Photography

To obtain a merit badge for Photography a scout must

1. Have a knowledge of the theory and use of lenses, of the construction of cameras, and the action of developers.

2. Take, develop, and print twelve separate subjects: three interiors, three portraits, three landscapes, and three instantaneous "action photos."

3. Make a recognizable photograph of any wild bird larger than a robin, while on its nest; or a wild animal in its native haunts; or a fish in the water.

Pioneering

To obtain a merit badge for Pioneering a scout must

1. Fell a nine-inch tree or pole in a prescribed direction neatly and quickly.

2. Tie six kinds of knots quickly.

3. Lash spars properly together for scaffolding.

4. Build a modern bridge or derrick.

5. Make a camp kitchen.

6. Build a shack of one kind or another suitable for three occupants.

Plumbing

To obtain a merit badge for Plumbing a scout must

1. Be able to make wiped and brazed joints.

2. Repair a burst pipe.

3. Mend a ball or faucet tap.

4. Understand the ordinary hot and cold water system of a house.

Poultry Farming

To obtain a merit badge for Poultry Farming a scout must

1. Have a knowledge of incubators, foster-mothers, sanitary fowl houses, and coops and runs.

2. Understand rearing, feeding, killing, and dressing birds for market.

3. Be able to pack birds and eggs for market.

4. Raise a brood of not less than ten chickens.

5. Report his observation and study of the hen, turkey, duck, and goose.

Printing

To obtain a merit badge for Printing a scout must

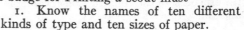

1. Know the names of ten different kinds of type and ten sizes of paper.

2. Be able to compose by hand or machines.

3. Understand the use of hand or power printing machines.

4. Print a handbill set up by himself.

5. Be able to read and mark proof correctly.

Public Health

To obtain a merit badge for Public Health a scout must

1. State what the chief causes of each of the following disease are: tuberculosis, typhoid, malaria.

2. Draw a diagram showing how the house-fly carries disease.

3. Tell what should be done to a house which has been occupied by a person who has had a contagious disease.

4. Tell how a scout may cooperate with the board of health in preventing disease.

5. Describe the method used in his community in disposing of garbage.

6. Tell how a city should protect its foods; milk, meat, and exposed foods.

7. Tell how to plan the sanitary care of a camp.

8. State the reason why school children should undergo a medical examination.

Scholarship

NOTE: The requirements for the merit badge for Scholarship had not been decided upon when this book was published. Information about same may be secured upon application to National Headquarters.

Sculpture

To obtain a merit badge for Sculpture a scout must

1. Make a clay model from an antique design.

2. Make a drawing and a model from nature, these models to be faithful to the original and of artistic design.

Seamanship

To obtain a merit badge for Seamanship a scout must

1. Be able to tie rapidly six different knots.

2. Splice ropes.

3. Use a palm and needle.

4. Fling a rope coil.

5. Be able to row, pole, scull, and steer a boat; also bring a boat properly alongside and make fast.

6. Know how to box the compass, read a chart, and show use of parallel rules and dividers.

7. Be able to state direction by the stars and sun.

8. Swim fifty yards with shoes and clothes on.

9. Understand the general working of steam and hydraulic winches, and have a knowledge of weather wisdom and of tides.

Signaling

To obtain a merit badge for Signaling a scout must

1. Send and receive a message in two of the following systems of signaling: Semaphore, Morse, or Myer, not fewer than twenty-four letters per minute.

2. Be able to give and read signals by sound.

3. Make correct smoke and fire signals.

Stalking

To obtain a merit badge for Stalking a scout must

1. Take a series·of twenty photographs of wild animals or birds from life, and develop and print them.

2. Make a group of sixty species of wild flowers, ferns, or grasses, dried and mounted in a book and correctly named.

3. Make colored drawings of twenty flowers, ferns, or grasses, or twelve sketches from life of animals or birds, original sketches as well as the finished pictures to be submitted.

Surveying

To obtain a merit badge for Surveying a scout must

1. Map correctly from the country itself the main features of half a mile of road, with 440 yards each side to a scale of two feet to the mile, and afterward draw same map from memory.

2. Be able to measure the height of a tree, telegraph pole, and church steeple, describing method adopted.

3. Measure width of a river.

4. Estimate distance apart of two objects a known distance away and unapproachable.

5. Be able to measure a gradient.

Swimming

To obtain a merit badge for Swimming a scout must

1. Be able to swim one hundred yards.

2. Dive properly from the surface of the water.

3. Demonstrate breast, crawl, and side stroke.

4. Swim on the back fifty feet.

Taxidermy

To obtain a merit badge for Taxidermy a scout must

1. Have a knowledge of the game laws of the state in which he lives.

2. Preserve and mount the skin of a game bird, or animal, killed in season.

3. Mount for a rug the pelt of some fur animal.

Life Scout

The life scout badge will be given to all first-class scouts who have qualified for the following five-merit badges: first aid, athletics, life-saving, personal health, and public health.

Star Scout

The star scout badge will be given to the first-class scout who has qualified for ten merit badges. The ten include the list of badges under life scout.

Eagle Scout

Any first-class scout qualifying for twenty-one merit badges will be entitled to wear the highest scout merit badge. This is an eagle's head in silver, and represents the all-round perfect scout.

Honor Medals

A scout who is awarded any one of the following medals is entitled to wear the same on the left breast:

Bronze medal. Cross in bronze with first-class scout badge superimposed upon it and suspended from a bar by a red ribbon. This is awarded to a scout who has saved life.

Silver Medal. Silver Cross with first-class scout badge  superimposed upon it and suspended from bar by blue ribbon. This medal is awarded to a scout who saves life with considerable risk to himself.

Gold Medal. Gold Cross with first-class scout badge superimposed upon it and suspended from bar by white ribbon. This medal is the highest possible award for service and heroism. It may be granted to a scout who has saved life at the greatest possible risk to his own life, and also to any one who has rendered service of peculiar merit to the Boy Scouts of America.

The Honor Medal is a national honor and is awarded only by the National Council. To make application for one of these badges the facts must first be investigated by the Court of Honor of the Local Council and presented by that body to the Court of Honor of the National Council.

The Local Court of Honor may at any time invite experts to share in their examinations and recommendations.

When the National Court of Honor has passed upon the application, the proper medal will be awarded.

Badges of Rank

The following devices are used to distinguish the various ranks of scouts:

Patrol Leader: The patrol leader's arm badge consists of two bars, $1\frac{1}{2}$-inches long and $\frac{3}{8}$-inch wide, of white braid worn on the sleeve below the left shoulder. In addition he may

Patrol Leader

wear an oxidized silver tenderfoot, second-class or first-class scout badge according to his rank. The assistant patrol leader wears one bar.

Service Stripes: For each year of service as a boy scout, he will be entitled to wear a stripe of white braid around the sleeve above the wrist, three stripes being changed for one red one. Five years of scouting would be indicated by one red stripe and two white stripes. The star indicates the position for wearing merit badges.

Service Stripes

Scout Master: The badge of the scout commissioner, scout master, and assistant scout master is the first-class scout's badge reproduced in blue, green, and red, respectively, and are worn on the sleeve below the left shoulder.

Chief Scout: The badge of the Chief Scout is the first-class scout badge with a five-pointed star above it embroidered in silver.

Scout Master

Chief Scout Surgeon: The badge of the Chief Scout Surgeon is the first-class scout badge with a caduceus above it embroidered in green. (The Chief Scout's staff wear the badge of rank in the same manner as the Chief Scout.)

Chief Scout

Chief Scout Surgeon

Chief Scout Woodsman: The badge of the Chief Scout Woodsman is the first-class scout badge with two crossed axes above it embroidered in green.

Chief Scout Stalker: The badge of the Chief Scout Stalker is the first-class scout badge with an oak leaf above it embroidered in blue.

Chief Scout Woodsman

Chief Scout Stalker

Chief Scout Director of Health: The badge of the Chief Scout Director of Health is the first-class scout badge with tongues of fire above it embroidered in red.

Chief Scout Camp Master: The badge of the

Chief Scout Camp
Master

Chief Scout Camp Master is the first-class scout badge with a moccasin above it embroidered in green.

Chief Scout Director of Athletics: The badge

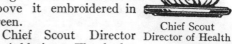

Chief Scout
Director of Health

of the Chief Scout Director of Athletics is the first-class scout badge with a winged Mercury foot above it embroidered in green.

Chief Scout Director of Chivalry: The badge of the Chief Scout Director of Chivalry is the first-class scout badge with the scout

Chief Scout Director of
Athletics

sign above it embroidered in gold.

Chief Scout Citizen: The badge of the Chief Scout Citizen is the first-class scout badge with the United States flag above it in silver.

Chief Scout
Citizen

Appropriate badges for national and local councilmen may be secured from the National Headquarters.

Equipment

It should be clearly understood by all interested in the Scout Movement that it is not necessary for a boy to have a uniform or any other special equipment to carry out the scout program. There are a great many troops in the country which have made successful progress without any equipment whatever.

However, for the convenience of boys who wish to secure a uniform or other equipment, the National Council has made arrangements with certain manufacturers to furnish such parts of the equipment as may be desired by the boys. Such arrangements have been made with these manufacturers only after a great number of representative firms have been given an opportunity to submit samples and prices; the prices quoted to be uniform throughout the country. These manufacturers are given the privilege of using for a limited period an imprint of the official badge as an indication that the Committee on Equipment is willing to recommend the use of that particular article. The official badge is fully protected by the U. S. Patent Laws and any one using it without expressed authority from National Headquarters is subject to prosecution at law.

Considerable difficulty has been experienced in the selection of the material used in making coats, breeches, and shirts. The material used in the boy scout coat, breeches, and shirt has been submitted to a thirty-day sun test, the acid and strength test and is guaranteed to be a fast color and durable. To show the result of the selection made, the manufacturer of these articles has been given the privilege of using the imprint of the official seal and the right to use the official buttons. We recommend the purchase of the articles having this imprint through any local dealer or through National Headquarters. However, where a local council exists, buttons will be supplied on order of the Executive Committee for use on such uniforms as the Committee may desire to have made locally. In communities where no local council has been formed, they may be supplied on order of a registered scout master. Prices of the buttons per set for coat is 15 cents and per set for shirt 10 cents.

Every effort is made to have all parts of the uniform and equipment available to scouts through local dealers. If such arrangements have not been made in a community, the National Headquarters will be glad to help in making such an arrangement. Many scout masters prefer to order uniforms and other supplies direct from National Headquarters. In order to cover the expense involved in handling these supplies, the manufacturers have agreed to allow National Headquarters the same trade discount allowed to local dealers. Trade through National Headquarters if sufficiently large will help to meet a part of the current expenses of the National Organization. Any combination desired may be made from this list. A fairly complete equipment may be secured at the very nominal sum of $2.15. For instance, the Summer equipment which consists of: Hat, 50 cents; Shirt, 75 cents; Shorts, 50 cents; Belt, 40 cents.

Where it is desired to equip the members of the troop with a standard uniform the following equipment is suggested: Hat, Shirt, Coat, Breeches or Knickerbockers, Belt, Leggings or Stockings, Shoes, Haversack.

Other combinations may be made according to the resources of the boys forming the troop.

However, it is recommended that each troop decide upon a definite combination to be worn by its members so that all of the scouts in the troop may dress alike. Each boy should pay for his own supplies and equipment. Soliciting donations for this purpose should be prohibited.

A complete list of all supplies and equipment with full information about places where same can be secured is given in the appendix of this book.

KNOTS EVERY SCOUT SHOULD KNOW

By Samuel A. Moffat, Boy Scouts of America

Every scout knows what rope is. From the earliest moment of his play life he has used it in connection with most of his games. In camp life and on hikes he will be called upon to use it again and again. It is therefore not essential to describe here the formation of rope; its various sizes and strength. The important thing to know is how to use it to the best advantage. To do this an intelligent understanding of the different knots and how to tie them is essential. Every day sailors, explorers, mechanics, and mountain-climbers risk their lives on the knots that they tie. Thousands of lives have been sacrificed to ill-made knots. The scout therefore should be prepared in an emergency, or when necessity demands, to tie the right knot in the right way.

There are three qualities to a good knot: 1. Rapidity with which it can be tied. 2. Its ability to hold fast when pulled tight, and 3. The readiness with which it can be undone.

The following knots, recommended to scouts, are the most serviceable because they meet the above requirements and will be of great help in scoutcraft. If the tenderfoot will follow closely the various steps indicated in the diagrams, he will have little difficulty in reproducing them at pleasure.

In practising knot-tying a short piece of hemp rope may be used. To protect the ends from fraying a scout should know how to "whip" them. The commonest method of "whipping" is as follows:

Lay the end of a piece of twine along the end of the rope.

Hold it to the rope with the thumb of your left hand while you wind the standing part around it and the rope until the

end of the twine has been covered. Then with the other end of the twine lay a loop back on the end of the rope and continue winding the twine upon this second end until all is taken up. The end is then pulled back tight and cut off close to the rope.

For the sake of clearness a scout must constantly keep in mind these three principal parts of the rope:

1. *The Standing Part* — The long unused portion of the rope on which he works;

2. *The Bight* — The loop formed whenever the rope is turned back upon itself; and,

3. *The End* — The part he uses in leading.

Before proceeding with the tenderfoot requirements, a scout should first learn the two primary knots: the overhand and figure-of-eight knots.

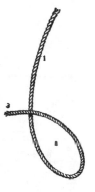

The Overhand Knot. Start with the position shown in the preceding diagram. Back the end around the standing part and up through the bight and draw tight.

The Figure of Eight Knot. Make a bight as before. Then lead the end around back of the standing part and down through the bight.

After these preliminary steps, the prospective tenderfoot may proceed to learn the required knots.

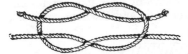

Square or Reef Knot. The commonest knot for tying two ropes together. Frequently used in first-aid bandaging. Never slips or jams; easy to untie.

False Reef or Granny. If the ends are not crossed correctly when making the reef knot, the false reef or granny is the result. This knot is always bad.

Sheet Bend or Weaver's Knot. This knot is used in bending the sheet to the clew of a sail and in tying two rope-ends together.

Make a bight with one rope *A*, *B*, then pass end *C*, of other rope up through and around the entire bight and bend it under its own standing part.

The Bowline. A noose that neither jams nor slips. Used in lowering a person from a burning building, etc.

Form a small loop on the standing part leaving the end long enough for the size of the noose required. Pass the end up through the bight around the standing part and down through the bight again. To tighten, hold noose in position and pull standing part.

Halter, Slip, or Running Knot. A bight is first formed and an overhand knot made with the end around the standing part.

Sheepshank. Used for shortening ropes. Gather up the amount to be shortened, then make a half hitch round each of the bends as shown in the diagram.

Scoutcraft

Clove Hitch. Used to fasten one pole to another in fitting up scaffolding; this knot holds snugly; is not liable to slip laterally.

Hold the standing part in left hand, then pass the rope around the pole; cross the standing part, making a second turn around the pole, and pass the end under the last turn.

The Fisherman's Bend. Used aboard yachts for bending on the gaff topsail halliards. It consists of two turns around a spar or ring, then a half hitch around the standing part and through the turns on the spar, and another half hitch above it around the standing part.

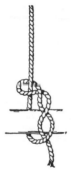

Timber Hitch. Used in hauling timber. Pass the end of the rope around the timber. Then lead it around its standing part and bring it back to make two or more turns on its own part. The strain will hold it securely

Two Half Hitches. Useful because they are easily made and will not slip under any strain.

Their formation is sufficiently indicated by the diagram.

Blackwall Hitch. Used to secure a rope to a hook. The standing part when hauled tight holds the end firmly.

Becket Hitch. For joining a cord to a rope. May be easily made from diagram.

The Fisherman's Knot. Used for tying silk-worm gut for fishing purposes. It never slips; is easily unloosed by pulling the two short ends.

The two ropes are laid alongside one another, then with each end an overhand knot is made around the standing part of the other. Pull the standing parts to tighten.

Carrick Bend. Used in uniting hawsers for towing. Is easily untied by pushing the loops inwards.

Turn the end of one rope *A* over its standing part *B* to form a loop. Pass the end of the other rope across the bight thus formed, back of the standing part *B* over the end *A*, then under the bight at *C*, passing it over its own standing part and under the bight again at *D*.

The Mariner's Compass

Boxing the Compass consists in enumerating the points, beginning with north and working around the circle as follows:

North	East by North
North by East	East
North, North-east	East by South
North-east by North	East, South-east
North-east	South-east by East
North-east by East	South-east
East, North-east	South-east by South

South, South-east
South by East
South
South by West
South, South-west
South-west by South
South-west
South-west by West
West, South-west
West by South

West
West by North
West, North-west
North-west by West
North-west
North-west by North
North, North-west
North by West
North

NOTES

Notes

Notes

Notes

CHAPTER II
WOODCRAFT

Woodlore

By Ernest Thompson Seton, Chief Scout

The Watch for a Compass*

The watch is often used to give the compass point exactly. Thus: Point the hour-hand to the sun; then, in the morning, half-way between the hour-hand and noon is due south. If afternoon, one must reckon half-way backward.

Thus: at 8 A. M., point the hour-hand to the sun and reckon forward half-way to noon; the south is at 10. If at 4 P. M., point the hour-hand at the sun and reckon back half-way. The south is at two o'clock.

The "half-way" is because the sun makes a course of twenty-four hours and the clock of but twelve If we had a rational timepiece of twenty-four hours, it would fit in much better with all nature, and with the hour-hand pointed to the sun would make 12 o'clock, noon, always south.

If you cannot see the sun, get into a clear, open space, hold your knife point upright on your watch dial, and it will cast a faint shadow, showing where the sun really is, unless the clouds are very heavy.

Finding Your Latitude by the Stars

The use of the stars to the scout is chiefly to guide him by showing the north, but the white man has carried the use a step farther: he makes the Pole-star tell him not only where the north is, but where he himself is. From the Pole-star, he can learn his latitude.

It is reckoned an exploit to take one's latitude from the North Star with a cart-wheel, or with two sticks and a bucket of water.

* From "Boy Scouts of America," by Ernest Thompson Seton. Copyright, 1910, by Doubleday, Page & Company

The first attempt I made was with two sticks and a bucket of water. I arranged the bucket in the daytime, so that it could be filled from rim to rim; that is, it was level, and that gave me the horizon line; next, I fastened my two sticks together at an adjustable angle. Then, laying one stick across the bucket as a base, I raised the other till the two sight notches on its upper edge were in straight line for the Pole-star. The sticks were now fastened at this angle and put away till the morning. On a smooth board — the board is allowable because it can be found either far on the plains when you have your wagon, or on the ship at sea — I mapped out, first a right angle, by the old plan of measuring off a triangle, whose sides were six, eight, and ten inches, and applied the star angle to this. By a process of equal subdivision I got 45 degrees, 22½ degrees, finally 40 degrees, which seemed to be the latitude of my camp; subsequent looking-up showed it to be 41 degrees 10 minutes.

Of course, it is hard to imagine that the boys will ever be so placed that it is important for them to take their latitude with home-made implements; but it is also hard to imagine circumstances under which it would be necessary to know that the sun is 92,000,000 miles away. It is very sure, however, that a boy who has once done this has a larger idea of the world and its geography, and it is likely to help him in realizing that

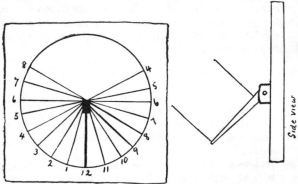

Sundial, or hunter's clock

there is some meaning to the lines and figures on the border of his school maps, and that they are not put there merely to add to his perplexities.

To make a scout's sundial, prepare a smooth board about fifteen inches across, with a circle divided into twenty-four equal parts, and a temporarily hinged pointer, whose upper edge is in the middle of the dial. Place on some *dead level*, solid post or stump in the open. At night fix the dial so that the twelve o'clock line points exactly to north, as determined by the Pole-star. Then, using two temporary sighting sticks of exactly the same height (so as to permit sighting clear above the edge of the board) set the pointer exactly pointing to the Pole-star; that is, the same angle as the latitude of the place, and fix it there immovably. Then remove the two sighting sticks. As a timepiece, this dial will be found roughly correct for that latitude. The angle of the pointer, or style, must be changed for each latitude.

Building a Log Cabin *

There are as many different kinds of log cabins as of any other architecture. It is best to begin with the simplest. The tools needed are a sharp ax, a crosscut saw, an inch auger, and a spade. It is possible to get along with nothing but an ax (many settlers had no other tool), but the spade, saw, and auger save much work.

For the site select a high, dry place, in or near the woods, and close to the drinking-water. It should be a sunny place, and with a view, preferably one facing south or east. Clear off and level the ground. Then bring your logs. These are more picturesque with the bark left on, but last longer peeled. Eight feet by twelve feet outside makes a good cabin for three or four boys.

Cut and carry about twelve logs, each ten feet long; and twelve more, each fourteen feet long. The logs should be at least six inches through. Soft wood is preferable, as it is easier to handle; the four ground logs or sills, at least, should be of cedar, chestnut, or other wood that does not rot. Lay two of the fourteen-foot logs on the ground, at the places for the long sides, and seven feet apart. Then across them, at the end, lay two short ones, eleven feet apart. This leaves about a foot projecting from each log. Roll the last two into their resting-places, and flatten them till they sit firmly. It is of prime importance that each log rest immovably on the one below. Now cut the upper part of each end log, to an edge over each corner. (Fig. 1.)

* From *Country Life in America*, May, 1905

Next put on two long logs, roll them onto the middle, taking care to change off, so the big end at a given corner may be followed next time by the small end and insure the corner rising evenly. Roll one of these large logs close to where it is to be

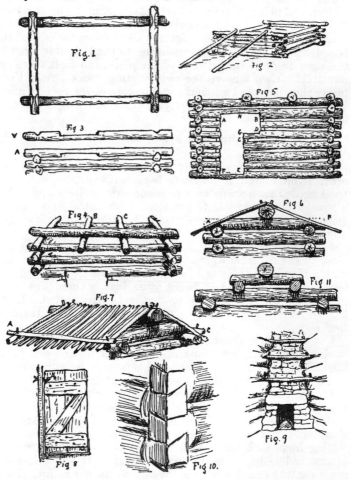

Fig. 1

Fig 2

Fig 3

Fig 5

Fig 4

Fig 6

Fig 11

Fig. 7

Fig 8

Fig 10.

Fig. 9

placed, then cut on its upper surface at each end a notch corresponding with the ridge on the log it is to ride on. When ready, half a roll drops it into place. The log should be one to three inches above the one under it, and should not touch except at the ends. Repeat the process now with the other sides, then the two ends, etc., *always keeping the line of the corner plumb*. As the walls rise, it will be found necessary to *skid* the larger logs; that is, roll them up on two long logs, or skids, leaning against the wall. (Fig. 2.)

When the logs are in place to the height of four and a half feet from the ground, it is time to decide where the door and window are to be; and at that place, while the next long log is lying on top, bottom up, cut out a piece four feet long and four inches deep. Roll this log into place. (Fig. 3.) One more log above this, or certainly two, will make your shanty high enough for boys. Put on final end logs, then two others across the shanty. (Fig. 4.) Roll up the biggest, strongest log of all for the ridge (sometimes two are used side by side); it should lie along the middle of the four cross pieces shown in Fig. 4.

The two cross logs, *B* and *C*, and the ridge log should be very strong, as the roof is heavy.

Now we are ready to cut the doorway and window.

First, drive in blocks of wood between each of the logs, all the way down from *A* to the ground, and from *B* down to *D*, and *C* to *E*. (Fig. 5.) Saw down now from *A* half-way through the ground log *F*. Then from *B* down to half-way through the log *D*; now continue from *G*, cutting down to half through the ground log. Use the ax to split out the upper half of the ground log, between the saw-cuts and also the upper half of the log *D*.

Hew a flat piece of soft wood, five or six inches wide, about two inches thick, and as long as the height of this doorway. Set it up against the ends of the logs *A* to *F*. Bore an auger hole through it into the end of each log (these holes must not be in line lest they split the jamb), including the top and bottom ones, and drive into each a pin of oak. This holds all safely. Do the same on the other side, *H* to *E*, and put a small one down *B*, *D*, which is the side of the window.

Now we are ready to finish the roof. Use the ax to bevel off the corners of the four cross-logs, *A* and *B*. (Fig. 6.) Then get a lot of strong poles, about five feet long, and lay them close together along the two sides of the roof till it is covered with poles; putting a very heavy one, or small log, on the outer edge of each, and fastening it down with a pin into the ridge log. Cut two long poles and lay one on each of the lower ends of the roof poles, as at *A*, *B*, and *C* (Fig. 7), pinning them to the side logs.

Cover this roof with a foot of hay or straw or grass, and cover that again evenly with about four inches of stiff clay. Pack this down. It will soon squeeze all that foot of straw down to little more than one inch, and will make a warm and water-tight roof. As the clay is very heavy, it is wise, before going inside, to test the roof by jumping on it. If it gives too much, it will be well to add a centre prop.

Now for the door: Hew out planks; two should be enough. Fasten these together with two cross-pieces and one angle-piece, using oak pegs instead of nails, if you wish to be truly primitive. For these the holes should be bored part way with a gimlet, and a peg used larger than the hole. The lower end of the back plank is left projecting in a point. (Fig. 8.) This point fits into a hole pecked with a point or bored with an auger into the door-sill.

Bore another hole near the top of the door (A), and a corresponding one through the door-jamb between two logs. Set the door in place. A strip of rawhide leather, a limber willow branch, or a strip of hickory put through the auger hole of the door and wedged into the hole in the jamb, makes a truly wildwood hinge. A peg in the front jamb prevents the door going too far out, and a string and peg inside answer for a latch.

The window opening may be closed with a glass sash, with a piece of muslin, or with the rawhide of an animal, scraped clear of hair and stretched on a frame.

It now remains to chink and plaster the place.

Chinking is best done from the inside. Long triangular strips and blocks of wood are driven in between the logs and fastened there with oak pins driven into the lower log till nothing but small crannies remain. Some cabins are finished with moss plugged into all the crannies, but mud worked into plaster does better.

It should be put on the outside first, and afterward finished form the inside. It is best done really with two plasterers working together, one inside and one out.

This completes the shanty, but a bunk and fireplace are usually added.

The fireplace may be in one corner, or in the middle of the end. It is easiest to make in the former.

Across the corner, peg three angle braces, each about three feet long. These are to prevent the chimney falling forward.

Now begin to build with stone, using mud as mortar, a fireplace this shape. (Fig. 9.) Make the opening about eighteen inches across; carry it up two feet high, drawing it in a little, then lay a long stone across the front, after which build up the flue behind the corner braces right up to the roof. The top corner-piece carries the rafter that may be cut off to let the flue out. Build the chimney up outside as high as the highest part of the ridge.

But the ideal fireplace is made with the chimney on the *outside* of the cabin, at the middle of the end farthest from the door. For this you must cut a hole in the end log, like a big, low window, pegging a jamb on the ends as before.

With stones and mud you now build a fireplace inside the shanty, with the big chimney carried up outside, always taking care that there are several inches of mud or stone between the fire and any of the logs.

In country where stone cannot be found, the fireplace is often built of mud, sustained by an outside cribbing of logs.

If the flue is fair size, that is, say one quarter the size of the fireplace opening, it will be sure to draw.

The bunk should be made before the chinks are plastered, as the hammering is apt to loosen the mud.

Cut eight or ten poles a foot longer than you need the bunk; cut the end of each into a flat board and drive these between the long logs at the right height and place for the bunk, supporting the other end on a crosspiece from a post to the wall. Put a very big pole on the outer side, and all is ready for the bed; most woodsmen make this of small fir boughs.

There are two other well-known ways of cornering the logs — one is simply flattening the logs where they touch. This, as well as the first one, is known in the backwoods of Canada as *hog-pen finish*. The really skilful woodsmen of the North always *dovetail* the corners and saw them flush: (Fig. 10)

Sometimes it is desirable to make a higher gable than that which one ridge log can make. Then it is made thus: (Fig. 11.)

This is as much slope as a clay roof should have; with any more, the clay would wash off.

This is the simplest way to build a log-cabin, but it illustrates all the main principles of log building. Shingle roofs and gables, broad piazzas outside, and modern fitting inside, are often added nowadays in summer camps, but it must be clear that the more towny you make the cabin, the less woodsy it is, and less likely to be the complete rest and change that is desired.

For fuller instructions, see "Log-Cabins and Cottages." By Wm. S. Wicks, 1900. (Pub. *Forest and Stream*, N. Y.)

Also, "The Jack of All Trades." By Dan C. Beard, Scribner's; and "Field and Forest Handy Book."

Measuring Distances *

The height of a tree is easily measured when on a level, open place, by measuring the length of its shadow, then comparing that with your own shadow, or that of a ten-foot pole.

Thus, the ten-foot pole is casting a fifteen-foot shadow, and the tree's shadow is one hundred and fifty feet long, apply the simple rule of three.

$$15 : 150 :: 10 : x = 100$$

But it is seldom so easy, and the good old rule of the triangle can be safely counted on: Get a hundred or more feet from your tree, on open ground, as nearly as possible on the level of its base. Set up a ten-foot pole (*A B*, page 65). Then mark the spot where the exact line from the top of the tree over the top of the pole touches the ground (*C*). Now measure the distance from that spot (*C*) to the foot of the ten-foot pole (*B*); suppose it is twenty feet. Measure also the distance from that spot (*C*) to the base of the tree (*D*); suppose it is one hundred and twenty feet, then your problem is:

$$20 : 10 :: 120 : x = 60$$

i.e., if at that angle twenty feet from the eye gives ten feet elevation, one hundred and twenty feet must give sixty.

To make a right angle, make a triangle whose sides are exactly six, eight, and ten feet or inches each (or multiples of these). The angle opposite the ten must be a true right angle. There are many ways of measuring distance across rivers, etc., without crossing. The simplest, perhaps, is by the equilateral triangle. Cut three poles of exactly equal length; peg them together into a triangle. Lay

To make a right angle

this on the bank of the river so one side points to some point on the opposite bank. Drive in three pegs to mark the exact points of this triangle (A,B,C). Then move it along the bank until you find a place (F,E,G) where its base is on line with the two pegs, where the base used to be, and one side in line with the point across the river (D). The width of the river is seven eighths of the base of this great triangle.

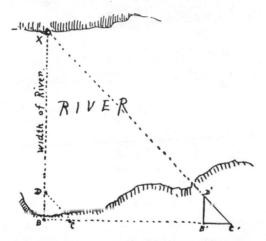

Another method is by the isosceles triangle. Make a right-angled triangle as above, with sides six, eight, and ten feet (A,B,C); then, after firmly fixing the right angle, cut down the

Measuring height of tree.

eight-foot side to six feet, and saw off the ten-foot side to fit. Place this with the side $D\ B$ on the river bank in line with the sight object (X) across. Put three pegs to mark the three corner places. Then take the triangle along the bank in the direction of C until C' D' are in line with the sight object,

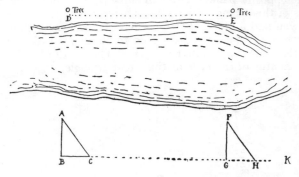

To climb a tree that is too thick — Place a small tree against it.

while B' C' is in line with the pegs B C. Then the length of the long base B C' will equal the distance from B to X.

To measure the space between two distant objects, D and E. Line A B on one, then move this right-angled triangle until F G is lined on the other, with B G in line with G H. B G equals the space between D and E then.

If the distance is considerable, it may be measured sometimes by sound. Thus, when a gun is fired, a man is chopping, or a dog barking, count the seconds between the sight and the hearing of the sound, and multiply by eleven hundred feet, which is the distance sound travels in a second.

Occasionally, the distance of an upright bank, cliff, or building can be measured by the echo. Half the seconds between shout and echo, multiplied by eleven hundred gives the distance in feet.

The usual way to estimate long distances is by the time they take to cover. Thus, a good canoe on dead water goes four to five miles an hour. A man afoot walks three and a half miles an hour on good roads. A packtrain goes two and a half miles an hour, or perhaps one and a half on the mountain trails.

A man's thumb is an inch wide.

Span of thumb and longest finger, nine inches.

Brisk walking pace is one yard for men.

What To Do When Lost in the Woods*

"Did you ever get lost in the woods?" I once asked a company of twenty campers. Some answered, "Yes; once or twice." Others said, "Many a time." Only two said, "No, never." Then I said, turning to the two, "I know that all the others here have had plenty of experience, and that you two are the tenderfeet, and never lived in the woods."

It is quite certain to come sooner or later; if you go camping, you will get lost in the woods. Hunters, Indians, yes, birds and beasts, get lost at times. You can avoid it for long by always *taking your bearings* and noting the landscape before leaving the camp, and this you should always do; but still you will get lost some time, and it is well to be ready for it by carrying matches, knife, and compass.

When you do miss your way, the first thing to remember is, like the Indian, "*You* are not lost; it is the *teepee* that is lost." It isn't serious. It cannot be so unless you do something foolish.

The first and most natural thing to do is to get on a hill, up a tree, or other high lookout, and seek for some landmark near camp. You may be sure of this much:

You are not nearly so far from camp as you think you are.

Your friends will soon find you.

You can help them best by signaling.

The worst thing you can do is to get frightened. The truly dangerous enemy is not the cold or the hunger so much as the *fear*. It is fear that robs the wanderer of his judgment and of his limb power; it is fear that turns the passing experience into a final tragedy. Only keep cool and all will be well.

*Ladies' Home Journal, October, 1902.

If there is snow on the ground, you can follow your back track.

If you see no landmark, look for the smoke of the fire. Shout from time to time, and wait; for though you have been away for hours it is quite possible you are within earshot of your friends. If you happen to have a gun, fire it off twice in quick succession on your high lookout; then wait and listen. Do this several times and wait plenty long enough — perhaps an hour. If this brings no help, send up a distress signal — that is, make two smoke fires by smothering two bright fires with green leaves and rotten wood, and keep them at least fifty feet apart, or the wind will confuse them. Two shots or two smokes are usually understood to mean "I am in trouble." Those in camp on seeing this should send up one smoke, which means, "Camp is here."

If you have a dog or a horse with you, you may depend upon it he can bring you out all right; but usually you will have to rely on yourself. The simplest plan, when there is fresh snow and no wind, is to follow your own track back. No matter how far around or how crooked it may be, it will certainly bring you out safely.

If you are sure of the general direction to the camp and determined to keep moving, leave a note pinned on a tree if you have paper; if not, write with charcoal on a piece of wood, and also make a good smoke, so that you can come back to this spot if you choose. But make certain that the fire cannot run, by clearing the ground around it and by banking it around with sods. And mark your course by breaking or cutting a twig every fifty feet. You can keep straight by the sun, the moon, or the stars, but when they are unseen you must be guided by the compass. I do not believe much in guidance by what are called nature's compass signs. It is usual to say, for example, that the north side of the tree has the most moss or the south side the most limbs, etc. While these are true in general, there are so many exceptions that when alarmed and in doubt as to which is north, one is not in a frame of mind to decide with certainty on such fine points.

If a strong west wind, for example, was blowing when you left camp, and has blown ever since, you can be pretty sure it is still a west wind; but the only safe and certain natural compass guides are the sun, moon, and stars.

The Pole or North Star, and the Great Bear (also called the Dipper and the Pointers), should be known to every boy as they are to every Indian. The Pointers always point out the

Pole-star. Of course, they go around it once in twenty-four hours, so this makes a kind of clock.

The stars, then, will enable you to keep straight if you travel. But thick woods, fog, or clouds are apt to come up, and without something to guide you are sure to go around in a circe.

Old woodsmen commonly follow down the streams. These are certain to bring you out somewhere; but the very worst traveling is along the edges of the streams, and they take you a long way around. All things considered, it is usually best to stay right where you are, especially if in a wild country where there is no chance of finding a farm house. Make yourself comfortable for the night by gathering plenty of good wood while it is daylight, and building a wind screen on three sides, with the fire in front, and something to keep you off the ground. Do not worry but keep up a good fire; and when day comes renew your two smokes and wait. A good fire is the best friend of a lost man.

I have been lost a number of times, but always got out without serious trouble, because I kept cool. The worst losing I ever got was after I had been so long in the West that I qualified to act as a professional guide, and was engaged by a lot of Eastern farmers looking for land locations.

This was in the October of 1883 on the Upper Assiniboin. The main body of the farmers had remained behind. I had gone ahead with two of them. I took them over hundreds of miles of wild country. As we went northward the country improved. We were traveling with oxen, and it was our custom to let them graze for two hours at noon. One warm day, while the oxen were feeding, we went in our shirt sleeves to a distant butte that promised a lookout. We forgot about the lateness till the sun got low. Even then I could have got back to camp, but clouds came up and darkness fell quickly. Knowing the general direction I kept on, and after half an hour's tramp we came to a cañon I had never seen before. I got out my compass and a match and found that I had been circling, as one is sure to do in the dark. I corrected the course and led off again. After another brief turn I struck another match and learned from the compass that I was again circling. This was discouraging, but with corrected course we again tramped. I was leading, and suddenly the dark ground ten feet ahead of me turned gray. I could not make it out, so went cautiously nearer. I lay down, reached forth, and then slowly made sure that we were on the edge of a steep precipice. I backed off, and frankly told the men I did not know where we were. I got out my match box and compass and found I had but one match left.

"Any of you got any matches?" I asked. "No; left 'em all in our coats," was their answer.

"Well," said I, "I have one. Shall I use it to get a new course from the compass, or shall we make a fire and stay here till morning?"

All voted to camp for the night. There was now a cold rain. We groped into a hollow where we got some dead wood, and by using our knives got some dry chips from the inside of a log. When all was ready we gathered close around, and I got out the one match. I was about to strike it when the younger of the men said:

"Say, Seton, you are not a smoker; Jack is. Hadn't you better give him that match?"

There was sense in this. I have never in my life smoked. Jack was an old stager and an adept with matches. I handed it to him. "*Rrrp-fizz*" — and in a minute we had a fire.

With the help of the firelight we now found plenty of dead wood; we made three blazing fires side by side, and after an hour we removed the centre one, then raked away all the hot ashes, and all lay down together on the warm ground. When the morning came the rain ceased. We stretched our stiffened limbs and made for camp. Yes, there it was in plain view two miles away across a fearful cañon. Three steps more on that gloomy night and we should have been over the edge of that cañon and dashed to the bottom.

How to Make Fire by Rubbing Sticks

"How do the Indians make a fire without matches?" asked a boy who loved to "play Indian." Most of us have heard the answer to this. "The Indians use a flint and steel, as our own fathers and mothers did one hundred years ago, and before they had flint and steel they used rubbing-sticks." We have all read about bringing fire out of two sticks by rubbing them together. I tried it once for an hour, and I know now I never would have got it in a thousand years as I was doing it. Others have had the same experience; consequently, most persons look upon this as a sort of fairy tale, or, if they believe it to be true, they think it so difficult as to be worth no second thought. All scouts, I find, are surprised and greatly interested to learn that not only is it possible, it is easy, to make a friction fire, if you know how; and hopeless, if you don't. I have taught many boys and men (including some Indians) to do it, and some have grown so expert that they make it nearly as quickly as with an old-fashioned sulphur match. When I first learned from Walter Hough, who learned from the Indians, it took me from five to ten minutes to get a blazing fire — not half an hour, as some books have it. But later I got it down to a minute, then to thirty-one seconds from the time of taking up the rubbing-sticks to having a fine blaze, the time in getting the first spark being about six seconds.

My early efforts were inspired by book accounts of Indian methods, but, unfortunately, I have never yet seen a book account that was accurate enough to guide any one successfully in the art of fire-making. All omit one or other of the absolute essentials, or dwell on some triviality. The impression they leave on those who know is that the writers did not.

The surest and easiest method of making a friction fire is by use of the bow-drill. Two sticks, two tools, and some tinder are needed.

The two sticks are the drill and the fire-board, or fire-block. The books generally tell us that these must be of different kinds of wood. This is a mistake. I have uniformly gotten the best results with two pieces of the same kind — all the better, indeed, if they are parts of the same stick.

What Kind of Wood

This is a very important question, as woods that are too hard, too soft, too wet, too oily, too gummy, or too resinous will not produce fire. The wood should be soft enough to wear away, else it produces no punk, and hard enough to wear slowly, or the heat is not enough to light the punk, and, of course, it should be highly inflammable. Those that I have had the best luck with are balsam fir, cottonwood roots, tamarack, European larch, red cedar, white cedar, Oregon cedar, basswood, cypress, and sometimes second-growth white pine. It should always be a dry, sound stick, brash, but not in the least punky.

In each part of the country there seems to be a kind of wood well suited for fire-making. The Eastern Indians used cedar; the Northern Indians, cedar or balsam fir; the plains Indians used cottonwood or sage-brush roots.

Perhaps the most reliable of all is dry and seasoned balsam fir; either the species in the North woods or in the Rockies will do. It gives a fine big spark or coal in about seven seconds.

When in the grinding the dust that runs out of the notch is coarse and brown, it means that the wood is too soft; when it is very fine and scanty it means that the wood is too hard.

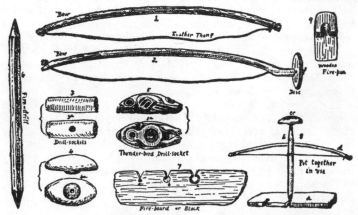

The rubbing-sticks for fire-making

1. The simplest kind of bow; a bent stick with a stout leather thong fastened at each end. It is about 27 inches long and ⅝ inch thick.

2. A more elaborate bow with a hole at each end for the thong. At the handle end it goes through a disc of wood. This is to tighten the thong by pressure of the hand against the disc while using.

3. Simplest kind of drill-socket; a pine or hemlock knot with a shallow hole or pit in it. 3a is under view of same. It is about 4½ inches long.

4. A more elaborate drill-socket; a pebble cemented with gum in a wooden holder. 4a is under view of same.

5. A very elaborate drill-socket; it is made of tulip wood, carved to represent the Thunderbird. It has eyes of green felspar cemented in with resin. On the under side (5a) is seen, in the middle, a soapstone socket let into the wood and fastened with pine gum, and on the head a hole kept filled with grease, to grease the top of the drill before use.

6. The drill; 12 to 18 inches long and about ¾ inch thick; it is roughly eight-sided so the thong will not slip, and pointed at each end. The best wood for the drill is old, dry brash, but not punky, balsam fir or cottonwood roots; but basswood, white cedar, red cedar, tamarack, and sometimes even white pine, will do.

7. Fire-board or block; about ¾ inch thick and any length handy; a is notch with pit just begun, b shows the pit after once using and in good trim for second time, c shows the pit bored through and now useless; the notch is ½ inch wide and ¾ inch deep.

8. Shows the way of using the sticks. The block (a) is held down with one foot, the end of the drill (b) is put in the pit, the drill-socket (c) is held on top in left hand, one end of the bow (d) is held in the right hand, while the bow is drawn back and forth.

9. Is a little wooden fire-pan, not essential but convenient; its thin edge is put under the notch to catch the powder that falls.

I have made many experiments to determine whether there is anything in the idea that it is better to have the block and the drill of different woods.

But no hybrid combination was so successful as "two of a kind."

The drill and the bow and socket are fully described in the illustration.

The preparing of the fire-board is one of the most important things. At the edge cut a notch half an inch wide and about three fourths of an inch deep; at the top of this notch make a pit or shallow hole, and the board is ready. The importance of this notch is such that it is useless to try fire-making without it.

While these are the essentials, it is well to get ready, also, some *tinder*. I have tried a great many different kinds of lint and punk, including a number that were artificially prepared, soaked with saltpetre or other combustibles. But these are not really fair play. The true woodcrafter limits himself to the things that he can get in the woods, and in all my recent fire-making I have contented myself with the tinder used for ages by the red men: that is, cedar wood finely shredded between two stones. Some use the fringes that grow on birch, improving it by rubbing in powdered charcoal.

Now that he has the tools and material ready, it will be an easy matter for the matchless castaway to produce a fire.

Pass the leather thong once around the drill — and this should make the thong taut; put the lower point of the drill in the pit at the top of the notch in the fire-board, and hold the socket with the left hand on top of the drill. The notch of the fire-board should be resting on a chip or thin wooden tray. Hold the bow by the handle end in the right hand, steady the board under the left foot, and the left arm against the left knee. Now draw the bow back and forth with steady, even strokes, its full length. This causes the drill to turn in the pit and bore into the wood; ground-up wood runs out of the side of the notch, falling on the chip or tray. At first it is brown; in two or three seconds it turns black, and then smokes; in five or six seconds it is giving off a cloud of smoke. A few more vigorous strokes of the bow, and now it will be found that smoke still comes from the pile of black wood-dust on the chip. Fan this gently with the hand; the smoke increases, and in a few seconds you see a glowing coal in the middle of the dust. (There are never any visible flying sparks.)

Now take a liberal pinch of the cedar tinder — about a teaspoonful; wrap this in some bark fibre or shredded rope to keep it from blowing away. Hold it down on the coal, and, lifting tray and all, blow or fan it until in a few seconds it blazes. Carefully pile over it the shreds of birch bark or splinters of fat pine prepared beforehand, and the fire is made.

If you have the right wood and still cannot get the fire, it is likely because you do not hold the drill steady, or have not cut the side notch quite into the middle point of the little fire pit.

The advantages of learning this method are threefold:

First : Fire-making by friction is an interesting experiment in woodcraft.

Second: A boy is better equipped having learned it. He can never afterward freeze to death for lack of matches if he has wood and an old shoe lace.

Third: For the very reason that it is difficult, compared with matches, it tends to prevent the boys making unnecessary fires, and thus reduces the danger of their setting the woods ablaze or of smoking the forbidden cigarette.

There is such a fascination in making the rubbing-stick fire that one of my Western cooks, becoming an expert, gave up the use of matches for a time and lit his morning fire with the fire-drill, and, indeed, he did not find it much slower than the usual way.

Walter Hough told me a story of an Apache Indian who scoffed at the matches of white men, and claimed that he could light a fire with rubbing-sticks faster than Hough could with matches. So each made ready. They were waiting for the word "go" when the Indian said:

"Wait. I see if him right." He gave a few strokes with the drill, and called —"Stop — stop him no good." He rearranged the sticks, and tried a few more strokes. Just as Mr. Hough was going to strike the match, he said: "Stop — stop — him no good." He did this three times before he called "Ready." Then the word "Go" was given. The white man struck the slow, sizzling match. The Indian gave half a dozen twirls to the drill — the smoke burst forth. He covered it with the tinder, fanned a few seconds, then a bright flame arose, just before the white man got his twigs ablaze. So the Indian won, but it was by an Indian trick; for the three times when he pretended to be trying it, he was really warming up the wood — that is, doing a large part of the work. I am afraid that, deft as he was, he would have lost in a fair race. Yet this incident shows at least that, in point of speed, the old rubbing-sticks are not very far behind the matches, as one might have supposed.

It is, indeed, a wonder that the soldiers at West Point are not taught this simple trick, when it is so easily learned, and might some day be the one thing to save the lives of many of them.

Archery

No woodcraft education is complete without a knowledge of archery. It is a pity that this noble sport has fallen into disuse. We shall find it essential to some of our best games.

The modern hunting gun is an irresistible weapon of wholesale murder, and is just as deadly no matter who pulls the trigger. It spreads terror as well as death by its loud discharge, and it leaves little clew as to who is responsible for the shot. Its deadly range is so fearfully great as to put all game at the mercy of the clumsiest tyro. Woodcraft, the oldest of all sciences and one of the best, has steadily declined since the coming of the gun, and it is entirely due to this same unbridled power that America has lost so many of her fine game animals.

The bow is a far less destructive weapon, and to succeed at all in the chase the bowman must be a double-read forester. The bow is silent and it sends the arrow with exactly the same power that the bowman's arm puts into it — no more, no less — so it is really his own power that speeds the arrow. There is no question as to which hunter has the right to the game or is responsible for the shot when the arrow is there to tell. The gun stands for little skill, irresistible force supplied from an outside source, overwhelming unfair odds, and sure death to the victim. The bow, on the other hand, stands for all that is clever and fine in woodcraft; so, no guns or fire-arms of any kind are allowed in our boy scout camp.

The Indian's bow was short, because, though less efficient, it was easier to carry than a long one. Yet it did not lack power. It is said that the arrow head sometimes appeared on the far side of the buffalo it was fired into, and there is a tradition that Wah-na-tah, a Sioux chief, once shot his arrow through a cow buffalo and killed her calf that was running at the other side.

But the long bow is more effective than the short one. The old English bowmen, the best the world has ever seen, always shot with the long bow.

The finest bows and arrows are those made by the professional makers, but there is no reason why each boy should not make his own.

According to several authorities the best bow woods are mulberry, osage-orange, sassafras, Southern cedar, black locust, apple, black walnut, slippery elm, ironwood, mountain ash, hickory, California yew, and hemlock.

Take a perfectly sound, straight, well-seasoned stick five or six feet long (your bow should be about as long as yourself); mark off a five-inch space in the middle for the handle; leave this round and a full inch thick; shave down the rest, flat on one side for the front and round on the other for the back, until it is about one inch wide and three fourths of an inch thick next the handle, tapering to about one half that at the ends, which are then "nocked," nicked, or notched as shown in Cut I. These notches are for the string, which is to be put on early. Draw the bow now, flat side out, not more than the proper distance, and note carefully which end bends the most; then shave down the other side until it bends evenly. The middle scarcely bends at all. The perfect shape, when bent, is shown in Cut II. Trim the bow down to your strength and finish smoothly with sand-paper and glass. It should be straight when unstrung, and unstrung when not in use. Fancy curved bows are weak affairs. The bow for our boy should require a power of fifteen or twenty pounds (shown on a spring balance) to draw the string twenty-three inches from the bow; not more. The best string is of hemp or linen; it should be about five inches from the middle of the bow when strung (Cut II). The notches for the string should be two thirds the depth of the string. If you have not a bought string make one of strong, unbleached linen thread twisted together. At one end the string, which is heaviest at the ends, should be fast knotted to the bow notch (Cut V); at the other it should have a loop as shown in Cut IV. In the middle it should be lashed with fine silk and wax for five inches, and the exact place marked where the arrow fits it.

The arrow is more important than the bow. Any one can make a bow; few can make an arrow, for, as a Seminole Indian expressed it to Maurice Thompson, "Any stick do for bow; good arrow much heap work, ugh." Hiawatha went all the way to Dakota to see the famous arrow maker. In England when the bow was the gun of the country, the bow maker was called a "bowyer," and the arrow maker a "fletcher" (from the Norman *flèche*, an arrow). So when men began to use surnames those who excelled in arrow making were proud to be called the "Fletchers"; but to make a good bow was not a notable achievement, hence few took "Bowyer" as their name.

The first thing about an arrow is that it must be perfectly straight. "Straight as an arrow" refers to the arrow itself, not to its flight; that is always curved.

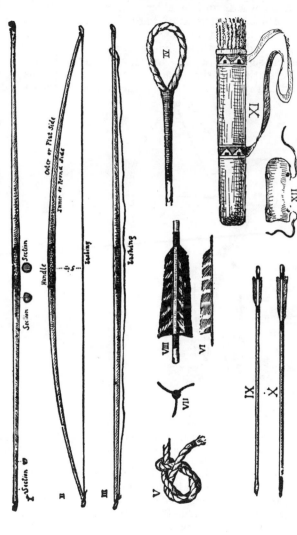

THE ARCHERY OUTFIT (Not all on scale.)

I. The five-foot bow as finished, with sections at the point shown.
II. The bow "braced," or strung.
III. The bow unstrung, showing the loop slipped down.
IV. The loop that is used on the upper end of the bow.
V. The timber hitch always used on the lower end or notch of the bow.
VI. A turkey feather with split midrib, all ready to lash on.
VII. End view of arrow, showing notch and arrangement of three feathers.
VIII. Part of arrow, showing feathering and lashing.
IX. Sanger hunting arrow with wooden point; 25 inches long.
X. Sanger war arrow with nail point and extra long feathers; it also is 25 inches long.
XI. Quiver with Indian design; 30 inches long.
XII. The "bracer" or arm guard of heavy leather for left arm, with two laces to tie it on. It is six inches long.

The Indians made arrows of reeds and of straight shoots of viburnum or arrow-wood, and of elder, but we make better arrows out of the solid heartwood of hard pine for target use, and of hickory or ash for hunting. The arrow should be twenty-five inches long, round, and three eighths of an inch thick, and have three feathers set as shown in Cut VI, about an inch from the notch. The feather *B*, that stands out at right angles to notch *A*, should always be away from the bow in shooting.

CORRECT FORM IN SHOOTING
The diagram at bottom is to show the centres of heels in line with target

This is called the cock-feather, and it is usually marked or colored in some way to be quickly distinguished.

Turkey and goose wing feathers are the best that grow in our country for arrow feathers. The Indians mostly use turkey. With a sharp knife cut a strip of the midrib on which is the vane of the feather; make three pieces, each two to three inches long. White men glue these on to the arrow. The Indians leave the midrib projecting at each end and by these lash the feathers without gluing. The lashed feathers stand the weather better than those glued. but do not fly so well. The Indians use sharp flint arrow heads for war and for big game, but for birds and small game they make arrow heads with a knob of hard wood or the knuckle bone of some small animal. The best arrow heads for our purpose are like the ferrule of an umbrella top; they receive the end of the shaft into them and keep it from splitting.

One of the best arrows I ever shot with was twenty-eight inches long, five sixteenths of an inch thick, had a ferrule head and very small feathers.

The finishing touch of an arrow is "painting" it. This is done for several purposes: First, to preserve it from damp which would twist the arrow and soften the glue that holds the feathers; second, each hunter paints all his arrows with his mark so as to know them; third, they are thus made bright-colored to help in finding them when lost.

There are four other things required by our archer: A smooth, hard arm-guard, or bracer, usually of hard leather. The Indians who use one make it of wood, grass, or rawhide. In photographs of famous Indians you may often see this on the left wrist, and will remember that it was there as a protection from the blow of the bow cord. Some archers can shoot with the wrist bent so as to need no guard. The three middle fingers of the right hand also need protection. An old leather glove, with thumb and little finger cut away, will do very well for this, though the ready-made tips at the archery stores are more convenient. Some archers who practise all their lives can shoot without protecting the fingers.

The bow case and quiver are important. Any kind of a cover that will keep them from the rain, and hang on your back, will do, but there are many little things that help to make them handy. When the cover is off the arrows should project three or four inches so that they may be more easily drawn out. The Indians often carried very beautiful quivers of buckskin ornamented with quills and beads.

One day out West I saw an Omaha brave with a bow case and quiver covered with very odd material — a piece of common red and white cotton print. When allowed to examine it, I felt some other material underneath the print. After a little dickering he sold me bow, arrows, quiver, and all for a couple of dollars. I then ripped open the print and found my first suspicions confirmed; for, underneath, the quiver was of buckskin, beautifully embroidered with red feathers and porcupine quills of deep red and turquoise blue. The Indian was as much puzzled by my preference for the quill work as I was by his for the cotton print.

The standard target for men is four feet across with a nine-inch bull's-eye, and around that four rings, each four and three quarter inches wide. The bull's-eye counts nine, the other rings seven, five, three, one. The bought targets are made of straw, but a good target may be made of a box filled with sods, or a bank covered with sacking on which are painted the usual rings.

The archer's grip

Now comes the most important point of all— how to shoot. There are several ways of holding an arrow, but only one good one. Most boys know the ordinary finger and thumb pinch, or grip. This is all very well for a toy bow, but a hunter's bow cannot be drawn that way. No one has strength enough in his fingers for it. The true archer's grip of the arrow is shown in the cut. The thumb and little finger have nothing to do with it.

As in golf and all such things, there is a right "form." You attend to your end of the arrow's flight and the other will take care of itself.

Stand perfectly straight. Plant your feet with the centres of the two heels in line with the target. (Cut page 78.) Grasp the bow in the middle with the left hand and place the arrow on the string at the left side of the bow. Hold the bow plumb, and draw as above till the notch of the arrow is right under your eye, and the head of the arrow back to the bow. The right elbow must be in the same line with the arrow. Let go the arrow by straightening the fingers a little, turning the hand outward at the bottom and drawing it back one inch. Always do this in exactly the same way and your shooting will be even. Your left hand should not move a hair's breadth until the arrow strikes the target.

To begin shooting put the target very near, within fifteen or twenty yards; but the proper shooting distance when the archer is in good practice is forty yards for a four-foot target and thirty yards for a three-foot target. A good shot, shooting twelve arrows at this, should score fifty.

The Indians generally used their bows at short range, so that it was easy to hit the mark. Rapid firing was important. In their archery competitions, therefore, the prize was given to the one who could have the most arrows in the air at once. Their record, according to Catlin, was eight.

The Stars

As Seen With the Naked Eye

The chief works referred to in this are C. Flammarion's "Popular Astronomy" (Gore's translation), and Garrett P. Serviss's "Astronomy with an Opera Glass." (Those who wish to go farther a-sky are referred to these books.)

Whether he expects to use them as guides or not, every boy should learn the principal constellations and the important stars. A non-scientific friend said to me once: "I am always glad that I learned the principal star groups when I was young. I have never forgotten them, and, no matter in what strange country I find myself, I can always look up at night, and see the old familiar stars that shone on me in my home in my own country."

All American boys know the Dipper or Great Bear. This is, perhaps, the most important star group in our sky, because of its size, peculiar form, and the fact that it never sets in our latitude, and last, that it always points out the Pole-star, and, for this reason, it is sometimes known as the Pointers. It is called the Dipper because it is shaped like a dipper with a long, bent handle. Why it is called the Great Bear is not so easy to explain. The classical legend has it that the nymph Calisto, having violated her vow, was changed by Diana into a bear, which, after death, was immortalized in the sky by Zeus. Another suggestion is that the earliest astronomers, the Chaldeans, called these stars "the shining ones," and their word happened to be very like the Greek *arktos* (a bear). Another explanation (I do not know who is authority for either) is that vessels in olden days were named for animals, etc. They bore at the prow the carved effigy of the namesake, and if the *Great Bear*, for example, made several very happy voyages by setting out when a certain constellation was in the ascendant, that constellation might become known as the *Great Bear's* constellation. Certainly, there is nothing in its shape to justify the name. Very few of the constellations, indeed, are like the thing they are called after. Their names were usually given for some fanciful association with the namesake, rather than for resemblance to it.

The Pole-star is really the most important of the stars in our sky; it marks the north at all times; it alone is fixed in the heavens: all the other stars seem to swing around it once in twenty-four hours. It is in the end of the Little Bear's tail. But the Pole-star, or Polaris, is not a very bright one, and it would be hard to identify but for the help of the Dipper, or Pointers.

The outside (Alpha and Beta) of the Dipper points nearly to Polaris, at a distance equal to three and one half times the space that separates these two stars of the Dipper's outer side.

Various Indians call the Pole-star the "Home Star," and "The Star that Never Moves," and the Dipper they call the "Broken Back."

The last star but one in the Dipper, away from the pole — that is, the star at the bend of the handle, — is known to astronomers as Mizar, one of the Horses. Just above it, and tucked close in, is a smaller star known to astronomers as Alcor, or the Rider. The Indians call these two the "Old Squaw and the Pappoose on Her Back." In the old world, from very ancient times, these have been used as tests of eyesight. To be able to see Alcor with the naked eye means that one has excellent eyesight. So also on the plains, the old folks would ask the children at night, "Can you see the pappoose on the old squaw's back?" And when the youngster saw it, and proved that he did by a right description, they rejoiced that he had the eyesight which is the first requisite of a good hunter.

The Great Bear is also to be remembered as the Pointers for another reason. It is the hour-hand of the woodman's clock. It goes once around the North Star in about twenty-four hours, the same way as the sun, and for the same reason — that it is the earth that is going and leaving them behind.

The time in going around is not exactly twenty-four hours, so that the position of the Pointers varies with the seasons, but, as a rule, this for woodcraft purposes is near enough. The bowl of the Dipper swings one and one half times the width of the opening (*i.e.*, fifteen degrees) in one hour. If it went a quarter of the circle, that would mean you had slept a quarter of a day, or six hours.

Each fifteen days the stars seem to be an hour earlier; in three months they gain one fourth of the circle, and in a year gain the whole circle.

According to Flammarion, there are about seven thousand stars visible to the naked eye, and of those but nineteen are stars of the first magnitude. Thirteen of them are visible in the latitude of New York, the other six belong to the South Polar Region of the sky. Here is Flammarion's arrangement of them in order of seeming brightness. Those that can be seen in the Southern Hemisphere only, are in brackets:

1. Sirius, the Dog-star.
2. [Canopus, of Argo.]
3. [Alpha, of the Centaur.]
4. Arcturus, of Boötes.
5. Vega, of the Lyre.
6. Rigel, of Orion's foot.
7. Capella, of Auriga.
8. Procyon, or the Little Dog-star.
9. Betelguese, of Orion's right shoulder.
10. [Beta, of the Centaur.]
11. [Achernar, of Eridanus.]
12. Aldebaran, of Taurus, the Bull's right eye.
13. Antares, of Scorpio.
14. [Alpha, of the Southern Cross.]
15. Altair, of the Eagle.
16. Spica, of Virgo.
17. Fomalhaut, of the Southern Fish.
18. [Beta, of the Southern Cross.]
19. Regulus, of the Lion.

Orion

Orion (O-ri-on), with its striking array of brilliant stars, Betelguese, Rigel, the Three Kings, etc., is generally admitted to be the finest constellation in the heavens.

Orion was the hunter giant who went to Heaven when he died, and now marches around the great dome, but is seen only in the winter, because, during the summer, he passes over during daytime. Thus he is still the hunter's constellation. The three stars of his belt are called the "Three Kings."

Sirius, the Great Dog-star, is in the head of Orion's hound, and following farther back is the Little Dog-star, Procyon.

In old charts of the stars, Orion is shown with his hound,
hunting the bull, Taurus.

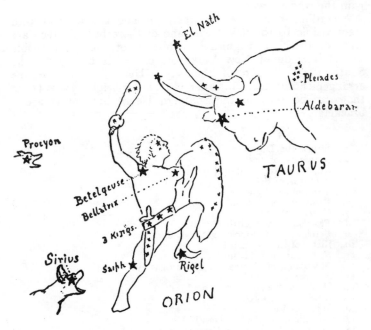

Pleiades

Pleiades (Ply-a-des) can be seen in winter as a cluster of
small stars between Aldebaran and Algol, or, a line drawn from
the back bottom, through the front rim of the Dipper, about
two Dipper lengths, touches this little group.   They are not
far from Aldebaran, being on the shoulder of the Bull, of which
Aldebaran is the right eye.   They may be considered the seven
arrow wounds made by Orion.   They are nearer the Pole-star
than Aldebaran is, and on the side away from the Dipper; also,
they are nearly on a line between Beta of the Dipper (front
bottom) and Capella.

Serviss tells us that the Pleiades have a supposed connection
with the Great Pyramid, because "about 2170 B. C., when the
beginning of spring coincided with the culmination of the
Pleiades at midnight, that wonderful group of stars was visible

just at midnight, through the mysterious southward-pointing passage of the Pyramid."

The Moon

The moon is one fifth the diameter of the earth, about one fiftieth of the bulk, and is about a quarter million miles away. Its course, while very irregular, is nearly the same as the apparent course of the sun. But "in winter the full moon is at an altitude in the sky near the limit attained by the sun in summer, . . . and even, at certain times, five degrees higher. It is the contrary in summer, a season when the moon remains very low" (F.).

The moon goes around the earth in $27\frac{1}{4}$ days. It loses nearly three fourths of an hour each night; that is, it rises that much later.

BIRDCRAFT

By the National Association of Audubon Societies

Any boy who cares enough for out-doors to be a scout is sure to want a good acquaintance with the birds. Even dull people cannot help taking notice of our "little brothers of the air," on account of their beauty, their songs, and their wondrous flight. But most folks never take the trouble to try and learn the names of any except a few common birds. Scouts whose eyes are sharp and ears are keen will find the study of birds a fascinating sport, which may prove to be the best fun that the woods provide.

Knowing the Birds

It is no easy matter, this trying to get to know the birds; but scouts are not looking for the easiest jobs, and it is great sport for them to follow some shy songster through the briery thicket until a really good look can be had, to sit stock still for half an hour to watch some unknown bird come home to her nest, or to wriggle on all fours through the grass to have a glimpse over the top of the knoll at the ducks in the pool beyond.

The only equipment necessary for bird study is an opera or field glass, a note-book and a good bird reference book. As soon as you get a good look at a strange bird, notice its colors and markings, and then, if it moves, follow it up until you have seen practically all of its most prominent features. It will be impossible to carry these facts in your head, and unless some definite memorandum is made at the time you will probably be hopelessly perplexed when you go to consult the bird book later. As it is hard to jot down satisfactory notes in the field, while catching fleeting glances of some timid bird, a handy little booklet has been prepared in which observations can be recorded very rapidly. These can be procured for fifteen cents apiece from the National Association of Audubon Societies, 1974 Broadway, New York City.

Location_____

Date_____ Hour_____

Weather_____ Wind_____

SIZE:

Smaller than wren

Between wren and sparrow

Between sparrow and robin

Between robin and crow

Larger than crow

SEEN

Near ground or high up

In heavy woods

Bushy places

Orchard

Garden

Swamp

Open country

Near water

Name_____

Order_____ Family_____

Genus_____ Species_____

Each booklet contains outline figures of the five leading types of birds: (1) small perching birds, (2) hawks, (3) snipes, (4) herons, (5) ducks. On the page opposite is a list of numbers corresponding to colors. You can quickly mark on the outline the proper numbers, and note with your pencil any marks on the bird. Then check the other data on the page, add any additional memoranda, and you have your "bird in the hand," ready to take back and look up at your leisure.

Careful Observation

Notice particularly the "range" of the birds in your reference book, and eliminate all those not stated as occurring in your territory. Notice too, dates of the birds' coming and going, and do not expect to find species at any other time of year than within the dates mentioned. By thus narrowing down the possibilities the task is much simplified. As a final resort, the National Association of Audubon Societies stands ready to help all scouts who are positively "stumped," and if the descriptive slips are mailed with return envelopes to the secretary of the association, 1974 Broadway, New York City, an identification will be made, if the information furnished renders it in any way possible.

The next time you see a bird that you have once identified, you will probably remember its name, and in this way you will be surprised to find how rapidly your bird acquaintance will grow. After a time even the flight of a bird or its song will be enough to reveal an old acquaintance, just as you can often recognize a boy friend by his walk or the sound of his voice, without seeing his face. And what a new joy in life there is for anybody that really knows the birds about him. He can pick from the medley of bird songs the notes of the individual singers; he knows when to look for old friends of the year before; no countryside is ever lonely for him, for he finds birds everywhere and knows that any moment he may make some rare discovery or see a bird before unknown to him.

Bird Lists

A scout should make a list of all the birds he has positively identified. This is his "life list" and is added to year by year. In addition he will keep daily lists of the birds seen on special trips in the field. Two or more patrols can enjoy a friendly rivalry by covering different regions and seeing which can observe the largest variety of birds. Hundreds of well-known ornithologists often have the fun of this kind of competition, sending in their lists to a central bureau. As many as one hundred and twenty different kinds of birds have been counted in a single day by one energetic band of bird-lovers. Such a list is, however, attainable only under exceptionally favorable circumstances and by skilled observers who know their country

Bob-white at feeding station

thoroughly. For most scouts, thirty to forty species on a summer day, and fifty to sixty during the spring migration, would be regarded as a good list.

Nesting Season

Undoubtedly the most interesting season to study birds is during the nesting period which is at its height in June. It takes a pair of sharp eyes to find most birds' nests in the first place, and once found, there are dozens of interesting little incidents which it is a delight to watch. Only a foolish scout would rob himself of his chance to observe the secrets of nest life by stealing the contents, or would take any delight in piling up a collection of egg shells whose value at its best is almost nothing, and whose acquisition is necessarily accompanied by genuine heart pangs on the part of the rightful owners. It is more exciting to try to hide yourself near the nest so skilfully that the birds will carry on their domestic duties as though you were not near. A blind made of green cloth and set up near the nest like a little tent will often give opportunity for very close observation. It is surprising how near many birds will allow one to come in this way. Even though the blind looks very strange and out of place, the birds soon seem to get used to it, so long as it is motionless and the inmate cannot be seen. A simple type of blind can be constructed by sewing the edges of long pieces of green cloth together, drawing in the top with a cord, and then draping it over an open umbrella.

How to Photograph

From such a hiding place, photographs can often be secured of timid birds at their nests. In attempting to take photo-

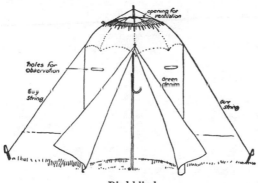

Bird blind

graphs it must be remembered that cameras of the pocket variety or fixed box type are almost useless. Most of them cannot be worked without special attachments at closer range than six feet, and, even if the focus is correctly guessed, the image is apt to be very small. In this work it is far better to invest in a cheap camera (second-hand if need be) with which one can obtain a definite image on the ground glass where the plate or film is to be. Focus the camera on some spot where it is expected the bird will come; usually this is on the nest or young, sometimes it is the food, a favorite perch, or some form of decoy. The next requisite is patience. If the coveted opportunity arrives, set off the shutter by hand in the blind, or, where this is not possible, by means of a long thread, after carefully hiding the camera with boughs, leaves, sods, etc.

How to Know

An idea of the details of a bird's life which a scout may come to know, may be had from the following table:

1. Description. (Size, form, color, and markings.)
2. Haunts. (Upland, lowland, lakes, rivers, woods, fields, etc.)
3. Movements. (Slow or active, hops, walks, creeps, swims, tail wagged, etc.)
4. Appearance. (Alert, listless, crest erect, tail drooped, etc.)
5. Disposition. (Solitary, flocking, wary, unsuspicious, etc.)
6. Flight. (Slow, rapid, direct, undulating, soaring, sailing, flapping, etc.)
7. Song. (Pleasing, unattractive, long, short, loud, faint, sung from the ground, from a perch, in the air, etc. Season of song.)
8. Call notes. (Of surprise, alarm, protest, warning, signaling, etc.)
9. Season. (Spring, fall, summer, winter, with times of arrival and departure in numbers.)
10. Food. (Berries, insects, seeds, etc.; how secured.)
11. Mating. (Habits during courtship.)
12. Nesting. (Choice of site, material, construction, eggs, incubation, etc.)
13. The young. (Food and care of, time in the nest, notes, actions, flight, etc.)

So varied is a bird's life that there is still plenty to be learned about even our common birds. It is quite possible for a scout to discover some facts that have never yet been published in books.

What One Boy Did

Red-breasted nuthatch

A boy once originated the idea of varying the usual "bird's nesting" craze into a systematic study of the breeding of our common birds. In one spring he found within the limits of a single village one hundred and seventy robins' nests. 'One hundred were in suitable situations on private places, forty-one were in woods, swamps and orchards, eight were placed under bridges (two being under the iron girders of the railroad bridge), four were in quarries, sixteen were in barns, sheds, under piazzas, etc., and one was on the ground at the foot of a bush."

In addition to searching out the birds in their natural haunts, there is a great fascination in trying to attract them to our homes. During winter evenings boy scouts can busy themselves making nesting boxes. Even an old cigar box or a tomato can with a hole in it the size of a quarter will satisfy a house wren. Other boxes which are suitable for bluebirds, chickadees, tree swallows, purple martins, and starlings, will, if set up in March, often have tenants the very first season. In many cases it is feasible to have hinged doors or sides on the nesting boxes, so that they may occasionally be opened and the progress of events within observed. It is needless to add, however,

Downy woodpecker

that great caution must be exercised to prevent desertion of the nest, or other disturbance of the birds' home life. Under favorable circumstances, even some of the shyer inhabitants of the woods, such as woodpeckers, owls, and ducks can be induced to patronize artificial cavities, if they are made right and erected right.

Caring for Birds

Another way of attracting birds in summer is by providing drinking and bathing places. A little artificial pool protected from cats, will be a source of joy to the birds and of delight to the observer from morning to night. Apply to the

Observation box, open

National Association of Audubon Societies for information as to where ready-made nest boxes and fountains can be procured, also books on this subject, as well as on the subject of making friends of the birds through feeding.

House wren and tomato-can house

The Bird Lunch Counter

How best to feed the birds is almost an art in itse f. A winter lunch counter spread with suet, nuts, hemp seed, meat, and crumbs will attract nuthatches, chickadees, downy and hairy woodpeckers, creepers, blue jays, etc. Canary seed, buckwheat, oats and haychaff scattered on the ground beneath will provide an irresistible banquet for other feathered boarders. A feeding place of this sort can be arranged for convenient observation from a window, and afford no end of diversion and instruction. But whether close to home or far afield, the great secret of success in such work is regularity. Begin to put the food out early in November, and let the birds get to know that they are always sure to find a supply of dainties in a certain spot, and the news will soon spread among them. In wintry weather, especially, it is amazing what can be accomplished by feeding the birds regularly, and at least the following birds have been induced to feed from the human hand: chickadee, white-breasted nuthatch, red-breasted nuthatch, brown creeper, Carolina wren, cardinal, evening grosbeak, tufted titmouse, Canada jay, Florida jay, Oregon jay, and redpoll. Even in spring untiring patience has resulted in the gratification of this supreme ambition of the bird-lover, and bluebird, robin, cat-bird, chipping sparrow, ovenbird, brown thrasher and yellow-throated vireo have been known to feed from the hand of a trusted friend, even with plenty of food all around. What scout can add to this list?

Birch-bark house

Protecting the Birds

Many a boy thinks that just because a bird is alive and moves it is a proper target for his air rifle or his sling shot.

Let us be thankful that there has now arisen a new class of boys, the scouts, who, like the knights of old, are champions of the defenceless, even the birds. Scouts are the birds' police, and wo betide the lad who is caught with a nest and eggs, or the limp corpse of some feathered songster that he has slaughtered. Scouts know that there is no value in birds that are shot, except a few scientific specimens collected by trained museum experts. Scouts will not commend a farmer for shooting a hawk or an owl as a harmful bird, even though it were seen to capture a young chicken. They will post themselves on the subject and find that most hawks and owls feed chiefly on field mice and large insects injurious to the farmer's crops, and that thus, in spite of an occasional toll on the poultry, they are as a whole of tremendous value. The way the birds help mankind is little short of a marvel. A band of nuthatches worked all winter in a pear orchard near Rochester and rid the trees of a certain insect that had entirely de-

White-breasted nuthatch

stroyed the crop of the previous summer. A pair of rose-breasted grosbeaks were seen to feed their nest of youngsters four hundred and twenty-six times in a day, each time with a billful of potato-bugs or other insects. A professor in Washington counted two hundred and fifty tent caterpillars in the stomach of a dead yellow-billed cuckoo, and, what appeals to us even more, five hundred bloodthirsty mosquitoes inside of one night-hawk.

Bluebird at entrance of nesting-box

It must not be forgotten that large city parks are among the best places for observing birds. As an example of what can be accomplished, even with limited opportunities, there was a boy who happened to know where some owls roosted.

Now all owls swallow their prey whole, and in digesting this food they disgorge the skulls, bones, fur, and feathers in the form of hard dry pellets. This boy used to go out on Saturday or Sunday afternoon and bring home his pockets full of pellets, and then in the evening he would break them apart. In this way he learned exactly what the owls had been eating (without killing them) and he even discovered the skulls of certain field mice that naturalists had never known existed in that region. He let the owl be his collector.

Patrol Work

It is a good idea to keep at patrol headquarters a large sheet on the wall, where a list of the year's bird observations can be tabulated. Each time a new bird is seen, its name is added, together with the initial of the observer, and after that its various occurrences are noted opposite its name. The keenest eyed scouts are those whose initials appear most frequently in the table In addition, the tables will show the appearance and relative abundance of birds in a given locality. For patrols of young boys, a plan of tacking up a colored picture of each bird, as soon as it is thoroughly known, has been found very successful, and the result provides a way to decorate the headquarters.

Such pictures can be obtained very cheaply from the Perry Pictures Co., Boston, Mass., or the National Association of Audubon Societies, 1974 Broadway, New York City.

MOLLUSCA—Shells and Shellfish

By Dr. William Healey Dall, of the United States Geological Survey

Among the shy and retiring animals which inhabit our woods and waters, or the borders of the sea, without making themselves conspicuous to man except when he seeks the larger ones for food, are the mollusca, usually confounded with crabs and crayfish under the popular name of "shellfish," except the few which have no external shell, which are generally called slugs. Hardly any part of the world (except deserts) is without them, but, shy as they are, it takes pretty sharp eyes to find them. Some come out of their hiding places

FIG. 1
White lipped snail
(*Polygyra albolabris*)

only at night, and nearly all our American kinds live under cover of some sort.

The mollusks can be conveniently divided into three groups: those which inhabit fresh water, those which breathe air and live on dry land, and lastly those which are confined to the sea. The land shells, or snails, have generally thin shells of spiral form and live upon vegetable matter, many of them laying small eggs which look like minute pearls. Their hiding places are under leaves in shady or moist places, under the bark of dead trees or stumps, or under loose stone. They creep slowly and are most active after rain. Some of our larger kinds are an inch or two in diameter, (see Fig. 1., the white-lipped) but from this size there are others diminishing in size to the smallest, which are hardly larger than the head of a pin. In collecting them the little ones may be allowed to dry up. The big ones must be killed in boiling water, when the animal can be pulled out with a hook made of a crooked pin, leaving the shell clean and perfect. The slugs are not attractive on account of the slime which they throw out and can

Fig. 2

Whelk (*Buccinum undatum*)

only be kept in spirits. Some of the species found in California are as large as a small cigar, but those of the states east of the Rocky Mountains are smaller and have mostly been introduced from Europe, where they do a lot of mischief by eating such garden plants as lettuce.

Many of the fresh-water snails are abundant in brooks and ponds, and their relations, the fresh-water mussels, are often very numerous in shallow rivers. They have a shell frequently beautifully pearly, white or purple, and sometimes have the brown outer skin prettily streaked with bright green.

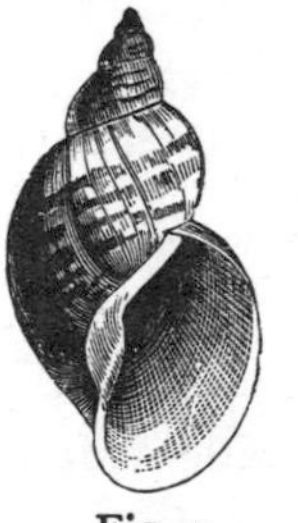

Fig. 3

Pond snail (*Lymnæa palustris*)

The principal fresh-water snails are the pond snail (*Lymnaea;* see Fig. 3); the *Physa* (see Fig. 6), which is remarkable for having the coil turned to the left instead of the right; and the orb-snail, (*Planorbis:* see Fig. 4) which has its coil flat. All of these lay minute eggs in a mass of transparent jelly, and are to be found on lily pads and other water plants, or crawling on the bottom, while the mussels bury themselves more or less in the mud or lie on the gravelly bottom of streams.   There is also a very numerous tribe of small bivalve shells, varying from

half an inch to very minute in size, which are also mud lovers and are known as *Sphærium* or *Pisidium*, having no "common" English names, since only those who hunt for them know of their existence.

On the seashore everybody knows the mussel (*Mytilus:* see Fig. 5), the soft clam, the round clam, and the oyster, as these are sought for food; but there is a multitude of smaller bivalves which are not so well known. The sea-snails best known on the coast north of Chesapeake Bay are the whelk (*Buccinum:* see Fig. 2), the sand snail or *Natica*, which bores the round holes often found in clam

Fig. 4
Orb-Shell (*Planorbis trivolvis*

shells on the beach, in order to suck the juices of its neighbors, and the various kinds of periwinkles (rock snails or *Littorina*) found by the millions on the rocks between tides. These, as well as the limpets, small boat-shaped or

Fig. 5
Black mussel (*Mytilus*)

slipper-shaped conical shells found in similar places, are vegetable feeders.   Altogether, there are several hundred

kinds found on the seashore and the water near the shore, and a collection of them will not only contain many curious, pretty, and interesting things, but will have the advantage of requiring no preservative to keep them in good condition after the animal has been taken out.

Fig. 6
Bubble snail
(*Physa heterostropha*)

The squids, cuttle-fishes, octopus, and their allies are also mollusks, but not so accessible to the ordinary collector, and can only be kept in spirits.

Books which may help the collector to identify the shells he may find are:

For the land and fresh-water shells:

"Mollusks of the Chicago Area" and "The Lymnæidæ of North America."
By F. C. Baker. Published by the Chicago Academy of Sciences.

For the American Marine Shells:

Bulletin No. 37. Published by the United States National Museum,
at Washington.

For shells in general:

"The Shell Book." Published by Doubleday, Page & Co., Garden City,
N. Y.

On the Pacific Coast the "West Coast Shells," by Prof.
Josiah Keep of Mills College, will be found very useful.

REPTILES

By Dr. Leonhard Stejneger, Curator National Museum

By reptiles we understand properly a certain class of verte-
brate or backboned animals, which, on the whole, may be
described as possessing scales or horny shields since most of
them may be distinguished by this outer covering, as the
mammals by their hair and the birds by their feathers. Such
animals as thousand-legs, scorpions, tarantulas, etc., though
often erroneously referred to as reptiles, do not concern us in
this connection. Among the living reptiles we distinguish
four separate groups, the crocodiles, the turtles, the lizards,
and the snakes.

The crocodiles resemble lizards in shape, but are very much
larger and live only in the tropics and the adjacent regions of the
temperate zone. To this order belongs our North American
alligator, which inhabits the states bordering the Gulf of Mexico
and the coast country along the Atlantic Ocean as far north
as North Carolina. They are hunted for their skin, which
furnishes an excellent leather for traveling bags, purses, etc.,
and because of the incessant pursuit are now becoming quite
rare in many localities where formerly they were numerous.
The American crocodile, very much like the one occurring in
the river Nile, is also found at the extreme southern end of
Florida.

The turtles are easily recognized by the bony covering which
encases their body, and into which most species can withdraw
their heads and legs for protection. This bony box is usually
covered with horny plates, but in a large group, the so-called
soft-shell turtles, the outer covering is a soft skin, thus forming a

notable exception to the rule that reptiles are characterized by being covered with scales or plates. While most of the turtles live in fresh water or on land, a few species pass their lives in the open ocean, only coming ashore during the breeding season to deposit their eggs. Some of these marine turtles grow to an enormous size, sometimes reaching a weight of over eight hundred pounds. One of them is much sought for on account of the delicacy of its flesh; another because of the thickness and beauty of its horny plates which furnish the so-called tortoise-shell, an important article of commerce. Turtles appear to reach a very old age, specimens having been known to have lived several hundred years. The box tortoise of our woods, the musk turtles, the snapping turtles are familiar examples of this order, while the terrapin, which lives in brackish ponds and swamps along our sea-coasts, is famous as a table delicacy.

The lizards are four-legged reptiles, usually of small size, living on the ground or in the trees, but very rarely voluntarily entering water. The so-called water lizards are not lizards at all, but belong to the salamanders and are distinguished by having a naked body not covered with scales. Most of the true lizards are of very graceful form, exceedingly quick at

Harlequin snake

running; others display the most gorgeous coloration which, in many of them, such as the chameleons, changes according to the light, or the temperature, or the mood of the animal. Not all of them have four legs, however, there being a strong tendency to develop legless species which then externally become so much like snakes that they are told apart with some difficulty. Thus our so-called glass-snake, common in the Southern states, is not a snake at all, but a lizard, as we may easily see by observing the ear openings on each side of the head, as no snake has ears. This beautiful animal is also known as the joint-snake, and both names have reference to the exceeding brittleness of its long tail, which often breaks in many pieces in the hands of the enemy trying to capture the lizard. That these pieces ever join and heal together is of course a silly fable. As a matter of fact, the body in a comparatively short time grows a new tail, which, however, is much shorter and stumpier than the old one. The new piece is often of a different color from the rest of the body and greatly resembles a "horn," being conical and pointed, and has thus given rise to another equally silly fable, *viz.*, that of the horn snake, or hoop snake, which is said to have a sting in its tail and to be deadly poisonous. The lizards are all perfectly harmless, except the sluggish Gila monster (pronounced Heela, named from the Gila River in Arizona) which lives in the deserts of Arizona and Mexico, and whose bite may be fatal to man. The poison glands are situated at the point of the lower jaw, and the venom is taken up by the wound while the animal hangs on to its victim with the tenacity of a bulldog. All the other lizards are harmless in spite of the dreadful stories told about the deadly quality of some of the species in various parts of the country.

The snakes form the last group of the reptiles. Universally legless, though some of the boas and pythons have distinct outer rudiments of hind limbs, they are not easily mistaken. And it is perhaps well so, for unless one is an expert at distinguishing between the poisonous and the harmless kind it is just as well to keep at a respectful distance from them. It is safest not to interfere with them, especially as those that are not poisonous are usually very useful in destroying rats and mice and other vermin, except perhaps those living in trees and feeding on eggs and young birds, which certainly do not deserve our protection. Of course the rattlesnake is not to be mistaken.

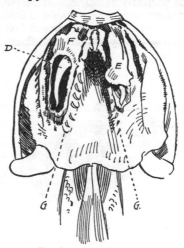

Rattlesnake palate

The horny appendix to its tail, with which it sounds the warning of its presence, is enough to distinguish it. It should here be explained that both lizards and snakes at various intervals shed the outer layer of their skin, the so-called epidermis. This transparent layer, after a certain length of time, loosens and is usually stripped off whole by the animal crawling out of it and turning it inside out, as a tight glove is turned. Now, at the end of a rattlesnake's tail there is a horny cap which is called the button, and being narrowed at the base and more strongly built than the rest of the epidermis it is not shed with the rest of the skin, but remains attached. Thus for each shedding a new joint or ring is added to the rattle. How often the shedding takes place depends on various circumstances and may occur an uncertain number of times each year. Such a rattle, loose-jointed as it is, is rather brittle and the tip of the sounding instrument is easily broken and lost. It will therefore be easily understood that the common notion that a rattlesnake's age can be told by the number of the rings in its rattle is absolutely erroneous. Another equally common and equally erroneous notion relates to the tongue of the snake, which the ignorant often term its "sting" and which they believe to be the death-dealing instrument. Of course, the soft, forked tongue which constantly darts out and in of the snake's mouth is perfectly harmless. It serves rather as a "feeler" than as a taste organ. The wound is inflicted by a pair of large, curved, teeth or fangs, in the upper jaw. These fangs are hollow and connected by a duct with the gland on the side of the head, in which the poison is formed. Pressure on this gland at the time

Copperhead

of the strike—for our poisonous snakes strike rather than bite — squirts the poison into the wound like a hypodermic syringe. The fangs when shed or damaged are replaced within a short time with new ones, so that a poisonous snake can only be made harmless for a short period by breaking them off. Only in exceptional cases need snake bites prove fatal. It is estimated that in North America only about two persons in a hundred bitten are killed by the poison, though many more die from carelessness or bad treatment, *the worst of which is the filling up with whiskey, which aids the poison rather than counteracts it.* The essential things in case of snake bite are: (1) keeping one's wits; (2) tying a string, or the like, tightly around the wounded limb between the wound and the heart, and loosening it about once in fifteen minutes, so as to admit the poison slowly into the circulation; (3) making the wound bleed freely by enlarging it with a knife or otherwise; (4) if permanganate of potash be handy it should at once be applied to the wound; (5) treat the wound as antiseptically as it is possible with the means at hand and hurry to a doctor. The danger depends greatly on the amount of the poison injected, hence upon the size of the snake. It is for this reason that the big Florida rattlesnakes which grow to six feet and over are more to be feared than are other poisonous snakes. Of these, we have in our country, besides the rattlesnakes, the water moccasin, or cotton mouth, the copperhead, and

Water moccasin

the coral snake. The latter is a bright-colored snake of red, yellow, and black rings found in the South, but it is usually small, and not aggressive, so that but few cases of poisoning are known. The other two are common enough, the former from Norfolk, Va., south, the other all over the eastern country from Texas to Massachusetts. They are usually confounded, however, with two perfectly harmless snakes, the cotton mouth with the common water snake, the copperhead with the so-called spreading adder, but as their differences have to be learned from actual inspection and are very hard to express in a description which would help to identify living specimens, it is wisest to keep away from all of them.

See "The Poisonous Snakes of North America." By Leonard Stejneger, published by Government Printing office, Washington.

INSECTS AND BUTTERFLIES*
United States Bureau of Entomology

There is an advantage in the study of insects over most other branches of nature, excepting perhaps plants, in that there is plenty of material. You may have to tramp miles to see a certain bird or wild animal, but if you will sit down on the first patch of grass you are sure to see something going on in the insect world.

Butterflies

Nearly all insects go through several different stages. The young bird is very much like its parent, so is the young squirrel or a young snake or a

Chrysalis

---

*Illustrations are copies from Comstock's "How to Know the Butterflies," through courtesy of D. Appleton & Company.

young fish or a young snail; but with most of the insects the young is very different from its parents. All butterflies and moths lay eggs, and these hatch into caterpillars which when full grown transform to what are called pupæ or chrysalids — nearly motionless objects with all of the parts soldered together under an enveloping sheath. With some of the moths, the pupæ are surrounded by silk cocoons spun by the caterpillars just before finally transforming to pupæ. With all butterflies the chrysalids are naked, except with one species which occurs in Central America in which there is a common silk cocoon. With the moths, the larger part spin cocoons, but some of them, like the owlet moths whose larvæ are the cut-worms, have naked pupæ, usually under the surface of the ground. It is not difficult to study the transformations of the butterflies and moths, and it is always very interesting to feed a caterpillar until it transforms, in order to see what kind of a butterfly or moth comes out of the chrysalis.

Take the monarch butterfly, for example: This is a large, reddish-brown butterfly, a strong flier, which is seen often flying about in the spring and again in the late summer and autumn. This is one of the most remarkable butterflies in America. It is found all over the United States. It is one of the strongest fliers that we know. It passes the winter in the Southern states as an adult butterfly, probably hidden away in cracks under

the bark of trees or elsewhere. When spring comes the butterflies come out and begin to fly toward the north. Wherever they find the milk-weed plant they stop and lay some eggs on the leaves. The caterpillars issue from the eggs, feed on the milkweed, transform to chrysalids; then the butter-flies issue and continue the northward flight, stopping to lay eggs farther north on other milkweeds. By the end of June or July some

Empty chrysalis and butterfly

of these Southern butterflies have found their way north into Canada and begin the return flight southward. Along in early August they will be seen at the summer resorts in the Catskill Mountains, and by the end of October they will have traveled far down into the Southern states where they pass the winter.

The caterpillar of the monarch or milkweed butterfly is a very striking creature. It is nearly two inches long when full grown. Its head is yellow striped with black; its body is white with narrow black and yellow cross-stripes on each segment. On the back of the second segment of the thorax there is a pair of black, whiplash-like filaments, and on the eighth joint there is a similar shorter pair. When this caterpillar gets ready to transform to chrysalis, it hangs itself up by its tail end, the skin splits and gradually draws back, and the chrysalis itself is re- vealed — pale pea-green in color with golden spots. Any one by hunting over a patch of milkweed anywhere in the United States during the sum- mer is quite apt to find these cater- pillars feeding. It will be easy to watch them and to see them trans- form, and eventually to get the butterfly.

Larva getting ready to transform

The same thing may be done with any one of the six hundred and fifty-two different kinds of butterflies found in the United States.

Full grown larva

Moths

When it comes to moths, there is a much greater variety.

Instead of six hundred and fifty-two, there are fifty-nine hundred and seventy in Doc- tor Dyar's big catalogue. Perhaps the most interesting of these caterpillars are the big native silk-worms, like those of the cecropia moth, the luna moth, the polyphemus moth, or the promethia moth. These caterpillars are very large and are to be found feeding upon the leaves of different trees, and all spin strong silken cocoons. People have tried to reel these cocoons, thinking that they might be able to use the silk to make silk cloth as with the domestic silk-worm of commerce, but thay have been unable to reel them properly. The polyphemus moth, for example, has been experimented with a great deal. It is found over a greater part of the United States, and its caterpillar feeds upon a great variety of trees and shrubs such as oak, butternut, hickory, basswood, elm, maple, birch, chestnut, sycamore, and many others. The caterpillar is light green and has raised lines of silvery white on the side. It grows to a very large size and spins a dense, hard cocoon, usually attached to leaves. There are two generations in the Southern states, and one in the Northern states. The moth which comes out of the cocoon has a wing spread of fully five inches. It is reddish-gray or some-

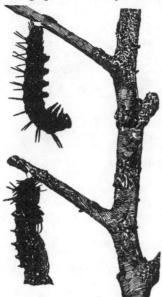

what buff in color with darker bands near the edge of the wings, which themselves are pinkish on the outside, and with a large clear spot near the centre of the forewing and a regular eyespot (clear in part and blue in the rest) in the centre of the hind wing.

One wishing to know about butterflies and moths should consult a book entitled, "How to Know the Butterflies," by Prof. J. H. Comstock of Cornell Univeristy and his wife, Mrs. Comstock, published by D. Appleton & Co., of New York, or, "The Butterfly Book," by Dr. W. J. Holland of Pittsburg, published by Doubleday, Page & Co., of New York, and "The Moth Book," also by Doctor Holland, and published by the same firm.

Caterpillar to chrysalis

Other Insects

There are many more different kinds of insects than there are of flowering plants, and if we were to add together all of the different kinds of birds, mammals, reptiles, fishes, crabs, mollusks, and all of the lower forms of animal life, they would not all together amount to so many different kinds as there are insects. This makes the classification of insects quite complicated. There are eighteen or nineteen main orders, and each one is subdivided almost indefinitely. There is not one of these that is not full of interest. The habits of ants, for example, living in communities by themselves, afford a tremendous opportunity for interesting observation. A good book about them has been recently written by Dr. W. M. Wheeler, of Harvard, entitled "Ants, their Structure, Development, and Behavior," published by the Columbia University Press, New York.

Many insects live in the water, and to follow their life histories in small home-made aquaria is one of the most interesting occupations one could have, and there is a lot to be learned about these insects. Go to any stagnant pool and you will find it swarming with animal life: Larvæ or "wigglers" of mosquitoes, and a number of other aquatic insects will be found, feeding upon these wigglers. Water bugs of different kinds will be found and the life histories of most of these were until quite recently almost unknown.

Beetles and Wasps

The order *Coleoptera*, comprising what we know as beetles, has thousands of species, each one with its own distinctive mode of life; some of them feeding upon other insects, others boring into wood, others feeding upon flowers, others upon leaves, and so on in endless variety.

The wasps also will bear study. Here, too, there is a great variety, some of them building the paper nests known to every one, others burrowing into the surface of the ground and storing up in these burrows grasshoppers and other insects for food for their young which are grub-like in form; others still burrowing into the twigs of bushes, and others making mud nests attached to the trunks of trees or to the clapboards of houses or outbuildings.

This is just a hint at the endless variety of habits of insects. The United States National Museum publishes a bulletin, by Mr. Nathan Banks, entitled "Directions for Collecting and Preserving Insects," which gives a general outline of the classification, and should be possessed by every one who wishes to take up the study from the beginning.

FISHES

By Dr. Hugh M. Smith, Deputy Commissioner United States Fisheries

There is no more fascinating and profitable study than the fish life of the lakes, ponds, rivers, brooks, bays, estuaries, and coasts of the United States; and no more important service can be rendered our American boys than to teach them to become familiar with our native food and game fishes, to realize their needs, and by example and precept to

Esox lucius
Common pike pickerel

Oncorhynchus tschawytscha
Chinook salmon

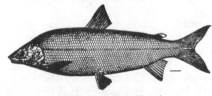

Coregonus clupeiformis
Common whitefish

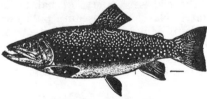

Salvelinus fontinalis
Brook trout: speckled trout

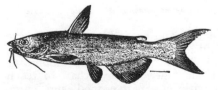

Ictalurus punctatus
The speckled catfish

endeavor to secure for the fishes fair consideration and treatment.

Classes of Fish

Fishes may be roughly classified as (1) fresh water, (2) migratory between fresh and salt water, and (3) marine. Among the families of American fresh-water fishes that are conspicuous on account of their size, abundance, or economic importance, or all of these, there may be mentioned the sturgeons, the catfishes, the suckers, the minnows or carps, the pikes, the killifishes, the trouts, salmons, and whitefishes, the perches, and the basses, and sun fishes.

Migratory Fish

The migratory fishes fall into two groups, the anadromous and the catadromous. The anadromous fishes pass most of their lives in the sea, run up stream only for the purpose of spawning, and constitute the most valuable of our river fishes. In this group are the shads and the alewives or river herrings, the white perch, the striped bass or rock fish, some of the sturgeons, and the Atlantic salmon, all of which go back to sea after spawning, and the Pacific salmons (five species), all of which die after spawning. Of the catadromous fishes there is a single example in our waters — the common eel. It spends most of its life in the fresh waters and sometimes becomes permanently landlocked there, and runs down to the sea to spawn, laying its eggs off shore in deep water.

Perca flavescens
Yellow perch

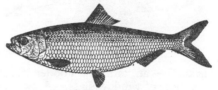

Pomolobus æstivalis
The alewife or river herring

Marine Fish

The marine fishes that are found in the coastal waters of the United States number many hundred species, some of them of great value as food. Among the most important are cod, haddock, hake, halibut, flounder, herring, bluefish, mackerel, weakfish or squeteague, mullet, snapper, drum, and rock fishes.

Micropterus salmoides
Large-mouth black bass

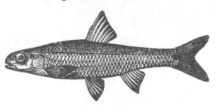

Notropis hudsonius
Minnow or shiner

Studying Fish

The study of living fishes is most entertaining and is rendered somewhat difficult by the medium in which they live, by their

Acipenser oxyrhynchus
The Atlantic sturgeon

shyness, and by the necessity of approaching closely in order
to obtain any accurate view.   The spawning, feeding, swimming
and other habits of very few of our fishes are so well known that
further information thereon is not needed; and the boy scout's
patience, skill, and powers of observation will be reflected in the
records that may be and should be kept about the different

Fundulus diaphanus
Killifish: top minnow

fishes met with.   Fishes
may be studied from
a bank, wharf, or boat,
or by wading; and the
view of the bottom
and the fishes on or
adjacent thereto may
be greatly improved
by the use of a "water

bucket" — an ordinary wooden pail whose bottom is replaced
by a piece of window glass.   A more elaborate arrangement for
observation is to provide at the bow of a row-boat a glass
bottom box over which may be thrown a hood so that the student is invisible to the fishes.

Identification of Specimens

While many of the fishes in a given section are easily recognizable, there are in every water fishes which, on account
of their small size, rarity, retiring habits, or close similarity
to other fishes, are unknown to the average boy.   These latter
fishes often afford the most interesting subjects for study; and
in all parts of the country it is possible for energetic observers
and collectors to add
to the list of fishes al-
ready recorded from
particular districts.

When fishes cannot
be identified in the
field, the larger ones
may be sketched and
notes taken on their
color, while the smaller

Catostomus commersonii
Common sucker: white sucker

ones may be preserved with salt, formalin, or any kind
of spirits.   Specimens and drawings may be forwarded for
identification to the zoölogical department of the local state
university, to the state fish commission, to the Bureau of Fisheries, Washington, D. C., or to the United States National
Museum in the same city.

Angling

This most delightful of outdoor pastimes requires for its enjoyment no elaborate or expensive paraphernalia: a rod cut on the spot, a cork float, an ordinary hook baited with angle-worm, grasshopper, grub, may-fly, or any of a dozen other handy lures, will answer for most occasions. At the same time, the joys of fishing will often be increased if one possesses and learns how to use a light, jointed rod, with reel, fine line, and artificial baits. The necessary equipment for scientific angling is so light and compact that it should form a part of the outfit of every one who spends much time in the open air.

It should be the invariable practice of anglers to return to the water all uninjured fish that are not needed for food or study. "It is not all of fishing to fish," and no thoughtful boy who has the interests of the country at heart, and no lover of nature, will go fishing merely for the purpose of catching the longest possible string of fish, thus placing himself in the class of anglers properly known as "fish hogs."

Special Service by Boy Scouts

Valuable service may be rendered by boy scouts in all parts of the country by bringing to the attention of the proper state, county, or municipal authorities matters affecting the welfare of the fishes. Among the subjects that should be reported to fish commissioners, fish wardens, or local legal officers are:

(1) All cases noticed where fish are being killed by dynamite, poisons, or other illegal and improper means.

(2) Threatened destruction of fish by the drying of streams or ponds.

(3) The existence of obstructions to the passage of fish on their way to their spawning grounds. All dams in streams in which are migratory fish should have fish-ways or fish-ladders.

Aquarium
William Leland Stowell, M. D.

Every boy should have an aquarium. The aquarium will give ten times as much pleasure as annoyance, and the longer time you have one undisturbed the greater will be its revelations.

A simple tank can be made from a large water bottle or demijohn. File a line around the top and carefully break it off. For the back yard, cut a paint barrel in two or coat a tub inside with spar varnish. Anything that will hold a few gallons of water, two inches of clean sand, and some water plants will be a suitable home for fish and other creatures. A boy handy with tools can make a frame, and with plate glass and proper cement construct a large tank.

Starting the Aquarium

You can balance your aquarium by plenty of plants. As they grow they give off oxygen which purifies the water and is breathed by the fish. The water need not be changed for years. The swamps and slow streams afford great numbers of plants. If you know the plants get pond weeds, Canadian water weed, ludwigia, willow moss, or tape grass. (Look in the dictionary for official

A balanced aquarium

names of the plants or get special books from the library.) Take some tape grass (*vallisneria*) to your teacher or doctor and ask him to show you under his microscope how the sap flows and the green coloring matter is deposited. The simplest form of vegetation is algæ which grows on the sides of the tank. Lest this grow too thick, put in a few snails. Watch the snails' eggs develop in clusters. Buy if you cannot find banded swamp snails that give birth to their young instead of laying eggs.

Any pond or stream will furnish fish that are beautiful or interesting to watch, *e.g.*, killies, sunfish, cat-fish, carp, shiners, blacknosed dace, minnows — the mud minnow that seems to stand on his tail — darters, etc. If you get your supply from dealers, buy gold fish, of which there are several varieties, fantailed, comets, fringe tails and telescope eyed. Mirror carp are lively. Paradise fish are as beautiful as butterflies.

Fish Nests

Every one knows something of birds' nests. Did you ever watch sticklebacks build their barrel-like nest, or the Paradise fish his floating nest, and the father fish take all the care of the young? Did you ever see the newt roll her eggs in small leaves, or the caddis fly make a case of bits of stick, leaves, and sand? For a real marvel watch a pair of diving spiders weave their balloon-like nest under water and actually carry air down to fill it, so that the young may be dry though submerged.

Put in a few fresh-water clams and insects in variety, water boatmen, diving spiders, and whirligigs. A tank of beetles will be full of interest. Always add two or three tadpoles as scavengers, and watch their legs grow out as the tail grows short and they become frogs. You can find or buy a variety of turtles which will soon be tame and eat from your fingers. Do not keep turtles with fish.

On every hike or tramp carry a wide-mouthed bottle for specimens and a piece of rubber cloth in which to bring home water plants. Fish can be carried wrapped in damp moss for hours and will be found well and lively when put in the aquarium.

Fish Food

Fish require very little food other than the minute creatures that develop in the water.

The dealers supply proper foods for aquaria, or you can prepare your own. Fine vermicelli is good for gold fish, scraped lean beef is just what the sunfish and Paradise fish want. Ant eggs suit many fish, and powdered dog biscuit will fill many mouths.

It is evident that an article so brief as this is only suggestive. The libraries contain many books of which two are recommended:

"Home Aquarium and How to Care For It." By Eugene Smith, 1902. Published by Dutton, New York.

"Book of Aquaria." By Bateman and Bennett, 1890. Published by L. Upcott Gill, 170 Strand, W. C., London.

ROCKS AND PEBBLES
United States Geological Survey

Geologists study the materials of the earth's crust, the processes continually changing its surface, and the forms and structures thus produced. In a day's tramp one may see much under each of these heads.

The earth's crust is made up chiefly of the hard rocks, which outcrop in many places, but are largely covered by thin, loose, surface materials. Rocks may be igneous, which have cooled from a melted condition; or sedimentary, which are made of layers spread one upon another by water currents or waves, or by winds.

Igneous rocks, while still molten, have been forced into other rocks from below, or poured out on the surface from volcanoes. They are chiefly made of crystals of various minerals, such as quartz, felspar, mica, and pyrite. Granite often contains large crystals of felspar or mica. Some igneous rocks, especially lavas, are glassy; others are so fine grained that the crystals cannot be seen.

In places one may find veins filling cracks in the rocks, and

Fold in stratified rock

Wearing the soft and hard beds by rain and wind

made of material deposited from solution in water. Many valuable minerals and ores occur in such veins, and fine specimens can sometimes be obtained from them.

Sedimentary rock are formed of material usually derived from the breaking up and wearing away of older rocks. When first deposited, the materials are loose, but later, when covered by other beds, they become hardened into solid rock. If the

Quartz vein in rock

layers were of sand, the rock is sandstone; if of clay, it is shale. Rocks made of layers of pebbles are called conglomerate or pudding-stone; those of limy material, derived perhaps from shells, are limestone. Many sedimentary rocks contain fossils, which are the shells or bones of animals or the stems and leaves of plants living in former times, and buried by successive beds of sand or mud spread over them. Much of the land is covered by a thin surface deposit of clay, sand, or gravel, which is yet loose material and which shows the mode of formation of sedimentary rocks.

Some rocks have undergone, since their formation, great pressure or heat and have been much changed. They are called metamorphic rocks. Some are now made of crystals though at first they were not; in others the minerals have become arranged in layers closely resembling the beds of sedimentary rocks; still others, like slate, tend to split into thin plates.

The earth's surface is continually being changed; the out-cropping hard rock is worn away by wind and rain, and is broken up by frost, by solution of some minerals, etc. The loose material formed is blown away or washed away by rain and deposited elsewhere by streams in gravel bars, sand beds, and mud flats. The streams cut away their beds, aided by the sand and pebbles washed along. Thus the hills are being worn down and the valleys deepened and widened, and the materials

Wave-cut cliff with beach and spit built by waves and currents

of the land are slowly being moved toward the sea, again to be deposited in beds.

Along the coast the waves, with the pebbles washed about, are wearing away the land and spreading out its materials in new beds elsewhere. The shore is being cut back in some places and built out in others. Rivers bring down sand and mud and build deltas or bars at their mouths.

Volcanoes pour out melted rock on the surface, and much fine material is blown out in eruptions. Swamps are filled by dead vegetable matter and by sand and mud washed in. These materials form new rocks and build up the surface. Thus the two processes, the wearing down in some places and the building up in others, are tending to bring the surface to a uniform level. Another process, so slow that it can be observed only through long periods of time, tends to deform the earth's crust and to make the surface more irregular. In times past, layers of rock once horizontal have been bent and folded into great arches and troughs, and large areas of the earth's surface have been raised high above sea-level.

At almost any rock outcrop the result of

Rock ledge rounded smooth and scratched by ice

Sand-dune with wind-rippled surface

Slab containing fossil shells

the breaking-up process may be seen; the outer portion is softer, more easily broken, and of different color from the fresh rock, as shown by breaking open a large piece. The wearing away of the land surface is well shown in rain gullies, and the carrying along and depositing of sand and gravel may be seen in almost any stream. In the Northern states and Canada, which at one time were covered by a great sheet of ice, moving southward and grinding off the surface over which it passed, most of the rock outcrops are smoothly rounded and many show scratches made by pebbles dragged along by the ice. The hills too have

Conglomerate or pudding-stone

smoother and rounder outlines, as compared with those farther south where the land has been carved only by rain and streams. Along the coast the wearing away of the land by waves is shown at cliffs, found where the coast is high, and by the abundant pebbles on the beaches, which are built of material torn from the land by the waves. Sand bars and tidal flats show the deposition of material brought by streams and spread out by currents. Sand dunes and barrens illustrate the carrying and spreading out of fine material by the wind.

In many regions the beds of sedimentary rocks, which must have been nearly horizontal when formed, are now found sloping at various angles or standing on edge, the result of slow deforming of these beds at an earlier time. As some beds are more easily worn away than others, the hills and valleys in such regions owe their form and position largely to the different extent to which the harder and softer beds have been worn down by weather and by streams. The irregular line of many coasts is likewise due to the different hardness of the rocks along the shore.

It is by the study of the rocks and of the remains of life found in them, by observing the way in which the surface of the earth is being changed and examining the results of those changes and by concluding that similar results were produced in former times in the same way, that geologists are able to read much of the past history of the earth, uncounted years before there were men upon it.

Plants, Ferns, and Grasses

By Dr. L. C. Corbett, Horticulturist, United States Bureau of Plant Industry

The appearance of the blossoms and fruits of the fields and forests in any locality note the advent and progress of the seasons more accurately than does the calendar. Plants and seeds which have lain asleep during the winter are awakened not by the birth of a month, but by the return of heat and moisture in proper proportions. This may be early one year and late another, but, no matter what the calendar says, the plants respond to the call and give evidence of spring, summer, or autumn as the case may be. The surface of the earth is not flat. We have valleys and we have mountains; we have torrid and we have temperate zones. The plant life of the world has been adjusted to these varied conditions, and as a result we have plants with certain characteristics growing in the tropics at sea-level, but a very different class of plants with different habits and characteristics inhabiting the elevated regions of this same zone. It must be remembered that even under the tropics some of the highest mountains carry a perpetual snow-cap. There is therefore all possible gradations of climate from sea-level to the top of such mountains, even at the equator, and plant life is as a result as varied as is climate. Each zone, whether determined by latitude or by altitude, possesses a distinctive flora.

But altitude and latitude are not the only factors which have been instrumental in determining the plants found in any particular locality. This old earth of ours has not always been as we see her to-day. The nature we know and observe is quite different from that which existed in earlier ages of the earth's history. The plants, the trees, and the flowers that existed upon the earth during the age when our coal was being deposited were very different from those we now have. There has been a change, but, strange as it may seem, there are in some places upon the earth to-day some of the same species of plants which were abundant during the coal-forming periods. These are among the oldest representatives of the plant world now extant. Then we are told that there was a period when the north temperate zone was covered with a great ice field which crowded down as far as southern Pennsylvania and central Ohio. This naturally brought about a profound change in the location and character of the plants of this region. There are in the Black Hills of Dakota species of plants which have no relatives anywhere in the prairie region, and no means is known by which these representatives of a Rocky Mountain family could find their way into the Black Hills, save that, previous to the ice age, this species was generally scattered over the territory, and that, during the ice age, the species was perpetuated in the hills, but was killed out between there and the Rocky Mountains where it is found in abundance. These are some of the natural reasons for the existence of varied plants in different localities. They are sufficient to explain the reason for the existence of local floras.

But nature has provided untold ways for the perpetuation as well as the dispersal of plants for the purpose of, so far as possible, enabling the plants of the world to take possession of all parts of the earth's surface. If this adjustment were complete, the plants would be practically alike all over the surface of the earth, but we have already explained why this cannot be and why we have a different flora in each zone, whether it be marked by lines of latitude or height of the

Pinkster Flower.—It shows its pink flowers in rocky woods and thickets during spring

White Pine.—Common evergreen tree of the Northeastern states. Needle-like leaves in bundles of five

Butterfly Weed.—The bright, orange colored flowers are conspicuous in dry meadows from June to September

Poison Ivy.—Can be distinguished from the harmless woodbine by its three-lobed leaves

mountains. Plants are perpetuated by seeds, by bulbs, and by woody parts. Some seeds are highly perishable and must be sown as soon as ripe; others remain years without losing their power to produce plants. Some grow as soon as they come in contact with the soil; others must fall, be buried and frozen before they will germinate. Some plants are perpetuated by bulbs, tubers, or roots in which a supply of food material is stored away to carry the plant over a period when its above-ground parts cannot thrive owing to frost or drought. Upon the return of favorable conditions, these resting parts throw out shoots and again make the round of growth, usually producing both seeds and underground parts for the preservation of the species. There are both wild and cultivated plants in nearly all sections which illustrate these methods of preservation. Besides plants which have bulbs, tubers, or perennial roots, we have the large, woody plants which live many years and so perpetuate themselves, not only as individuals the same as plants with perennial roots; but they, too, as a rule, produce seed for the multiplication of their kind.

The agencies which serve to spread plants about over the earth's surface are very varied and interesting. Nature has provided seeds with many appendages which assist in their dispersal. Some seeds have wings, and some parachutes to take advantage of the wind. Some seeds are provided with hooks and stickers by which they become attached to the fur of animals and are in this way enabled to steal a free ride. Other seeds are provided with edible coverings which attract birds, but the seeds themselves are hard and not digestible; the fruit is eaten and the seeds rejected and so plants are scattered. Besides these methods of perpetuation and dispersal, some plants are perpetuated as well as dispersed by vegetative reproduction, i. e., by cuttings as in the case of willows; by runners as in the case of the strawberry; and by stolons as with the black raspberry. (For further information on this point see Bailey's "Lessons with Plants.")

Some plant characteristics, however, of greatest interest to the scout may be enumerated. Plants not only mark zones, but they indicate soils with certain characteristics, and the crop wise say that the soil on which chestnut abounds is suitable for buckwheat or peaches. Plants also indicate the influence of local conditions such as lakes, ponds, or even variations in contour. A knowledge of the local flora of a region will at once tell one whether he is upon a northern or a southern hillside by the plants of the area. The creek bottom will abound with species not to be found on the hillsides, but species common to both plain and mountain will mark the progress of the season up the slope.

In the north temperate zone the moss if any will be found growing upon the north side of the tree trunk. Each hundred feet of elevation in a given latitude makes from one to two days difference in time of blooming of plants. The character of the vegetation of a region is an index to its climate. Certain plants are adapted to frigid regions, others to temperate, and still others to tropical areas. Some plants are adapted to humid sections, while others are admirably adjusted to desert conditions. A knowledge of these differences in plants will be of the greatest value to the scout, and if this is supplemented by information about the value and uses of the various plant products many hardships can be avoided. Many plants produce valuable juices, gums, and resins, while others yield us valuable timber for building and cabinet uses.

While it is impossible to even suggest the great variety of plants found within the confines of the United States, the following books on botany will be found helpful in each of the different sections for which they are designed.

Bibliography

For the botany of the Northeastern United States use:

"New Manual of Botany," 7th ed. Asa Gray.
"Illustrated Flora of the United States and Canada." N. L. Britton and Hon. Addison Brown.

For the botany of the Southern United States use:

"Flora of the Southern United States." A. W. Chapman.
"Southern Wild Flowers and Trees." Alice Lounsberry.

For the Botany of the Rocky Mountain region use:

"New Manual of Botany of the Central Rocky Mountains." John M. Coulter; Revised by Aven Nelson.
"Rocky Mountain Wild Flower Studies." Burton O. Longyear.
"The Trees of California." Willis Linn Jepson.

For general information regarding the shrubby plants of the United States use:

"Our Shrubs of the United States." Austin C. Apgar.
"Our Northern Shrubs." Harriet Louise Keeler.

For the wild flowers outside of those already mentioned for the Southern United States and the Rocky Mountain region use:

"Our Garden Flowers." Harriet Louise Keeler.
"How to Know the Wild Flowers." Frances Theodora Parsons.
"Field Book of American Wild Flowers." F. Schuyler Mathews.

For the ferns and grasses it will be found worth while to consult:

"How to Know the Ferns."   Frances Theodora Parsons.
"The Fern Collector's Guide."   Willard Nelson Clute.
"New England Ferns and Their Common Allies."   Helen Eastman.
"The Grasses, Sedges, and Rushes of the North United States."
Edward Knobel.

For the study of the monarchs of our forests the following books will all be found exceedingly useful:

"Manual of the Trees of North America."   Charles Sprague Sargent.
"Trees of the Northern United States."   Austin C. Apgar.
"Handbook of the Trees of the Northern United States and Canada."
Romeyn Beck Hough.
"North American Trees."   N. L. Britton.
"Familiar Trees and Their Leaves."   1911.   F. Schuyler Mathews.

Besides these, several states have issued through their state experiment stations bulletins dealing with the local plant inhabitants.   In some instances these publications cover forest trees, grasses, and shrubs, either native or introduced.   Several of the educational institutions, as well as the experiment stations, now regularly issue nature study leaflets or bulletins which treat of popular subjects of interest in connection with outdoor things.   It would be well to write the state experiment station in your state for literature of this nature.

MUSHROOMS, FUNGI, OR TOADSTOOLS

By Ernest Thompson Seton, Chief Scout

Revised by Dr. C. C. Curtis

There are thousands of different kinds of toadstools or mushrooms in the world; most of them are good to eat, yet all have a bad reputation, because some are deadly poisonous.

False tests.   First of all let us dispose of some ancient false tests that have led many into disaster.

Cooking or otherwise trying with silver proves absolutely nothing.   It is believed by many that the poisonous mushrooms turn silver black.   Some do; some do not; and some eatable ones do.   There is nothing in it.

Bright colors on the cap also mean nothing; many gorgeous toadstools are wholesome food.   But the color of the pores means a great deal, and this is determined by laying the fungus cap gills down on gray paper for six or eight hours under a glass.

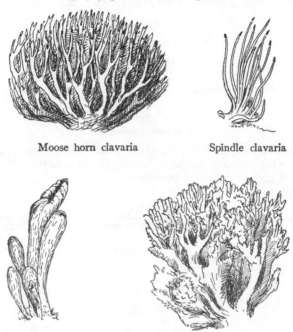

Moose horn clavaria

Spindle clavaria

Club clavaria

Golden clavaria

Poisonous Toadstools

Of all the poisonous kinds the deadliest are the Amanitas. Not only are they widespread and abundant, but they are unhappily much like the ordinary table mushrooms. They have however one or two strong marks: Their stalk always grows out of a "*poison cup*" which shows either as a cup or as a bulb; they have white or yellow gills, and *white spores*. The worst of these are:

Deathcup, Destroying Angel, Sure=death, or Deadly Amanita

(*Amanita phalloides*)

One and one half to five inches across the cup; three to seven inches high; white, green, yellowish olive, or grayish brown;

smooth but sticky when moist; gills white; spores white; on the stem is an annulus or ring just below the cap.

Fly Amanita

(*Amanita muscaria*)

About the same size; mostly yellow, but ranging from orange red to or almost white; usually with raised white spots or scales on the top; gills white or tinged yellow; spores white; flesh white.

Hated Amanita

(*Amanita spreta*)

Four to six inches high; cap three to five inches across; white, tinged with brown in places especially in the middle of the cap, where it has sometimes a bump.

Deadly amanita   Fly amanita   Hated amanita

There are over a score more of amanitas varying in size and color, but all have the general style of mushrooms, and the label marks of poison, viz., white or yellow gills, a poison cup, and white spores.

Emetic Russula

(*Russula emetica*)

In a less degree this russula is poisonous. It is a short-stemmed mushroom, two to four inches high, about the size of the Fly Amanita; its cap is rosy red, pinkish when young, dark red when older, fading to straw color in age; its gills and spores white. Its peppery taste when raw is a fair notice of danger.

Symptoms of Poisoning: Vomiting and purging, "the discharge from the bowels being watery with small flakes suspended and sometimes containing blood," cramps in the extremities. The pulse is very slow and strong at first but later weak and rapid, sometimes sweat and saliva pour out. Dizziness, faintness, and blindness, the skin clammy, cold, and bluish, or livid; temperature low with dreadful tetanic convulsions, and finally stupor.

Remedy: "Take an emetic at once, and send for a physician with instructions to bring hypodermic syringe and atropine sulphate. The dose is $\frac{1}{180}$ of a grain, and doses should be continued heroically until $\frac{1}{20}$ of a grain is administered, or until, in the physician's opinion, a proper quantity has been injected. Where the victim is critically ill, the $\frac{1}{20}$ of a grain may be administered." (McIllvaine & Macadam.)

Emetic russula: russula emetica
(after Marshall)

Mushrooms

WHOLESOME TOADSTOOLS

IMPORTANT NOTE.—Experimenting with mushrooms is dangerous; it is better not to eat them unless gathered under expert direction.

The Common Mushroom

(*Agaricus campestris*)

Known at once by its general shape and smell, its pink or brown gills, white flesh, brown spores and solid stem.

Coprinus

Also belonging to the gilled or true mushroom family are the *ink-caps* of the genus.

They grow on dung piles and rich ground. They spring up over night and perish in a day. In the last stage the gills turn as black as ink.

Inky Coprinus

(*Coprinus atramentarius*)

This is the species illustrated. The example was from the woods; often it is less tall and graceful. The cap is one inch to three inches in diameter, grayish or grayish brown, sometimes tinged lead color. Wash and stew: Stew or bake from twenty to thirty minutes after thorough washing, being the recognized mode.

All the *Clavarias* or *Coral Mushrooms* are good except *Clavaria dichotoma* which is *white*, and has its branches *divided in pairs* at each fork. It grows on the ground under beeches and is slightly poisonous; it is rare.

The Delicious Morel

(*Morchella deliciosa*)

One and a half to three inches high; greenish with brown hollows. There are

Inky coprinus

Morel

several kindred species of various colors. This is known by the cylindrical shape of its cap. Wash, slice, and stew.

Puffballs

(*Lycoperdaceæ*)

The next important and *safe* group are the *puffballs* before they begin to puff. All our puffballs when young and *solid white inside* are good, wholesome food. Some of them, like

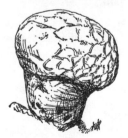

Brain puffball   Pear puffball   Cup puffball

the *brain puffball* or the *giant puffball*, are occasionally a foot in diameter, and yield flesh enough to feed a dozen persons.

They are well known to all who live in the country, their smooth rounded exterior, without special features except the roots, and their solid white interior are easily remembered. Peel, slice, and fry.

Bibliography

The following are standard and beautifully illustrated works on mushrooms and toadstools. They have been freely used for guidance and illustrations in the preparation of the above:

"Edible Fungi of New York." By Charles H. Peck. Published by New York State Museum, Albany, 1900.

"The Mushroom Book." By Nina L. Marshall. Published 1902 at New York by Doubleday, Page & Co. $3.50.

"One Thousand American Fungi." By McIllvaine and Macadam. Published by the Bobbs-Merrill Company of Indianapolis, 1902. $3.00. Add 40 cents express.

"Mushrooms." G. F. Atkinson. Holt & Co.

"The Mushroom." M. E. Hard. The Ohio Library Co., Columbus, Ohio.

COMMON NORTH AMERICAN TREES
White Pine
(Pinus strobus)

A noble evergreen tree, up to 175 feet high. This is the famous pine of New England, the lumberman's prize. Its leaves are in bunches of five, and are 3 to 5 inches long;

White pine

Hemlock

Red cedar

cones 4 to 6 inches long. Wood pale, soft, straight-grained, easily split. Newfoundland to Manitoba and south to Illinois.

There are many different kinds of pines. They are best distinguished by their cones.

Hemlock

(*Tsuga Canadensis*)

Evergreen. Sixty to seventy feet high. Wood pale, soft, coarse, splintery, not durable. Bark full of tannin. Leaves $\frac{1}{2}$ to $\frac{3}{4}$ inches long; cones about the same. Its knots are so hard that they quickly turn the edge of an axe or gap it as a stone might; these are probably the hardest vegetable growth in our woods. Its topmost twig usually points easterly. Nova Scotia to Minnesota, south to Delaware and Michigan.

Red Cedar

(*Juniperus Virginiana*)

Evergreen. Any height up to 100 feet. Wood, heart a beautiful bright red; sap wood nearly white; soft, weak, but extremely durable as posts, etc. Makes a good bow. The

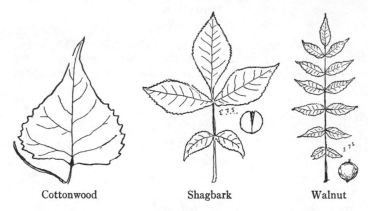

Cottonwood   Shagbark   Walnut

tiny scale-like leaves are 3 to 6 to the inch; the berry-like cones are light blue and $\frac{1}{4}$ of an inch in diameter. It is found in dry places from Nova Scotia to Florida and west to British Columbia.

Cottonwood

(*Populus deltoides*)

Small and rare in the Northeast, but abundant and large

in West; even 150 feet high.   Leaves 3 to 6 inches long. Found from Quebec to Florida and west to the mountains.

Shagbark or White Hickory
(*Hicoria ovata*)

A tall forest tree up to 120 feet high.   Known at once by the great angular slabs of bark hanging partly detached from its main trunk, forced off by the growth of wood, but too tough to fall.   Its leaves are 8 to 14 inches long, with 5 to 7 broad leaflets.

Black Walnut
(*Juglans nigra*)

A magnificent forest tree up to 150 feet high.   Wood, a dark purplish-brown or gray; hard, close-grained, strong, very durable in weather or ground work, and heavy; fruit round, 1¾ nches through.   Leaflets 13 to 23, and 3 to 5 inches long. ?ound from Canada to the Gulf.

White Walnut or Butternut
(*Juglans cinerea*)

A much smaller tree than the last, rarely 100 feet high, with much smoother bark, leaves similar but larger and coarser, compound of fewer leaflets, but the leaflet stalks and the new twigs are covered with sticky down.   Leaves 15 to 30 inches long, leaflets 11 to 19 in number and 3 to 5 inches long; fruit oblong, 2 to 3 inches long.   New Brunswick and Dakota and south to Mississippi.

Common Birch or Aspen-leaved Birch
(*Betula populifolia*)

A small tree on dry and poor soil, rarely 50 feet high.   Wood soft, close-grained, not strong, splits in drying, useless for weather or ground work.   A cubic foot weighs 36 pounds. Leaves 2 to 3 inches long.   It has a black triangular scar at each armpit.   The canoe birch is without these black marks. New Brunswick to Ontario to Pennsylvania and Delaware.

Black Birch, Sweet Birch, or Mahogany Birch
(*Betula lenta*)

The largest of the birches; a great tree, in Northern forests up to 80 feet high.   The bark is scarcely birchy, rather like that of cherry, very dark, and aromatic. Leaves $2\frac{1}{2}$ to 6 inches long. Newfoundland to Western Ontario and south to Tennessee.

Beech

(*Fagus Americana*)

In all North America there is but one species of beech. It is a noble forest tree, 70 to 80 and occasionally 120 feet high, readily distinguished by its smooth, ashy-gray bark. Leaves

 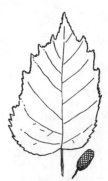 

| Ashen-leaved birch | Black birch | Beech |

3 to 4 inches long. It shares with hickory and sugar maple the honor of being a perfect firewood. Nova Scotia to Wisconsin, south to Florida and Texas.

Chestnut

(*Castanea dentata*)

A noble tree, 60 to 80 or even 100 feet high. The most delicious of nuts. Leaves 6 to 8 inches long. Maine to Michigan and south to Tennessee.

Red Oak

(*Quercus rubra*)

A fine forest tree, 70 to 80 or even 140 feet high. Hard, strong, coarse-grained, heavy. It checks, warps, and does not stand for weather or ground work. The acorn takes two seasons to ripen. Leaves 4 to 8 inches long. Nova Scotia to Minnesota, south to Texas and Florida.

White Oak

(*Quercus alba*)

A grand forest tree, over 100 up to 150 feet high. Wood pale, strong, tough, fine-grained, durable and heavy, valuable timber. Called white from pale color of bark and wood. Leaves 5 to 9 inches long. Acorns ripen in one season. Maine to Minnesota, Florida and Texas.

White Elm or Swamp Elm

(*Ulmus Americana*)

A tall, splendid forest tree, commonly 100, occasionally 120 feet high. Wood reddish-brown, hard, strong, tough,

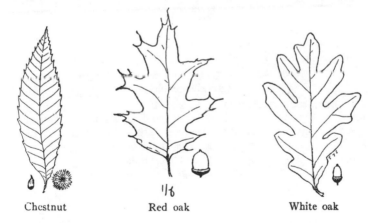

Chestnut   Red oak   White oak

very hard to split, coarse, heavy. Soon rots near the ground. Leaves 2 to 5 inches long. Flowers in early spring before leafing. Abundant, Newfoundland and Manitoba to Texas.

Sycamore, Plane Tree, Buttonball or Buttonwood

(*Platanus occidentalis*)

One of the largest of our trees; up to 140 feet high; commonly hollow, Little use for weather work. Famous for shedding its bark as well as its leaves; leaves 4 to 9 inches long.   Canada to Gulf.

Black or Yellow Locust, Silver Chain
(*Robinia pseudacacia*)

A tall forest tree up to 80 feet high; leaves 8 to 14 inches long; leaflets 9 to 19, 1 to 2 inches long, pods 2 to 4 inches long, 4 to 7 seeded.   This is the common locust so often seen about old lawns.

White elm   Sycamore   Black locust

Red, Scarlet, Water, or Swamp Maple
(*Acer rubrum*)

A fine, tall tree, often over 100 feet high.   Noted for its flaming crimson foliage in fall, as well as its red leaf stalks, flowers, and fruit, earlier.   Leaves 2 to 6 inches long.   Like all the maples it produces sugar, though in this case not much. Western North America.

The sugar maple is a larger, finer tree.

Red maple

White Ash
(*Fraxinus Americana*)

White ash

A fine tree on moist soil.   Seventy to 80 or even 130 feet high.   Yellow in autumn; noted for being last to leaf and first to shed in the forest. Called white for the silvery under sides of the leaves; these are 8 to 12 inches long, each leaflet 3 to 6 inches long. Nova Scotia to Texas.

For a full unbotanical account of one hundred and twenty of our finest trees with their uses as wood, their properties, and the curious and interesting things about them see:

"The Forester's Manual: or Forest Trees That Every Scout Should Know." By Ernest Thompson Seton.

NATIVE WILD ANIMALS

Every scout ought to know the principal wild animals that are found in North America. He need not know them as a naturalist, but as a hunter, as a camper. Here is a brief account of twenty-four of them, and those who wish to know more will find the fullest possible account in "Life Histories of North America," by E. T. Seton. (Scribners, 1909.) These two volumes are found in all large libraries.

Elk

Elk or Wapiti
(*Cervus canadensis*)

This is smaller than the moose. It stands four to five feet at the shoulder and weighs four hundred to eight hundred pounds. It is known by its rounded horns and the patch of yellowish-white on the rump and tail. At one time this splendid animal was found throughout temperate America from the Atlantic to the Pacific, north to Massachusetts, the Ottawa River, the Peace River, and British Columbia; and south to Georgia, Texas, and southern California. It is now exterminated except in Manitoba, Saskatchewan, Alberta; Vancouver Island, Washington, Wyoming and a few localities in the mountain states and in parks where it has been reintroduced.

The elk of Washington is very dark in color; that of the Southwest is very pale and small.

White-tailed Deer

(Odocoileus virginianus)

This is the best known of the common deer of America. It is distinguished by the forward bend of the horns, with the snags pointing backward, and by its long tail which is brown or blackish above and pure white below. Its face is gray, its throat white. A fair sized buck weighs two hundred pounds, live weight. A few have been taken of over three hundred and fifty pounds weight. In the Southern states they run much smaller. Several varieties have been described. It was found formerly in all of the timber states east of the Rockies; also in Ontario south of Lake Nipissing, in south Quebec and south New Brunswick. At present it is exterminated in the highly cultivated states of the Middle West, but has spread into northern Ontario, New Brunswick, and Manitoba.

White-tailed deer

Mule deer

Mule Deer

(Odocoileus hemionus)

This is the commonest deer of the hill country in the centre of the continent. It is found in the mountains

Moose

from Mexico to British Columbia and northeasterly to the Saskatchewan and the Lake of the Woods. It is known by its double-forked horns, its large ears, the dark patch on the forehead, the rest of the face being whitish. Also by its tail which is white with a black bunch on the end. This is a larger deer than the White-tail. There are several varieties of it in the South and West.

Moose

(*Alces americanus*)

This is the largest of the deer tribe. It stands five and a half to six and a half feet at the withers and weighs eight hundred to one thousand pounds. It is readily distinguished by its flat horns and pendulous, hairy muzzle. It is found in all the heavily timbered regions of Canada and Alaska and enters the United States in Maine, Adirondacks, Minnesota, Montana, Idaho, and northwestern Wyoming. Those from Alaska are of gigantic stature.

In all our deer the antlers are grown and shed each year, reaching perfection in autumn for the mating season. They are found in the males only, except in the caribou, in which species the females also have small horns.

Antelope

(*Antilocapra americana*)

Antelope

The antelope is famous as the swiftest quadruped native in America. It is a small creature, less than a common deer; a fair-sized buck weighs about one hundred pounds. It is known by its rich buff color with pure white patches, by having only two hoofs on each foot, and by the horns which are of true horn, like those of a goat, but have a snag or branch and are shed each year. In the female the horns are little points about an inch long.

Formerly the antelope abounded on all the high plains from Manitoba to Mexico and west to Oregon and California. It is now reduced to a few straggling bands in the central and wildest parts of the region.

Mountain Goat

(*Oreamnos montanus*)

The mountain goat is known at once by its pure white coat of wool and hair, its black horns, and peculiar shape. It is above the size of a common deer; that is, a full grown male weighs two hundred and fifty to three hundred pounds; the female a third less.

It is famous for its wonderful power as a rock climber and mountaineer. It is found in the higher Rockies, chiefly above timber lines, from central Idaho to Alaska.

Goat

Woodchuck
(*Marmota monax*)

The common woodchuck is a grizzly brown on the back, chestnut on the breast, blackish on the crown and paws, and whitish on the cheeks. Its short ears and bushy tail are important characteristics. It measures about twenty-four inches of which the tail is five and a half inches and weighs five to ten pounds.

It is found in all the wooded parts of Canada from the Rockies to the Atlantic and south in the eastern states to about 40 degrees latitude.

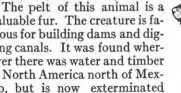
Woodchuck

Beaver
(*Castor canadensis*)

The beaver is known by its great size — weighing from twenty-five to fifty pounds— its chestnut color, darker on the crown, its webbed feet, and its broad, flat, naked, scaly tail.

The pelt of this animal is a valuable fur. The creature is famous for building dams and digging canals. It was found wherever there was water and timber in North America north of Mexico, but is now exterminated in most highly settled regions.

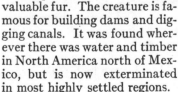
Beaver

Muskrat
(*Fiber zibethicus*)

The muskrat is about the size of a cat; that is, it is twenty-one inches long, of which the tail is ten inches. In color it somewhat resembles the beaver, but its feet are not conspicuously webbed, its tail is long and flattened vertically, not horizontally. This abundant animal is found throughout North America within the limit of trees wherever there is fresh water. It is the most abundant fur on the market.

Muskrat

Black-tailed jack rabbit

Jack Rabbit
(*Lepus Californicus*)

The jack-rabbit, famous for its speed and its ears, is known by its size, which about doubles that of a common rabbit and the *jet black stripe* running from its back into its tail. It is found on the plains from Nebraska to Oregon and south to Mexico. There are several different varieties.

Cottontail
(*Sylvilagus floridanus*)

The common eastern cottontail is known from the snowshoe by its smaller feet and its much larger, longer tail, which is gray

Cottontail

above, and snow-white underneath. Sometimes the common tame rabbit resembles the cottontail in general color, but the latter has the top of its tail black.

The cottontails do not turn white in winter. They are found in most parts of the United States, entering Canada only in the Ontario peninsula and southern Saskatchewan.

Cougar or Panther
(*Felis couguar*)

The cougar has been called the American lion; it is the largest cat in the western world except the jaguar or American tiger. It is known by its unspotted brown coat, its long, heavy tail, and its size. A male cougar weighs one hundred and fifty to two hundred pounds; a few have been taken over that. The females are a third smaller. The young in first coat have black spots.

Cougar

The cougar never attacks man but preys on deer, horses, calves, etc. There are several different forms; one or other of these is (or was) found from Ottawa, Minnesota, and Vancouver Island to Patagonia.

Wild Cat or Bob Cat
(*Lynx rufus*)

Lynx

This is somewhat like the Canada lynx but is more spotted, has smaller feet, and the tail has several dark bars above and is pure white on the under side of the tip. There are several species of bob cats; they cover the timbered states and enter Canada in Ontario, going north to Lake Simcoe.

Wild cat or bob cat

Fox
(*Vulpes fulvus*)

The fox is about four feet from snout to tail tip; of this the tail is sixteen inches or more; it stands about fifteen inches at the shoulder. It rarely weighs over fifteen pounds and sometimes barely ten. The fox is known by its bright, sandy-red coat, black ears and paws, its white throat, and the white tip at the end of the tail. At a distance the fox's ears and tail look very large. The silver or black fox is a mere color freak with black coat and white tail tip. Red foxes are found throughout the heavily timbered parts of North America north of latitude thirty-five degrees.

Gray Wolf
(*Canis occidentalis*)

The wolf is simply a big wild dog with exceptionally strong jaws and general gray color, becoming dirty white on the nder part. The wolf is found in all parts of North America, except where settlement has driven it out, and varies in color with locality. The Florida wolves are black, Texan wolves are reddish, and Arctic wolves are white. Wolves weigh from seventy-five to one hundred and twenty pounds and are distinguishable from coyotes by the heavy muzzle and jaws, greater size, and comparatively small tail, which is often held aloft. Wolves nowadays rarely molest man.

Coyote
(*Canis latrans*)

The common coyote is like a small and delicate edition of the gray wolf. It is much smaller, weighing only twenty to thirty pounds, and is distinguished by its sharp, fox-like muzzle and large bushy tail, which is rarely raised to the level. In color it is much like the ordinary gray wolf but usually more tinged with yellow. It is found in all the interior country from Wisconsin to Oregon and from Mexico to Great Slave Lake. There are several different varieties. It never attacks man.

Otter
(*Lutra canadensis*)

Otter

The otter is a large water weasel with close, dense, shiny fur and webbed feet. It is known by its color — dark brown above shaded into dark gray below and white on the cheeks without any markings — and by its size. It is about forty inches long and weighs about twenty pounds. It is found throughout North America within the limit of trees. Its fur is very valuable. It feeds on fish.

Weasel
(*Putorius noveboracensis*)

The common weasel of New England is about the size of a big rat; that is, it is sixteen inches long and all brown with the exception of white chin, throat, breast, and paws, and black tip to the tail. In winter it turns white except the tail tip; that does not change.

The whole continent is inhabited by weasels of one kind

Weasel

or another. To the north there is a smaller kind with shorter tail; on the prairies a large kind with a very long tail; but all are of the same general style and habits. A very small one, the least weasel, is only six inches long. It is found chiefly in Canada.

Mink
(*Putorius vison*)

The mink is simply a water weasel. It is known by its size, larger than that of a common weasel, as it is twenty-four inches

Mink

long of which the tail is seven inches; also by its deep brown color all over except the throat and chin which are pure white. Its fur is brown, harder and glossier than that of the marten, and worth about a quarter as much. It does not turn white in the winter. One form or another of mink is found over all the unarid parts of North America from the north limit of trees to the Gulf of Mexico.

Skunk
(*Mephitis mephitica*)

The skunk is known at once by its black coat with white

Skunk

stripes, its immense bushy tail *tipped with white*, and its size, nearly that of a cat. It weighs three to seven pounds. It ranges from Virginia to Hudson Bay. In the Northwest is a larger kind weighing twice as much and with black tip to tail. Various kinds range over the continent south of latitude 55 degrees. It is harmless and beautiful. The smell gun for which it is famous is a liquid musk; this is never used except in the extreme of self-defence.

Badger
(*Taxidea taxus*)

The common badger is known by its general whitish-gray

Badger

color, the black and white markings on the head, the black paws, and the strong claws for digging. It weighs from twelve to twenty-two pounds. That is, it is about the size of a 'coon.

It is found in all the prairie and plains country from the Saskatchewan Valley to Mexico and from Wisconsin to the Pacific.

Raccoon
(*Procyon lotor*)

Coon

The 'coon looks like a small gray bear with a *bushy ringed tail* and a large black patch on each eye. Its paws look like hands, and it has the full number of five fingers or toes on each extremity. It is found in all wooded regions from Manitoba south to Mexico and from Atlantic to Pacific, except the desert and Rocky Mountain region.

Opossum
(*Didelphis marsupialis*)

Opossum

The opossum is famous for carrying its young in a pouch in front of the body. It may be known by its dirty-white woolly fur, its long, naked, prehensile tail, its hand-like paws, its white face and sharp muzzle, and the naked pink and blue ears. In size it resembles a cat. The 'possum is found from Connecticut to Florida and westerly to California.

Gray-squirrel
(*Sciurus carolinensis*)

Gray-squirrel

America is particularly rich in squirrels. Not counting ground-squirrels or chipmunks, we have over seventy-five different forms on this continent. The widest spread is probably the red-squirrel; but the best known in the United States is the common gray-squirrel. Its gray coat white breast, and immense bushy tail are familiar to all eastern children. It is found in most of the hardwood timber east of the Mississippi and south of the Ottawa River and the State of Maine. Most of the nut trees in the woods of this region were planted by the gray-squirrel.

Black Bear

(*Ursus americanus*)

This is the common bear of America. It is known at once by its jet black color and brown nose. Its claws are short, rarely over an inch long, and curved, serving better as climbers than do the long claws of the grizzly. Two hundred pounds would be a good sized female, three hundred a male; but Florida black bears have been taken weighing five hundred pounds. Sometimes freaks with cinnamon-brown coats are found.

This bear is found throughout North America wherever there is timber.

NOTES

Notes

Notes

CHAPTER III

CAMPCRAFT*

Hiking and Over-night Camp

By H. W. Gibson, Boys' Work Secretary, Young Men's Christian Association Massachusetts and Rhode Island

Several things should be remembered when going on a hike: First, avoid long distances. A foot-weary, muscle-tired and temper-tried, hungry group of boys is surely not desirable. There are a lot of false notions about courage and bravery and grit that read well in print, but fail miserably in practice, and long hikes for boys is one of the most glaring of these notions. Second, have a leader who will set a good easy pace, say two or three miles an hour, prevent the boys from excessive water drinking, and assign the duties of pitching camp, etc. Third, observe these two rules given by an old woodsman: (1) Never walk over anything you can walk around; (2) never step on anything that you can step over. Every time you step on anything you lift the weight of your body. Why lift extra weight when tramping? Fourth, carry with you only the things absolutely needed, rolled in blankets, poncho army style.

Before starting on a hike, study carefully the road maps, and take them with you on the walk for frequent reference. The best maps are those of the United States Geological Survey, costing five cents each. The map is published in atlas sheets, each sheet representing a small, quadrangular district. Send to the superintendent of documents at Washington, D. C., for a list.

For tramping the boy needs the right kind of a shoe, or the trip will be a miserable failure. A light-soled or a light-built shoe is not suited for mountain work or even for an ordinary hike. The feet will blister and become "road weary." The shoe must be neither too big, too small, nor too heavy, and be amply broad to give the toes plenty of room. The shoe should be water-tight. A medium weight, high-topped lace shoe is about right. Bathing the feet at the springs and streams along the road will be refreshing, if not indulged in too frequently.

*In treating of camping there has been an intentional omission of the long-term camp. This is treated extensively in the books of reference given at the close of this chapter.

145

See Chapter on "Health and Endurance" for care of the feet and proper way of walking.

It is well to carry a spare shirt hanging down the back with the sleeves tied around the neck.   Change when the shirt you are wearing becomes too wet with perspiration.

The most practical and inexpensive pack is the one made for the Boy Scouts of America.   (Price 60 cents.)   It is about 14 x 20 inches square, and 6 inches thick, made of water-proof canvas with shoulder-straps, and will easily hold everything needed for a tramping trip.

A few simple remedies for bruises, cuts, etc., should be taken along by the leader.   You may not need them and some may poke fun at them, but, as the old lady said, "You can't always sometimes tell."   The amount and kind of provisions must be determined by the locality and habitation.

The Lean-to

Reach the place where you are going to spend the night in plenty of time to build your lean-to, and make your bed for

Fig. 1.   Frame of lean-to

Campcraft

the night. Select your camping spot with reference to water, wood, drainage, and material for your lean-to. Choose a dry, level place, the ground just sloping enough to insure the water running away from your lean-to in case of rain. In building your lean-to look for a couple of good trees standing from eight to ten feet apart with branches from six to eight feet above the ground. By studying the illustration (No. 1) you will be able to build a very service-able shack, affording protection from the dews and rain. While two or more boys are building the shack, an-other should be gather-ing firewood and pre-paring the meal, while

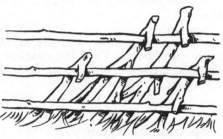

Fig. 2. Method of thatching

another should be cutting and bringing in as many soft, thick tips of trees as possible, for the roof of the shack and the beds.

How to thatch the lean-to is shown in illustration No. 2.

If the camp site is to be used for several days, two lean-tos may be built facing each other, about six feet apart. This will make a very comfortable camp, as a small fire can be built between the two thus giving warmth and light.

The Bed

On the floor of your lean-to lay a thick layer of the fans or branches of a balsam or hemlock, with the convex side up, and the butts of the stems toward the foot of the bed. Now thatch this over with more fans by thrusting the butt ends through the first layer at a slight angle toward the head of the bed, so that the soft tips will curve toward the foot of the bed, and be sure to make the head of your bed away from the opening of the lean-to and the foot toward the opening. Over this bed spread your rubber blankets or ponchos with rubber side down, your sleeping blanket on top, and you will be surprised how soft, springy, and fragrant a bed you have, upon which to rest your "weary frame" and sing with the poet:

> "Then the pine boughs croon me a lullaby,
> And trickle the white moonbeams
> To my face on the balsam where I lie
> While the owl hoots at my dreams."
>
> — *J. George Frederick.*

Hot-Stone Wrinkle

If the night bids fair to be cold, place a number of stones about six or eight inches in diameter near the fire, so that they will get hot. These can then be placed at the feet, back, etc., as needed, and will be found good "bed warmers." When a stone loses its heat, it is replaced near the fire and a hot one taken. If too hot, wrap the stone in a shirt or sweater or wait for it to cool off.

Boys desire adventure. This desire may be gratified by the establishment of night watchers in relays of two boys each, every two hours. Their imaginations will be stirred by the resistless attraction of the camp-fire and the sound of the creatures that creep at night.

Observation Practice

Many boys have excellent eyes, but see not, and good ears but hear not, all because they have not been trained to observe or to hear quickly. A good method of teaching observation while on a hike or tramp is to have each boy jot down in a small note-book or diary of the trip, the different kinds of trees, birds, animals, tracks, nature of roads, fences, peculiar rock formation, smells of plants, etc., and thus be able to tell what he saw or heard to the boys upon his return to the permanent camp or to his home.

Camera Snap Shots

One of the party should take a small folding camera. Photographs of the trip are always of great pleasure and memory-revivers. A practical and convenient method of carrying small folding cameras represents an ordinary belt to which a strap with a buckle has been attached, which is run through the loops at the back of the camera case. The camera may be pushed around the belt to the point where it will be least in the way.

Camp Lamp

A very convenient lamp to use on a hike is the Baldwin Camp Lamp made by John Simmons Co., 13 Franklin Street, New York City. It weighs only five ounces when full; is charged with carbide and is but $4\frac{3}{4}$ inches high. It projects a strong light 150 feet through the woods. A stiff wind will not blow it out. It can be worn comfortably in your hat or belt.

Handy Articles

A boy of ingenuity can make a number of convenient things. A good drinking cup may be made from a piece of bark cut in parallelogram shape twisted into pyramid form and fastened with a split stick. A flat piece of bark may serve as a plate. A pot lifter may be made from a green stick about 18 inches long, allowing a few inches of a stout branch to remain. By reversing the same kind of stick and driving a small nail near the other end or cutting a notch in it, it may be used to suspend a kettle over a fire. A novel candlestick is made by opening the blade of a knife and jabbing it into a tree; upon the other upturned blade put a candle. A green stick having a split which will hold a piece of bread or meat makes an excellent broiler. Don't pierce the bread or meat. Driving a good-sized stake into the ground at an angle of 45 degrees and cutting a notch on which may be suspended a kettle over a fire will provide a way of boiling water quickly.

Building the Fireplace

Take two or three stones and build a fireplace, a stick first shaved and then whittled for shavings, a lighted match, a little blaze, some bark and dry twigs added, a few small sticks, place the griddle over the fire and you are ready to cook the most appetizing griddle-cakes. After the cakes are cooked, fry slices of bacon upon the griddle; in the surplus fat fry slices of bread, then some thinly sliced raw potatoes done to a delicious brown. Here is a breakfast capable of making the mouth of a camper water.

Another way: Place the green logs side by side, closer together at one end than the other. Build the fire between. On the logs over the fire you can rest a frying-pan, kettle, etc. To start the fire have some light, dry wood split up fine. When sticks begin to blaze, add a few more of larger size and continue until you have a good fire. To prevent the re-kindling of the fire after it is apparently out, pour water over it and soak the earth for the space of two or three feet around it. This is very important, for many forest fires have started through failure to observe this caution.

COOKING RECEIPTS

Cooking for Hikes and Over-night Camps

The following tested receipts are given for those who go on hikes and over-night camps:

Griddle-cakes

Beat one egg, tablespoonful of sugar, one cup diluted condensed milk or new milk. Mix enough self-raising flour to make a thick cream batter. Grease the griddle with rind or slices of bacon for each batch of cakes. Be sure to have the griddle hot.

Bacon

Slice bacon quite thin; remove the rind, which makes slices curl up. Fry on griddle or put on a sharp end of a stick and hold over the hot coals, or better yet remove the griddle, and put on a clean, flat rock in its place. When hot lay the slices of bacon on the rock and broil. Keep turning so as to brown on both sides.

Canned Salmon on Toast

Dip slices of stale bread into smoking hot lard. They will brown at once. Drain them. Heat a pint of salmon, picked into flakes, season with salt and pepper and turn in a tablespoonful of melted butter. Heat in a pan. Stir in one egg, beaten light, with three tablespoonfuls evaporated milk not thinned. Pour the mixture on the fried bread.

Roast Potatoes

Wash and dry potatoes thoroughly, bury them deep in a good bed of coals, cover them with hot coals until well done. It will take about forty minutes for them to bake. Then pass a sharpened hard-wood sliver through them from end to end, and let the steam escape and use immediately as a roast potato soon becomes soggy and bitter.

Baked Fresh Fish

Clean well. Small fish should be fried whole with the back bone severed to prevent curling up; large fish should be cut into pieces, and ribs loosened from back bone so as to lie flat in pan. Rub the pieces in corn meal or powdered crumbs, thinly and evenly (that browns them), fry in plenty of hot fat to a golden brown, sprinkling lightly with salt just as the color turns. If fish has not been wiped dry it will absorb too much grease. If the frying fat is not very hot when fish are put in, they will be soggy with it.

Frogs' Legs

First, after skinning, soak them an hour in cold water to which vinegar has been added, or put them for two minutes into scalding water that has vinegar in it. Drain, wipe dry, and cook.

To fry: roll in flour, season with salt and pepper, and fry not too rapidly, preferably in butter or oil. Water-cress is a good relish with them. To griddle: Prepare three tablespoonsful melted butter, one half tablespoonful salt, and a pinch or two of pepper, into which dip the frogs' legs, then roll in fresh bread crumbs and broil for three minutes on each side.

Eggs

Boiled: Have water to boiling point. Place eggs in carefully. Boil steadily for three minutes if you wish them soft. If wanted hard boiled, put them in cold water, bring to a boil, and keep it up for twenty minutes. The yolk will then be mealy and wholesome.

Fried: Melt some butter or fat in frying-pan; when it hisses drop in eggs carefully. Fry them three minutes.

Scrambled: First stir the eggs up and after putting some butter in the frying-pan, stir the eggs in it after adding a little condensed milk.

Poached: First put in the frying-pan sufficient diluted condensed milk which has been thinned with enough water to float the eggs in, and let them simmer three or four minutes. Serve the eggs on slices of buttered toast, pouring on enough of the milk to moisten the toast.

Coffee

For every cup of water allow a tablespoonful of ground coffee, then add one extra. Have water come to boiling point first, add coffee, hold it just below boiling point for five minutes, and settle with one fourth of a cup of cold water. Serve. Some prefer to put the coffee in a small muslin bag loosely tied.

Cocoa

Allow a teaspoonful of cocoa for every cup of boiling water. Mix the powdered cocoa with water or boiled milk, with sugar to taste. Boil two or three minutes.

These receipts have been tried out. Biscuit and bread making have been purposely omitted. Take bread and crackers with you from camp. "Amateur" biscuits are not conducive to good digestion or happiness. Pack butter in small jar: cocoa, sugar, and coffee in small cans or heavy paper; also salt and pepper. Wrap bread in a moist cloth to prevent drying up:

bacon and dried or chipped beef in wax paper. Pickles can be purchased put up in small bottles. Use the empty bottle as candle-stick.

Sample Menu for an Over-night Camp and a Day Hike or Tramp

Breakfast

Griddle-Cakes
Fried Bacon and Potatoes
Bread   Coffee   Preserves

Dinner

Creamed Salmon on Toast
Baked Potatoes   Bread   Pickles
                          Fruit

Supper

Fried Eggs
Creamed or Chipped Beef   Cheese
              Bread   Cocoa

Ration List for Six Boys, Three Meals

2 pounds bacon (sliced thin)
1 pound butter
1 dozen eggs
½ pound cocoa
½ pound coffee
1 pound sugar
3 cans salmon
24 potatoes
2 cans condensed milk
1 small package of self-raising flour
Salt and pepper

Utensils

Small griddle
Small stew pan
Small coffee-pot
Large spoon
Plate and cup
Matches and candle.

Dish Washing

First fill the frying-pan with water, place over the fire, and let it boil. Pour out water and you will find the pan has practically cleaned itself. Clean the griddle with sand and water. Greasy knives and forks may be cleaned by jabbing them into the ground. After all grease is gotten rid of, wash in hot water and dry with cloth. Don't use the cloth first and get it greasy.

Leadership

The most important thing about a camping party is that it should always have the best of leadership. No group of boys should go camping by themselves. The first thing a patrol of scouts should do when it has determined to camp is to insist upon the scout master accompanying the members of the patrol. The reason for this is that there is less likely to be accidents of the kind that will break up your camp and drive you home to the town or city. When the scout master is one of the party, all of the boys can go in swimming when the proper time comes for such exercise, and the scout master can stay upon the bank or sit in the boat for the purpose of preventing accidents by drowning. There are also a hundred and one things which will occur in camp when the need of a man's help will show itself. A scout ought to insist on his scout master going to camp. The scout master and patrol leader should be present, in order to settle the many questions which must of necessity arise, so that there may be no need of differences or quarrels over disputed points, which would be sure to spoil the outing.

Scout Camp Program

In a scout camp there will be a regular daily program, something similar to the following :

6:30 A.M.	Turn out, bathe, etc.
7:00 A.M.	Breakfast
8:00 A.M.	Air bedding in sun, if possible, and clean camp ground
9:00 A.M.	Scouting games and practice
11:00 A.M.	Swimming
12:00 M.	Dinner
1:00 P.M.	Talk by leader
2:00 P.M.	Water games, etc.
6:00 P.M.	Supper
7:30 P.M.	Evening council around camp fire.

Order of Business

1. Opening Council
2. Roll-call
3. Record of last council
4. Reports of scouts
5. Left over business
6. Complaints
7. Honors
8. New scouts
9. New business
10. Challenges
11. Social doings, songs, dances, stories
12. Closing Council (devotional services when desired) 8:45 lights out

Water Supply

Dr. Charles E. A. Winslow, the noted biologist, is authority for the following statement: "The source of danger in water is always human or animal pollution. Occasionally we find water which is bad to drink on account of passage through the ground or on account of passage through lead pipes, but the danger is never from ordinary decomposing vegetable matter. If you have to choose between a bright clear stream which may be polluted at some point above and a pond full of dead leaves and peaty matter, but which you can inspect all around and find free from contamination, choose the pond. Even in the woods it is not easy to find surface waters that are surely protected and streams particularly are dangerous sources of water supply. We have not got rid of the idea that running water purifies itself. It is standing water which purifies itself, if anything does, for in stagnation there is much more chance for the disease germs to die out. Better than either a pond or stream, unless you can carry out a rather careful exploration of their surroundings, is ground water from a well or spring; though that again is not necessarily safe. If the well is in good, sandy soil, with no cracks or fissures, even water that has been poluted may be well purified and safe to drink. In a clayey or rocky region, on the other hand, contaminating material may travel for a considerable distance under the ground. Even if the well is protected below, a very important point to look after is the pollution from the surface. I believe more cases of typhoid fever from wells are due to surface pollution than to the character of the water itself. There is danger which can, of course, be done away with by protection of the well from surface drainage, by seeing that the surface wash is not allowed to drain toward it, and that it is protected by a tight covering from the entrance of its own waste water. If good water cannot be secured in any of these ways, it must in some way be purified. . . . Boiling will surely destroy all disease germs."

The Indians had a way of purifying water from a pond or swamp by digging a hole about one foot across and down about six inches below the water level, a few feet from the pond. After it was filled with water, they bailed it out quickly, repeating the bailing process about three times. After the third bailing the hole would fill with filtered water. Try it.

Sanitation

A most important matter when in camp, and away from modern conveniences is that of sanitation. This includes not only care as to personal cleanliness, but also as to the water supply and the proper disposal of all refuse through burial or burning. Carelessness in these matters has been the cause of serious illness to entire camps and brought about many deaths. In many instances the loss of life in the armies has been greater through disease in the camp than on the battlefields.

Typhoid fever is one of the greatest dangers in camping and is caused by unclean habits, polluted water, and contaminated milk, and food. The armies of the world have given this disease the most careful study with the result that flies have been found to be its greatest spreaders. Not only should all sources of water supply be carefully examined, an analysis obtained if possible before use, but great care should also be taken when in the vicinity of such a supply, not to pollute it in any way. In districts where typhoid is at all prevalent it is advisable for each scout to be immunized before going to camp.

A scout's honor will not permit him to disobey in the slightest particular the sanitary rules of his camp. He will do his part well. He will do everything in his power to make his camp clean, sanitary, and healthful from every standpoint.

General Hints

Two flannel shirts are better than two overcoats.

Don't wring out flannels or woolens. Wash in cold water, very soapy, hang them up dripping wet, and they will not shrink.

If you keep your head from getting hot and your feet dry there will be little danger of sickness.

If your head gets too hot put green leaves inside of your hat.

If your throat is parched, and you cannot get water, put a pebble in your mouth. This will start the saliva and quench the thirst.

Water Hints

If you work your hands like paddles and kick your feet, you can stay above water for some time even with your clothes on. It requires a little courage and enough strength not to lose your head.

Ready for the hike

Many boy swimmers make the mistake of going into the water too soon after eating. The stomach and digestive organs are busy preparing the food for the blood and body. Suddenly they are called upon to care for the work of the swimmer. The change is too quick for the organs, the process of digestion stops, congestion is apt to follow, and then paralyzing cramps.

Indian Bathing Precaution

The Indians have a method of protecting themselves from cramps. Coming to a bathing pool, an Indian swimmer, after stripping off, and before entering the water, vigorously rubs the pit of the stomach with the dry palm of his hands. This rubbing probably takes a minute, then he dashes cold water all over his stomach and continues the rubbing for another minute, and after that he is ready for his plunge. If the water in which you are going to swim is cold, try this method before plunging into the water.

Good Bathing Rule

The rule in most camps regarding entering the water is as follows: "No one of the party shall enter the water for swimming or bathing except at the time and place designated, and in the presence of a leader." Laxity in the observance of this rule will result disastrously.

Clouds

Every cloud is a weather sign. Low clouds, swiftly moving, indicate coolness and rain; hard-edged clouds, wind; rolled or jagged clouds, strong wind; "mackerel" sky, twelve hours day.

Look out for rain when

> A slack rope tightens.
> Smoke beats downward.
> Sun is red in the morning.
> There is a pale yellow or greenish sunset.

Rains

> Rain with east wind is lengthy.
> A sudden shower is soon over.
> A slow rain lasts long.
> Rain before seven, clear before eleven.
> A circle round the moon means "storm."

> "The evening red, the morning gray
> Sets the traveler on his way;
> The evening gray, the morning red
> Brings down showers upon his head."

"When the grass is dry at night
Look for rain before the light."

"When the grass is dry at morning light
Look for rain before the night."

Clear

"When the dew is on the grass
Rain will never come to pass."

A heavy morning fog generally indicates a clear day.

East wind brings rain.
West wind brings clear, bright, and cool weather.
North wind brings cold.
South wind brings heat.

Direction of the Wind

The way to find which way the wind is blowing is to throw up little bits of dry grass, or to hold up a handful of light dust and let it fall, or to suck your thumb, wet it all around and let the wind blow over it, and the cold side of it will then tell you which way the wind is blowing.

Weather Flags

The United States Weather Bureau publishes a "Classification of Clouds" in colors, which may be had for the asking. If you are near one of the weather signal stations, daily bulletins will be sent to camp upon request; also the weather map.

A set of flag signals run up each day will create interest. The flags are easily made or may be purchased.

Keep a daily record of temperature. A boy in charge of the "weather bureau" will find it to be full of interest as well as offering an opportunity to render the camp a real service. He will make a weather vane, post a daily bulletin, keep a record of temperature, measure velocity of wind, and rainfall.

How to Get Your Bearings

If you have lost your bearings, and it is a cloudy day, put the point of your knife blade on your thumb nail, and turn the blade around until the full shadow of the blade is on the nail. This will tell you where the sun is, and decide in which direction the camp is.

Face the sun in the morning, spread out your arms straight

from body. Before you is the east; behind you is the west; to your right is the south; the left hand is the north.

Grass turns with the sun. Remember this when finding your way at night.

Building a Camp Fire

There are ways and ways of building a camp fire. An old Indian saying runs, "White man heap fool, make um big fire — can't git near! Injun make um little fire — git close! Ugh! good!"

Make it a service privilege for a tent of boys to gather wood and build the fire. This should be done during the afternoon. Two things are essential in the building of a fire — kindling and air. A fire must be built systematically. First, get dry, small, dead branches, twigs, fir branches, and other inflammable material. Place these on the ground. Be sure that air can draw under it and upward through it. Next place some heavier sticks and so on until you have built the camp fire the required size. An interesting account of "How to Build a Fire by Rubbing Sticks," by Ernest Thompson Seton, will be found in Chapter II. In many camps it is considered an honor to light the fire.

Never build a large camp fire too near the tent or inflammable pine trees. Better build it in the open.

Be sure and use every precaution to prevent the spreading of fire. This may be done by building a circle of stones around the fire, or by digging up the earth, or by wetting a space around the fire. Always have the buckets of water near at hand. To prevent the re-kindling of the fire after it is apparently out, pour water over it and soak the earth for a space of two or three feet around it. This is very important, for many forest fires have started through failure to observe this caution.

Things to remember: First, *it is criminal to leave a burning fire;* second, *always put out the fire with water or earth.*

"A fire is never out," says Chief Forester H. S. Graves, "until the last spark is extinguished. Often a log or snag will smolder unnoticed after the flames have apparently been conquered only to break out afresh with a rising wind."

Be sure to get a copy of the laws of your state regarding forest fires, and if a permit is necessary to build a fire, secure it, before building the fire.

Kephart, in his book on "Camping and Woodcraft" (p. 28), says: "When there is nothing dry to strike it on, jerk the head

FOREST FIRES!

The great annual destruction of forests by fire is an injury to all persons and industries. The welfare of every community is dependent upon a cheap and plentiful supply of timber, and a forest cover is the most effective means of preventing floods and maintaining a regular flow of streams used for irrigation and other useful purposes.

To prevent forest fires Congress passed the law approved May 5, 1900, which—

Forbids setting fire to the woods, and

Forbids leaving any fires unextinguished.

This law, for offenses against which officers of the FOREST SERVICE can arrest without warrant, provides as maximum punishment—

A fine of $5,000, or imprisonment for two years, or both, if a fire is set maliciously, and

A fine of $1,000, or imprisonment for one year, or both, if fire results from carelessness.

It also provides that the money from such fines shall be paid to the school fund of the county in which the offense is committed.

THE EXERCISE OF CARE WITH SMALL FIRES IS THE BEST PREVENTIVE OF LARGE ONES. Therefore all persons are requested—

1. Not to drop matches or burning tobacco where there is inflammable material.

2. Not to build larger camp fires than are necessary.

3. Not to build fires in leaves, rotten wood, or other places where they are likely to spread.

4. In windy weather and in dangerous places, to dig holes or clear the ground to confine camp fires.

5. To extinguish all fires completely before leaving them, even for a short absence.

6. Not to build fires against large or hollow logs, where it is difficult to extinguish them.

7. Not to build fires to clear land without informing the nearest officer of the FOREST SERVICE, so that he may assist in controlling them.

This notice is posted for your benefit and the good of every resident of the region. You are requested to cooperate in preventing its removal or defacement, which acts are punishable by law.

JAMES WILSON,
Secretary of Agriculture.

The above is a copy of one of a series of notices posted in forests by the U. S. Department of Agriculture, directing attention to U. S. laws on this important subject.

of the match forward through the teeth.   Or, face the wind.
Cup your hands back toward the wind, remove the right hand
just long enough to strike the match on something very close
by, then instantly resume former position.   Flame of match
will run up stick instead of blowing away from it.

The Camp Fire

"I cannot conceive of a camp that does not have a big fire.
Our city houses do not have it, not even a fireplace.   The
fireplace is one of the greatest schools the imagination has ever

Around the camp fire

had or can ever have.   It is moral, and it always has a tremendous stimulus to the imagination, and that is why stories
and fire go together.   You cannot tell a good story unless you
tell it before a fire.   You cannot have a complete fire unless you
have a good story-teller along!

"There is an impalpable, invisible, softly stepping delight
in the camp fire which escapes analysis.   Enumerate all its
charms and still there is something missing in your catalogue.

"Any one who has witnessed a real camp fire and participated
in its fun as well as seriousness will never forget it.   The huge
fire shooting up its tongue of flame into the darkness of the
night, the perfect shower of golden rain, the company of happy

boys, and the great dark background of piny woods, the weird light over all, the singing, the yells, the stories, the fun, and then the serious word at the close, is a happy experience long to be remembered."

Camp-fire Stunts

The camp fire is a golden opportunity for the telling of stories — good stories told well. Indian legends, war stories, ghost stories, detective stories, stories of heroism, the history of life, a talk about the stars. Don't draw out the telling of a story. Make the story life-like.

College songs always appeal to boys. Let some leader start up a song in a natural way, and soon you will have a chorus of unexpected melody and harmony. As the fire dies down, let the songs be of a more quiet type like "My Old Kentucky Home," and ballads of similar nature.

When the embers are glowing is the time for toasting marsh-mallows. Get a long stick sharpened to a point, fasten a marsh-mallow on the end, hold it over the embers, not in the blaze, until the marsh-mallow expands. Oh, the deliciousness of it! Ever tasted one? Before roasting corn on the cob, tie the end of the husk firmly with string or cord; soak in water for about an hour; then put into the hot embers. The water prevents the corn from burning and the firmly tied husks enable the corn to be steamed and the real corn flavor is thus retained. In about twenty minutes the corn may be taken from the fire and eaten. Have a bowl of melted butter and salt at hand. Also a pastry brush to spread the melted butter upon the corn. Try it.

Story Telling

For an example of a good story to be told around the camp fire this excellent tale by Prof. F. M. Burr is printed by permission:

How Men Found the Great Spirit

In the olden time, when the woods covered all the earth except the deserts and the river bottoms, and men lived on the fruits and berries they found and the wild animals which they could shoot or snare, when they dressed in skins and lived in caves, there was little time for thought. But as men grew stronger and more cunning and learned how to live together, they had more time to think and more mind to think with.

Men had learned many things. They had learned that cold weather followed hot; and spring, winter; and that the sun got up in the morning and went to bed at night. They said that the great water was kindly when the sun shone, but when the sun hid its face and the wind blew upon it, it grew black and angry and upset their canoes. They found that knocking flints together or rubbing dry sticks would light the dry moss and that the flames which would bring back summer in the midst of winter and day in the midst of night were hungry and must be fed, and when they escaped devoured the woods and only the water could stop them.

These and many other things men learned, but no one knew why it all was or how it came to be. Man began to wonder, and that was the beginning of the path which led to the Great Spirit.

In the ages when men began to wonder there was born a boy whose name was Wo, which meant in the language of his time, "Whence." As he lay in his mother's arms she loved him and wondered: "His body is of my body, but from whence comes the life — the spirit which is like mine and yet not like it?" And his father seeing the wonder in the mother's eyes, said, "Whence came he from?" And there was no one to answer, and so they called him Wo to remind them that they knew not from whence he came.

As Wo grew up, he was stronger and swifter of foot than any of his tribe. He became a mighty hunter. He knew the ways of all the wild things and could read the signs of the seasons. As he grew older they made him a chief and listened while he spoke at the council board, but Wo was not satisfied. His name was a question and questioning filled his mind.

"Whence did he come? Whither was he going? Why did the sun rise and set? Why did life burst into leaf and flower with the coming of spring? Why did the child become a man and the man grow old and die?"

The mystery grew upon him as he pondered. In the morning he stood on a mountain top and stretching out his hands cried, "Whence?" At night he cried to the moon "Whither?" He listened to the soughing of the trees and the song of the brook and tried to learn their language. He peered eagerly into the eyes of little children and tried to read the mystery of life. He listened at the still lips of the dead, waiting for them to tell him whither they had gone.

He went out among his fellows silent and absorbed, always looking for the unseen and listening for the unspoken. He sat so long silent at the council board that the elders questioned him. To their questioning he replied like one awakening from a dream:

"Our fathers since the beginning have trailed the beasts of the woods. There is none so cunning as the fox, but we can trail him to his lair. Though we are weaker than the great bear and buffalo, yet by our wisdom we overcome them. The deer is more swift of foot, but by craft we overtake him. We cannot fly like a bird, but we snare the winged one with a hair. We have made ourselves many cunning inventions by which the beasts, the trees, the wind, the water and the fire become our servants.

"Then we speak great swelling words: 'How great and wise we are! There is none like us in the air, in the wood, or in the water!'

"But the words are false. Our pride is like that of a partridge drumming on his log in the wood before the fox leaps upon him. Our sight is like that of the mole burrowing under the ground. Our wisdom is like a drop of dew upon the grass. Our ignorance is like the great water which no eye can measure.

"Our life is like a bird coming out of the dark, fluttering for a heart-beat in the tepee and then going forth into the dark again. No one can tell whence it comes or whither it goes. I have asked the wise men and they cannot answer I have listened to the voice of the trees and wind and water, but I do not know their tongue; I have questioned the sun and the moon and the stars, but they are silent.

"But to-day in the silence before the darkness gives place to light, I seemed to hear a still small voice within my breast, saying to me, 'Wo, the questioner, rise up like the stag from his lair; away, alone, to the mountain of the sun. There thou shalt find that which thou seekest.' I go, but if I fail by the trail another will take it up. If I find the answer I will return."

Waiting for none, Wo left the council of his tribe and went his way toward the mountain of the sun. For six days he made his way through the trackless woods, guided by the sun by day and the stars by night. On the seventh day he came to the great mountain — the mountain of the sun, on whose top, according to the tradition of his tribe, the sun rested each night. All day long he climbed saying to himself, "I will sleep to-night in the teepee of the sun, and he will tell me whence I come and whither I go."

But as he climbed the sun seemed to climb higher and higher; and, as he neared the top, a cold cloud settled like a night bird on the mountain. Chilled and faint with hunger and fatigue, Wo struggled on. Just at sunset he reached the top of the mountain, but it was not the mountain of the sun, for many days' journey to the west the sun was sinking in the Great Water.

A bitter cry broke from Wo's parched lips. His long trail was useless. There was no answer to his questions. The sun journeyed farther and faster than men dreamed, and of wood and waste and water there was no end. Overcome with misery and weakness he fell upon a bed of moss with his back toward the sunset and the unknown.

And Wo slept, although it was unlike any sleep he had ever known before, and as he slept he dreamed. He was alone upon the mountain waiting for the answer. A cloud covered the mountain but all was silent. A mighty wind rent the cloud and rushed roaring through the crags, but there was no voice in the wind. Thunder pealed, lightning flashed, but he whom Wo sought was not there.

In the hush that followed up the storm Wo heard a voice, low and quiet, but in it all the sounds of earth and sky seemed to mingle — the song of the bird, the whispering of the trees, and the murmuring of the brook.

"Wo, I am he whom thou seekest. I am the Great Spirit. I am the All Father. Ever since I made man of the dust of the earth, and so child of the earth and brother to all living, and breathed into his nostrils the breath of life, thus making him my son, I have waited for a seeker who should find me. In the fullness of time thou hast come, Wo the questioner, to the answerer.

"Thy body is of the earth and to earth returns; thy spirit is mine; it is given thee for a space to make according to thy will; then it returns to me better or worse for thy making.

"Thou hast found me because thy heart was pure, and thy search for me tireless. Go back to thy tribe and be to them the voice of the Great Spirit. From henceforth I will speak to thee, and the seekers that come after thee in a thousand voices and appear in a thousand shapes. I will speak in the voices of the woods and streams and of those you love. I will appear to you in the sun by day and the stars by night. When thy people and mine are in need and wish for the will of the Great Spirit, then shall my spirit brood over thine and the words that thou shalt speak shall be my words."

And Wo awoke, facing the east and the rising sun. His body was warmed by its rays. A great gladness filled his soul. He had sought and found and prayer came to him like the song to the bird.

"O Great Spirit, father of my spirit, the sun is thy messenger, but thou art brighter than the sun. Drive thou the darkness before me. Be thou the light of my spirit." As Wo went down the mountain and took the journey back to the home of his people, his face shone, and the light never seemed to leave it, so that men called him "He of the shining face."

When Wo came back to his tribe, all who saw his face knew that he had found the answer, and they gathered again about the council fire to hear. As Wo stood up and looked into the eager faces in the circle of the fire, he remembered that the Great Spirit had given him no message and for a moment he was dumb. Then the words of the Great Spirit came to him again. "When thy people and mine shall need to know my will, my spirit shall brood over thine and the words that thou shalt speak shall be my words." Looking into the eager faces of longing and questioning, his spirit moved within him and he spoke:

"I went, I sought, I found the Great Spirit who dwells in the earth as your spirits dwell in your bodies. It is from Him the spirit comes. We are His children. He cares for us more than a mother for the child on her breast, or the father for the son that is his pride. His love is like the air we breathe: it is about us; it is within us.

"The sun is the sign of His brightness, the sky of His greatness and mother-love and father-love, and the love of man and woman are the signs of His love. We are but His children; we cannot enter into the council of the Great Chief until we have been proved, but this is His will, that we love one another as He loves us; that we bury forever the hatchet of hate, that no man shall take what is not his own and the strong shall help the weak."

The chiefs did not wholly understand the words of Wo, but they took a hatchet and buried it by the fire saying, "Thus bury we hate between man and his brother," and they took an acorn and put it in the earth saying, "Thus plant we the love of the strong for the weak." And it became the custom of the tribe that the great council in the spring should bury the hatchet and plant the acorn. Every morning the tribe gathered to greet the rising sun, and with right hand raised and left upon their hearts prayed: "Great Spirit hear us; guide us to-day; make our wills Thy will, our ways Thy way."

And the tribe grew stronger and greater and wiser than all the other tribes — but that is another story.

Tent Making Made Easy*

By H. J. Holden

The accompanying sketches show a few of the many different tents which may be made from any available piece of cloth or canvas. The material need not be cut, nor its usefulness for other purposes impaired, except that rings or tapes are attached at various points as indicated. For each tent the sketches show a front elevation, with a ground plan, or a side view; also a view of the material laid flat, with dotted lines to indicate where creases or folds will occur. Models may be made from stiff paper and will prove as interesting to the kindergartner in geometry as to the old campaigner in camping. In most of the tents a ring for suspension is fastened at the centre of one side. This may be supported by a pole or hung by means

---

*Reprinted from *Recreation*, Apr.1, 1911, by permission of the Editor.

of a rope from any convenient fastening; both methods are shown in the sketches. Guy ropes are required for a few of the different models, but most of them are pegged down to the ground.

After making paper models, find a stack cover, a tarpaulin, a tent fly, an awning, or buy some wide cotton cloth, say 90-inch. All the shapes may be repeatedly made from the same piece of material, if the rings for changes are left attached. In Nos. 3, 4, 6, 7, 8, 9, 11, a portion of the canvas is not used and may be turned under to serve as sod-cloth, or rolled up out of the way. If your material is a large piece, more pegs and guy lines will be required than is indicated in the sketches. The suspension ring, $1\frac{1}{2}$ inches or 2 inches in diameter, should be well fastened, with sufficient reinforcement to prevent tearing out; 1-inch rings fastened with liberal lengths of tape are large enough for the pegs and guy lines. Also reinforce along the lines of the strain from peg to pole.

Fig. 1.—A square of material hung by one corner, from any convenient support, in a manner to make a comfortable shelter; it will shed rain and reflect heat. This square makes a good fly or a good ground cloth for any of the tents.

Fig. 2.— A rectangle equal to two squares. A shelter roomy and warm, with part of one side open toward the fire.

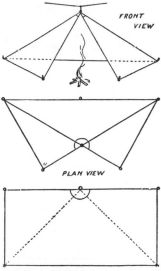

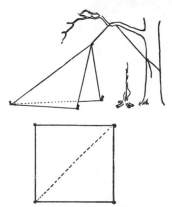

Fig. 1. Tent from a square of canvas. A 7 x 7 sheet is ample for a one-man shelter; 9 x 9 will house two

Fig. 2. Rectangle tent

Fig. 3.— Here the rectangle is folded to make a "lean-to" shelter, with the roof front suspended from a rope or from a horizontal pole by means of cords. The two corners not in use are folded under, making a partial ground cloth. A square open front is presented toward the camp fire.

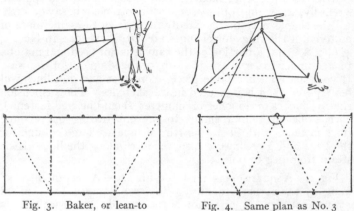

Fig. 3. Baker, or lean-to   Fig. 4. Same plan as No. 3

Fig. 4.— Same in plan as No. 3, but has a triangular front and only one point of suspension.

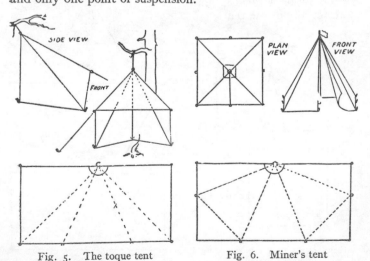

Fig. 5. The toque tent   Fig. 6. Miner's tent

Campcraft

167

Fig 5.— Uses all the cloth, has a triangular ground plan, a square front opening, plenty of head room at the back and requires two or more guy lines. This shelter resembles a "toque."

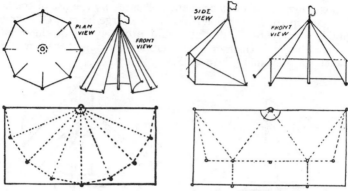

Fig. 7.   Conical tent, or wigwam

Fig. 8.   So-called canoe tent.
Requires three guy lines, and can be
supported by a rope instead of a pole

Fig. 6.— Square or "miner's" tent.   Two corners are turned under.   This tent is enclosed on all sides, with a door in front.

Fig. 7.   Conical tent or "wigwam," entirely enclosed, with door in front.   Two corners of the canvas are turned under.

Fig. 8.— Has a wall on one side and is called a "canoe tent" in some catalogues.   It requires two or more guy lines and is shown with a pole support.   The front has a triangular opening.

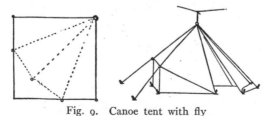

Fig. 9.   Canoe tent with fly

Fig. 9.— A combination of No. 8, with No. 1 in use as an awning or fly.   This sketch shows both tent and fly suspended by means of a rope.   The "awning" may be swung around to any angle.

Fig. 10.— Combination of Nos. 1 and 2; they may be fastened together by a coarse seam or tied with tapes. The ground plan is an equal-sided triangle, with a door opening on one side, as shown. There is no waste cloth.

Fig. 11.— No. 10 changed to a conical shape and suspended as a canopy. The circular shape is secured by the use of small-size gas pipe or limber poles bent into a large hoop. Of course guy lines may be used, but would probably be in the way. Notice that a little more material for making a wall would transform the canopy into a "Sibley" tent.

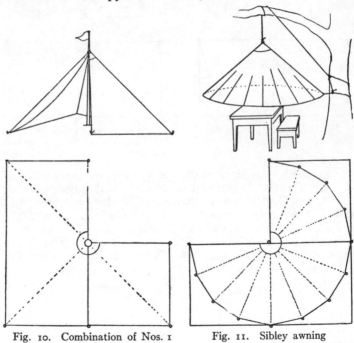

Fig. 10. Combination of Nos. 1 and 2   Fig. 11. Sibley awning

There are other shapes and combinations, but perhaps these sketches are enough in the line of suggestion.

The diagram Fig. 12 shows a method for laying out, on your cloth, the location of all the rings to make the tents and shelters. No dimensions are given and none is required. The diagram is good for any size. Most of the fastenings are found on radial lines, which are spaced to divide a semi-circle into eight equal angles, 22½ degrees each; these intersect other construction lines and locate the necessary loops and rings. Figures are given at each ring which refer back to the sketch numbers.

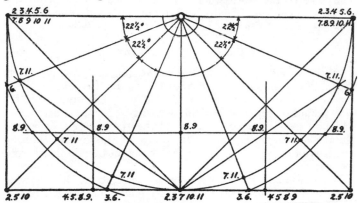

Fig. 12. Showing how ten different tents can be made with but one piece of canvas

Suppose the material at hand is the widest unbleached cotton cloth, 90 inches wide, 5 yards long, or 7½ feet by 15 feet. The accompanying table will give the dimensions for the various shapes from Fig. 1 to Fig. 11.

If in doubt about the location of rings on your canvas, suspend the tent by the centre ring and fasten the loops temporarily by means of safety pins, draw the tent into shape and shift the fastenings as required. The guy lines should have hooks or

TABLE OF DIMENSIONS, 90 IN. MATERIAL

Size	Area, Sq. Ft.	Height, Ft.	Remarks
1........7½ ft. triangle	25	6¼	One side open
2........6½ x 15 ft.	65	6¼	" " "
3........6 x 7½ ft.	45	4½	" " "
4........7½ x 8 ft.	60	5½	" " "
5........7½ ft. triangle	25	7½	" " "
6........6¼ x 6¼ ft.	39	7	Enclosed
7........7½ ft. diam.	44	6½	"
8........5 x 7½ ft.	37½	6½	2½ ft. wall
9........7½ x 8 ft.	60	6½	No. 8, with fly
10.......15 ft. triangle	97	6¼	Enclosed
11.......11¼ ft. circle	108	5	Canopy, no sides

snaps at one end for ready attachment and removal; the other end should be provided with the usual slides for "take up." The edge of the cloth where the large ring for suspension is fastened should be bound with tape or have a double hem, for it is the edge of the door in most of the tents shown.

Waterproofing a Tent

Dissolve half a pound of alum in two quarts of boiling water; then add two gallons of pure cold water. In this solution place the material and let it remain for a day. Dissolve a quarter of a pound of sugar of lead in two quarts boiling water, then add two gallons of cold water. Take the material from the alum solution, wring it lightly, place in the second solution and leave for five or six hours; then wring out again lightly and allow it to dry.

If you want to avoid trouble with a leaky tent, the following solution is a "sure cure;" Take a gallon or two gallons of turpentine and one or two cakes of paraffin, drug store size. Chip the paraffin fairly fine; dump it into the turpentine. Place the turpentine in a pail and set same in a larger pail or a tub of *hot water*. The hot water will heat the turpentine, and the turpentine will melt the paraffin. Stir thoroughly, and renew your supply of hot water if necessary. Then pile your tent into a tub and pour in the turpentine and paraffin mixture. Work the tent all over thoroughly with your hands, so that every fiber gets well saturated. You must work fast, however, as the paraffin begins to thicken as it cools; and work out of doors, in a breeze if possible, as the fumes of the turpentine will surely make you sick if you try it indoors. When you have the tent thoroughly saturated, hang it up to dry. It is not necessary to wring the tent out when you hang it up. Just let it drip. If you use too much paraffin the tent may look a little dirty after it dries, but it will be all right after you have used it once or twice.

An Open Outing Tent

By Warren H. Miller, Editor "Field and Stream."

To make an open outing tent, get thirteen yards of 8 oz. duck canvas, which can be bought at any department store or dry goods store for seventeen or eighteen cents a yard. This makes your total expense $2.21 for your tent. Lay out the strip of canvas on the floor and cut one end square; measure up 8 inches along the edge and draw a line to the other corner.

From this corner lay off 7 ft. 8 in. along the edge and on the opposite side, lay off 5 ft. 9 in. beginning at the end of your 8-in. measurement. Now take a ruler and draw another diagonal across the canvas at the ends of these measurements and you have the first gore of your tent. Cut it across, turn the gore over, lay it down on the strip so as to measure off

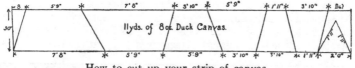

11yds. of 8 oz. Duck Canvas.

How to cut up your strip of canvas

another one exactly like it. This is the corresponding gore for the other side of the tent. To make the second pair of gores, lay off 5 ft. 9 in. along one side of the remaining strip of canvas beginning at the pointed end, and 3 ft. 10 in. on the other side. Join these points with a diagonal and you have a second gore, a duplicate of which is then cut by using it as a

Forester tent pattern

Forester tent with hood

pattern, reversing and laying it down on the strip of canvas. To make the third gore, lay off 3 ft. 10 in, on one edge of your strip beginning at the point, and 1 ft. 11 in. on the other side. Draw a diagonal across and you have the third gore.

You have now used up all but two yards of your canvas, plus a little left-over piece of about two feet long. Out of this little left-over piece make a triangle 1 ft. 11 in. on the side, which will form the back triangle of your tent. Now pin your three gores together to make the side of your tent, just as in the illustrations, and pin the two sides together along the ridge. Then sew this tent up. Sew in the little back triangle and hem all around the edges. Leave a hole at the peak of the little triangle through which the ridge pole must go.

To set it up, cut three small saplings, one of which should be twelve feet long and the other two, ten feet long. Tie these two together at the ends making what the sailors call a "shears." Take the twelve-foot pole and run it down the ridge inside the tent, and out through the hole in the back. Now raise the ridge pole with one end stuck in the ground and the front end resting on the two shear poles and tie all three of them together. At the end of each seam along the hem you must work in a little eyelet hole for a short piece of twine to tie to the tent pegs. Stretch out the back triangle, pegging it down at the two corners

Forester tent with hood

on the ground, and then peg out each hole along the foot until the entire tent stretches out taut as in our illustrations. Three feet from the peak along the front edge you must have another eyelet hole with a little piece of twine and you tie this out to the shear pole on each side which gives the tent the peculiar gambrel roof which it has, and which has the advantage of giving you lots more room inside than the straight tent would. You now have what is known as the "open" forester tent.

If a thunder storm comes up with a driving rain it will surely rain in at the front unless you turn the tent around by moving the poles one at a time. If you don't want to do this you can make a hood for the front out of the two yards of canvas you have left. Simply draw a diagonal from one corner to the other of this two-yard piece of duck and cut it down the diagonal, making two thin triangles which are sewed to the front edges of the open forester tent, making a hood of the shape shown in our picture. This prevents the rain beating in the opening of your tent but still lets the heat of your fire strike in and at the same time it keeps the heat in the tent as it will not flow out along the ridge pole as it does in the open type.

This tent weighs six pounds and packs into a little package fourteen inches long by seven inches wide by six inches thick, and can be carried as a shoulder strap or put in a back pack or any way you wish to take it. It will sleep three boys, or two men and a boy, very comfortably indeed. While it really does not need to be water-proofed, as it immediately shrinks tight after the first rain, you can water-proof it if you wish by making a solution of ten ounces of quick lime with four ounces of alum in ten quarts of water. Stir occasionally until the lime has slackened. Put the tent in another pail and pour the solution over it, letting it stand twelve hours. Take out and hang it on the clothes-line to dry. It will then be entirely water-proof.

To make a good night fire in front of the tent, drive two stout stakes three feet long in the ground about three feet from the mouth of the tent; pile four logs one on top of the other against these stakes or take a large flat stone and rest it against it. Make two log andirons for each side of the fire and build your fire in the space between them. It will give you a fine cheerful fire and all the heat will be reflected by the back logs into the tent, making it warm and cheerful. Inside you can put your browse bags stuffed with balsam browse; or pile up a mountain of dry leaves over which you can stretch your blankets. Pile all the duffle way back in the peak against the little back triangle where it will surely keep dry and will form a sort of back for your pillows. You will find the forester tent lighter and warmer than the ordinary lean-to, as it reflects the heat better. After a couple of weeks in it you will come home with your lungs so full of ozone that it will be impossible to sleep in an ordinary room without feeling smothered.

Canoeing, Rowing and Sailing*

The birch-bark canoe is the boat of the North American Indians, and our modern canvas canoes are made, with some

*Prepared with the coöperation of Mr. Arthur A. Carey, Scout Master, Boy Scout ship *Pioneer*; Mr. Carleton E. Sholl, Captain Lakanoo Boat Club Crew; Mr. Frederick K. Vreeland, Camp-Fire Club of America, and Mr. R. F. Tims, Vice-Commodore, American Canoe Association.

variations, on the Indian model. With the possible exception of the Venetian gondola, the motion of a canoe is more graceful than that of any other boat propelled by hand; it should be continuous and gliding, and so silent that it may be brought up in the night to an animal or enemy, Indian fashion, without making any sound, and so take them by surprise.

Many accidents happen in canoes — not because they are unsafe when properly handled, but because they are unsafe when improperly handled — and many people do not take

Canoeing stroke (a)

the trouble even to find out the proper way of managing a canoe. Many canoes have seats almost on a level with the gunwale, whereas, properly speaking, the only place to sit in a canoe is on the bottom; for a seat raises the body too high above the centre of gravity and makes the canoe unsteady and likely to upset. It is, however, difficult to paddle while sitting in the bottom of a canoe, and the best position for paddling is that of kneeling and at the same time resting back against one of the thwarts. The size of the single-blade paddle should be in proportion to the size of the boy who uses it — long enough to reach from the ground to the tip of his nose. The bow paddle may be a little shorter. The canoeman should learn to paddle equally well on either side of a canoe. When paddling on the

left side the top of the paddle should be held by the right hand,
and the left hand should be placed a few inches above the beginning of the blade.   The old Indian stroke, which is the most
approved modern method for all-round canoeing, whether racing or cruising, is made with the arms almost straight — but
not stiff — the arm at the top of the paddle bending only slightly
at the elbow.   This stroke is really a swing from the shoulder,
in which there is little or no push or pull with the arm.   When
paddling on the left side
of the canoe the right
shoulder swings forward
and the whole force of
the body is used to push
the blade of the paddle
through the water, the left
hand acting as a fulcrum.
While the right shoulder
is swung forward, the right
hand is at the same time
twisted at the wrist so
that the thumb goes down;
this motion of the wrist
has the effect of turning
the paddle around in the
left hand — the left wrist
being   allowed   to   bend
freely — so that, at the
end of the stroke, the blade
slides out of the water almost horizontally.   If you

Canoeing stroke   (b)

should twist the paddle in the opposite direction it would force
the head of the canoe around so that it would travel in a circle.
At the recovery of the stroke the right shoulder swings back and
the paddle is brought forward in a horizontal position, with the
blade almost parallel to the water.   It is swung forward until
the paddle is at right angles across the canoe, then the blade
is dipped edgewise with a slicing motion and a new stroke
begins.   In paddling on the right side of the canoe the position of the two hands and the motion of the two shoulders are
reversed.

Something should also be said about double paddles — that
is, paddles with two blades — one at each end — as their use
is becoming more general every year.   With the double paddle
a novice can handle a canoe head on to a stiff wind, a feat which

requires skill and experience with a single blade. The doubles give greater safety and more speed and they develop chest, arm and shoulder muscles not brought into play with a single blade. The double paddle is not to be recommended to the exclusion of the single blade, but there are many times when there is an advantage in its use.

In getting in or out of a canoe it is especially necessary to step in the very centre of the boat; and be careful never to lean on any object — such as the edge of a wharf — outside of the

Canoeing stroke   (*c*)

boat, for this disturbs your balance and may capsize the canoe. Especially in getting out, put down your paddle first, and then, grasping the gunwale firmly in each hand, rise by putting your weight equally on both sides of the canoe. If your canoe should drift away sideways from the landing-place, when you are trying to land, place the blade of your paddle flat upon the water in the direction of the wharf and gently draw the canoe up to the landing-place with a slight sculling motion.

When it is necessary to cross the waves in rough water, always try to cross them "quartering," *i. e.* at an oblique angle, but not at right angles. Crossing big waves at right angles is difficult and apt to strain a canoe, and getting lengthwise between the waves is dangerous. Always have more weight aft than in the bow; but, when there is only one person in the canoe, it may be convenient to place a weight forward as a balance; but it should always be lighter than the weight aft. A skillful canoeman will paddle a light canoe even in a strong wind by kneeling at a point about one third of the length from the stern.

For the purpose of sailing in a canoe the Lateen rig is the safest, most easily handled, and the best all-round sailing outfit. For a seventeen-foot canoe a sail having forty square feet of surface is to be recommended, and, in all except very high winds, this can be handled by one man.

The Lateen sail is made in the form of an equilateral triangle,

Canoe with sail

and two sides are fastened to spars which are connected at one end by a hinge or jaw. The mast — which should be set well forward — should be so long that, when the sail is spread and the slanting upper spar is swung from the top of the mast, the lower spar will swing level about six to eight inches above the gunwale and hang clear above all parts of the boat in going about. The sail is hoisted by a halyard attached at, or a little above, the centre of the upper spar, then drawn through a block attached to the brace which holds the mast in position, and thus to the cleats — within easy reach of the sailor. The sheet line is fastened to the lower spar, about two feet from the outer end; and, when not held in the hand, may be fastened to another cleat. Both halyard and sheet should at all times be kept clear, so as to run easily, and with knots about the cleats that can be instantly slipped.

The leeboard is a necessary attachment to the sailing outfit. It is made with two blades — about three feet long and ten inches wide would furnish a good-sized surface in the water — one dropping on each side of the canoe and firmly supported by a bar fastened to the gunwale. The blades should be so rigged that, when striking an object in the water, they will quickly release, causing no strain on the canoe. The leeboard, like a centre board, is of course intended to keep the canoe from sliding off when trying to beat up into the wind. When running free before the wind the board should be raised. The general rules for sailing larger craft apply to the canoe.

The paddle is used as a rudder and may be held by the sailor, but a better plan is to have two paddles, one over each side, made fast to the gunwale or the brace. The sailor can then grasp either one as he goes about and there is no danger of losing the paddles overboard. In sailing, the sailor sits on the bottom, on the oppsite side from the sail, except in a high wind, when he sits on the gunwale where he can the better balance the sail with his weight. The combination of sail, leeboards, and the balancing weight of the sailor, will render the canoe stiff and safe, with proper care, in any wind less than a gale. A crew may consist of two or three in a seventeen foot canoe.

The spars and mast of a sailing outfit should be of spruce or some other light but strong wood, while cedar or some non-splitting wood is best for the leeboards. Young canoeists will enjoy making their own sailing outfits; or a complete Lateen rig as made by various canoe manufacturers can be purchased either directly from them or through almost any dealer.

In case of an upset the greatest mistake is to leave the boat. A capsized canoe will support at least four persons as long as they have strength to cling to it. A single man or boy, in case of upsetting beyond swimming distance to land, should stretch himself flat upon the bottom of the canoe, with arms and legs spread down over the tumblehome toward the submerged gunwales. He can thus lie in safety for hours till help arrives. When two persons are upset, they should range themselves one on each side of the over-turned boat; and, with one hand grasping each other's wrists across the boat, use the other hand to cling to the keel or the gunwale. If the canoe should swamp,

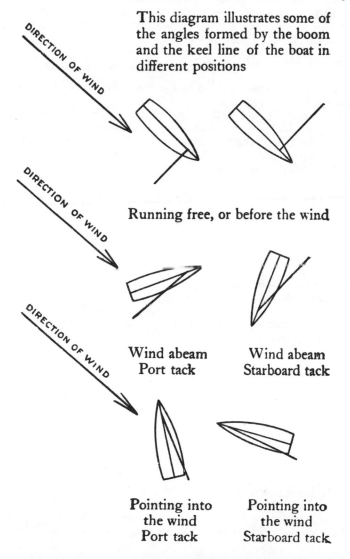

This diagram illustrates some of the angles formed by the boom and the keel line of the boat in different positions

Running free, or before the wind

Wind abeam
Port tack

Wind abeam
Starboard tack

Pointing into
the wind
Port tack

Pointing into
the wind
Starboard tack

fill with water, and begin to sink, it should be turned over in the water. It is the air remaining under the inverted hull that gives the craft sufficient buoyancy to support weight.

Never overload a canoe. In one of the ordinary size — about seventeen feet in length — three persons should be the maximum number at any time, and remember never to change seats in a canoe when out of your depth.

Row-boats

There is a certain caution in the use of boats which you will always find among sailors and fishermen and all persons who are using them constantly. Such a person instinctively steps into the middle of the boat when getting in, and always sits in the middle of the thwart or seat. This is a matter of instinct with seafaring people, and so is the habit of never fooling in a boat. Only landlubbers will try to stand up in a small boat while in motion; and, as for the man who rocks a boat "for fun," he is like the man "who didn't know the gun was loaded."

Rowing

Row-boats are propelled either by rowing or by sculling; and rowing is either "pulling" or "backing water." The usual way of rowing is to "pull" and to do so, you sit with your back to the bow and propel the boat by pulling the handles toward your body and so pressing the blades of the oars against the water toward the stern, while pushing with your feet against a brace. In backing water you reverse the action of the oars, pushing the handles away from your body and pressing the blades of the oars against the water toward the bow.

Turning

To turn your boat to the right, when pulling, you row only with the left oar; or, if you wish to make a sharp turn "pull" with the left oar and "back water" with the right. To turn your boat to the left the action of the oars is reversed.

Feathering

To prevent the momentum of the boat from being checked by the wind blowing on the blades of the oars, the blades must be turned into a horizontal position as they leave the water. In "pulling" this is done by turning the hands backward at the wrist, and in backing water it is done by turning the hands forward at the wrist.

Sculling

To scull is to propel a boat by a single oar at the stern. The boat must be provided with rowlock or a semicircular scoop in the stern, and the boat is propelled by working the oar at the stern, obliquely from side to side. This is a convenient way of doing when you are working among boats in the water, and have to go short distances without the necessity of speed.

Steering

When rowing a boat without the use of a rudder, instead of constantly turning the head around to see where you are going, it is convenient to fix upon some object in the landscape on an imaginary line with the middle of the stern and the middle of the bow; you can then keep your boat approximately in the right position, without the trouble of turning your head, by keeping the object selected on a line with the middle of the stern board.

Coming Alongside

When coming alongside of a boat or wharf always approach on the leeward side or that opposite from which the wind is blowing, and come up so that the boat will be headed into the wind and waves. Stop rowing at a convenient distance from the landing-place and come up with gentle headway; then take in the oar nearest the landing, and, if necessary, back water with the other oar.

Keeping Stroke

When two or more are rowing together the length and speed of the stroke are set by the man sitting nearest the stern.

Rough Weather

Always try to row as nearly as possible into the waves at right angles. In this way you are likely to ship less water and to avoid capsizing.

Going Ashore

When going ashore always leave your oars lying flat on the thwarts on either side of your boat.

The Salute

To salute a passing vessel or boat, hold the oars up at right angles with the water.

Every row-boat should be provided with a rough sponge and a tin dipper to be used in bailing out the water. Always bail out the water after a rain and keep your boat clean and tidy.

Sailing in Small Boats

The most convenient kind of a boat to learn to sail in is a cat-boat, which is a boat with a single fore and aft sail held in place by a boom at the bottom and a gaff at the top.

To understand the principle of sailing we must realize that a sail-boat, without the use of a rudder, acts in the water and wind very much the way a weather vane acts in the air. The bow of the boat naturally turns toward the wind, thus relieving the sail of all pressure and keeping it shaking. But if by keeping the main sheet in your hand you hold the sail in a fixed position, and, at the same time, draw the tiller away from the sail, it will gradually fill with air beginning at the hoist or mast end of the sail and impel the boat in the direction in which you are steering. Given a certain direction in which you want to travel, the problem is, by letting out or hauling in your main-sheet, to keep the sail as nearly as possible at right angles with the direction of the wind. We must remember, also, that, while the sail must be kept full, it should not be kept more than full; that is, its position must be such that, by the least push of the tiller toward the sail, the sail will begin to shake at the hoist. It is even desirable in a strong wind, and especially for beginners, to always let the sail, close to the mast, shake a little without losing too much pressure. When you are sailing with the wind coming over the boat from its port side you are sailing on the port tack, and when you are sailing with the wind coming across the boat on its starboard side you are sailing on the starboard tack. The port side of the boat is the left hand side as you face the bow while standing on board, and the starboard side is the right hand side. An easy way of remembering this is by recalling the sentence, "Jack left port."

Direction of Wind

Of course, you will see that, if you should forget which way the wind is blowing, you could not possibly know the right position for your sail; and this is one of the first requirements for a beginner. It is quite easy to become confused with regard to the direction of the wind, and therefore every boat should be provided with a small flag or fly at its mast-head and you should keep watching it at every turn of the boat until the habit has become instinctive. It is convenient to remember that the fly should always point as nearly as possible to the end of the gaff, except when you are sailing free or before the wind.

Close to Wind

Sailing with the boat pointing as nearly as possible against the wind is called sailing close to the wind; when you have turned your bow to the right or left so that the wind strikes both boat and sail at right angles you are sailing with the wind abeam; as you let out your sheet so that the boom makes a larger angle with an imaginary line running from the mast to the middle of the stern you are sailing off the wind; and, when your sail stands at right angles to this same line, you are sailing free or before the wind.

Before the Wind

Sailing free, or before the wind, is the extreme opposite of sailing close hauled or on the wind, and the wind is blowing behind your back instead of approaching the sail from the direction of the mast. If you are sailing free on the port tack, with the boom at right angles to the mast on the starboard side, and you should steer your boat sufficiently to starboard, the wind would strike the sail at its outer edge or leech and throw the sail and boom violently over to the port side of the mast. This is called jibing and is a very dangerous thing; it should be carefully guarded against whenever sailing before the wind.

Reefing

If you find that the wind is too strong for your boat, and that you are carrying too much sail, you can let her come up into the wind and take in one or two reefs.   This is done by letting out both the throat and peak halliards enough to give sufficient slack of sail, then by hauling the sail out toward the end of the boom, and afterward by rolling the sail up and tying the points under and around it, but not around the boom.   Always use a square or reef knot in tying your reef points.

In case of a squall or a strong puff of wind, remember that you can always ease the pressure on your sail by turning the bow into the wind, and if for any reason you wish to shorten suddenly you can drop your peak by loosening the peak halliards.

Ready About

Before "going about," or turning your bow so that the wind will strike the other side of the sail at its mast end, the man at the helm should always give warning by singing out the words, "ready about." "Going about" is just the opposite of jibbing.

Right of Way

When two boats approach each other in opposite directions, close hauled, the boat on the starboard tack has the right of way and should continue her course. The responsibility of avoiding a collision rests with the boat sailing on the port tack. But a boat running before the wind must always give way to a boat close hauled.

When sailing through high waves, always try as far as possible to head into them directly at right angles. Always steer as steadily as possible. If you are careful to keep the boat on her course and do not let your mind wander, only a slight motion of the tiller from side to side will be necessary.

Flying the Flag

While the "fly" or "pennant" is carried at the top of the mast, the flag is carried at the peak or upper corner of the sail at the end of the gaff. The salute consists of tipping or slightly lowering the flag and raising it again into position.

Notes

Notes

CHAPTER IV

TRACKS, TRAILING AND SIGNALING

By Ernest Thompson Seton, Chief Scout

"I wish I could go West and join the Indians so that I should have no lessons to learn," said an unhappy small boy who could discover no atom of sense or purpose in any one of the three R's.

"You never made a greater mistake," said the scribe. "For the young Indians have many hard lessons from their earliest days — hard lessons and hard punishments. With them the dread penalty of failure is 'go hungry till you win,' and no harder task have they than their reading lesson. Not twenty-six characters are to be learned in this exercise, but one thousand; not clear straight print are they, but dim, washed-out, crooked traces; not in-doors on comfortable chairs, with a patient teacher always near, but out in the forest, often alone and in every kind of weather, they slowly decipher their letters and read sentences of the oldest writing on earth — a style so old that the hieroglyphs of Egypt, the cylinders of Nippur, and the drawings of the cave men are as things of to-day in comparison — the one universal script — the tracks in the dust, mud, or snow.

"These are the inscriptions that every hunter must learn to read infallibly, and be they strong or faint, straight or crooked, simple or overwritten with many a puzzling, diverse phrase, he must decipher and follow them swiftly, unerringly if there is to be a successful ending to the hunt which provides his daily food.

"This is the reading lesson of the young Indians, and it is a style that will never become out of date. The naturalist also must acquire some measure of proficiency in the ancient art. Its usefulness is unending to the student of wild life; without it he would know little of the people of the wood."

There Are Still Many Wild Animals

It is a remarkable fact that there are always more wild animals about than any but the expert has an idea of. For example, there are, within twenty miles of New York City, fully fifty different kinds — not counting birds, reptiles, or fishes — one quarter of which at least are abundant. Or more particularly within the limits of Greater New York there are at least a dozen species of wild beasts, half of which are quite common.

"Then how is it that we never see any?" is the first question of the incredulous. The answer is: Long ago the beasts learned the dire lesson — man is our worst enemy; shun him at any price. And the simplest way to do this is to come out only at night. Man is a daytime creature; he is blind in the soft half-light that most beasts prefer.

While many animals have always limited their activity to the hours of twilight and gloom, there are not a few that moved about in daytime, but have given up that portion of their working day in order to avoid the arch enemy.

Thus they can flourish under our noses and eat at our tables, without our knowledge or consent. They come and go at will, and the world knows nothing of them; their presence might long go unsuspected but for one thing, well known to the hunter, the trapper, and the naturalist: wherever the wild four-foot goes, it leaves behind a record of its visit, its name, the direction whence it came, the time, the thing it did or tried to do, with the time and direction of departure. These it puts down in the ancient script. Each of these dotted lines, called the trail, is a wonderful, unfinished record of the creature's life during the time it made the same, and it needs only the patient work of the naturalist to decipher that record and from it learn much about the animal that made it, without that animal ever having been seen.

Savages are more skilful at it than civilized folk, because tracking is their serious life-long pursuit and they do not injure their eyes with books. Intelligence is important here as elsewhere, yet it is a remarkable fact that the lowest race of mankind, the Australian blacks, are reputed to be by far the best trackers; not only are their eyes and attention developed and disciplined, but they have retained much of the scent power that civilized man has lost, and can follow a fresh track, partly at least by smell.

It is hard to over-value the powers of the clever tracker. To him the trail of each animal is not a mere series of similar footprints; it is an accurate account of the creature's life, habit, changing whims, and emotions during the portion of life whose record is in view. These are indeed autobiographical chapters,

Tracks, Trailing and Signaling

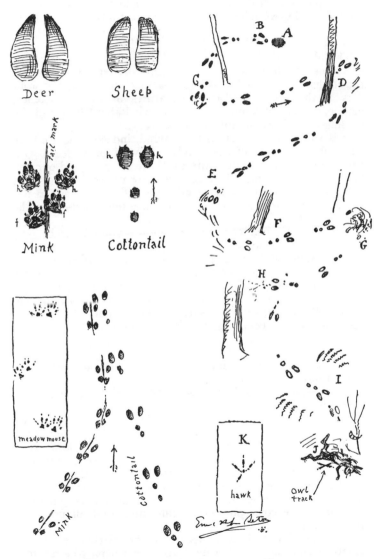

Deer

Sheep

Mink

Cottontail

meadow mouse

Mink

Cottontail

hawk

Owl track

No. 1

No. 2

and differ from other autobiographies in this — they cannot tell
a lie. We may get wrong information from them, but it is our
fault if we do; we misread the document that cannot falsify.

When to Learn Tracking

The ideal time for tracking, and almost the only time for
most folk, is when the ground is white. After the first snow
the student walks forth and begins at once to realize the wonders of the trail. A score of creatures of whose existence,
maybe, he did not know, are now revealed about him, and the
reading of their autographs becomes easy.

It is when the snow is on the ground, indeed, that we take
our four-foot census of the woods. How often we learn with
surprise from the telltale white that a fox was around our hen
house last night, a mink is living even now under the wood pile,
and a deer — yes! there is no mistaking its sharp-pointed un-
sheep-like footprint — has wandered into our woods from the
farther wilds.

Never lose the chance of the first snow if you wish to become
a trailer. Nevertheless, remember that the first morning after
a night's snow fall is not so good as the second. Most creatures
"lie up" during the storm; the snow hides the tracks of those
that do go forth; and some actually go into a "cold sleep"
for a day or two after a heavy downfall. But a calm, mild
night following a storm is sure to offer abundant and ideal
opportunity for beginning the study of the trail.

How to Learn

Here are some of the important facts to keep in view, when
you set forth to master the rudiments:

First. — No two animals leave the same trail; not only
each kind but each individual, and each individual at each
stage of its life, leaves a trail as distinctive as the creature's
appearance, and it is obvious that in that they differ
among themselves just as we do, because the young know their
mothers, the mothers know their young, and the old ones know
their mates, when scent is clearly out of the question.

Another simple evidence of this is the well known fact that
no two human beings have the same thumb mark; all living
creatures have corresponding peculiarities, and all use these
parts in making the trail.

Second. — The trail was begun at the birthplace of that
creature and ends only at its death place; it may be recorded
in visible track or perceptible odor. It may last but a few

hours, and may be too faint even for an expert with present equipment to follow, but evidently the trail is made, wherever the creature journeys afoot.

Third. — It varies with every important change of impulse, action, or emotion.

Fourth. — When we find a trail we may rest assured that, if living, *the creature that made it is at the other end.* And if one can follow, it is only a question of time before coming up with that animal. And be sure of its direction before setting out; many a novice has lost much time by going backward on the trail.

Fifth. — In studying trails one must always keep probabilities in mind. Sometimes one kind of track looks much like another; then the question is, "Which is the likeliest in this place."

If I saw a jaguar track in India, I should know it was made by a leopard. If I found a leopard in Colorado, I should be sure I had found the mark of a cougar or mountain lion. A wolf track on Broadway would doubtless be the doing of a very large dog, and a St. Bernard's footmark in the Rockies, twenty miles from anywhere, would most likely turn out to be the happen-so imprint of a gray wolf's foot. To be sure of the marks, then, one should know all the animals that belong to the neighborhood.

These facts are well known to every hunter. Most savages are hunters, and one of the early lessons of the Indian boy is to know the tracks of the different beasts about him. These are the letters of the old, old writing.

A First Try

Let us go forth into the woods in one of the North-eastern states when there is a good tracking snow, and learn a few of these letters of the wood alphabet.

Two at least are sure to be seen — the track of the blarina and of the deer mouse. They are shown on the same scale in Figs. 1 and 2, page 198.

In Fig. 3 is the track of the meadow mouse. This is not unlike that of the blarina, because it walks, being a ground animal, while the deer mouse more often bounds. The delicate lace traceries of the masked shrew, shown in Fig. 4, are almost invisible unless the sun be low; they are difficult to draw, and impossible to photograph or cast satisfactorily but the sketch gives enough to recognize them by.

The meadow mouse belongs to the rank grass in the lowland

near the brook, and passing it toward the open, running water we may see the curious track of the muskrat; its five-toed hind foot, its four-toed front foot, and its long keeled tail, are plainly on record. When he goes slowly the tail mark is nearly straight; when he goes fast it is wavy in proportion to his pace. Page 193.

The muskrat is a valiant beast; he never dies without fighting to the last, but he is in dread of another brookland creature whose trail is here — the mink. Individual tracks of this animal are shown in No. 1, page 161. Here he was bounding; the forefeet are together, the hindfeet track ahead, and tail mark shows, and but four toes in each track, though the creature has five on each foot. He is a dreaded enemy of poor Molly Cottontail, and more than once I have seen the records of his relentless pursuit. One of these fits in admirably as an illustration of our present study.

A Story of the Trail

It was in the winter of 1900, I was standing with my brother, a business man, on Goat Island, Niagara, when he remarked, "How is it? You and I have been in the same parts of America for twenty years, yet I never see any of the curious sides of animal life that you are continually coming across."

"Largely because you do not study tracks," was the reply. "Look at your feet now. There is a whole history to be read."

"I see some marks," he replied, "that might have been made by some animal."

"That is the track of a cottontail," was the answer. "Now, let us read the chapter of his life. See, he went in a general straight course as though making some well-known haunt, his easy pace, with eight or ten inches between each set of tracks, shows unalarm. But see here, joining on, is something else."

"So there is. Another cottontail."

"Not at all, this new track is smaller, the forefeet are more or less paired, showing that the creature can climb a tree; there is a suggestion of toe pads and there is a mark telling evidently of a long tail; these things combined with the size and the place identify it clearly. This is the trail of a mink. See! he has also found the rabbit track, and finding it fresh, he followed it. His bounds are lengthened now, but the rabbit's are not, showing that the latter was unconscious of the pursuit."

After one hundred yards the double trail led us to a great pile of wood, and into this both went. Having followed his

Dog tracks,
front and back
(½ life-size)

Cat tracks,
front and back
(½ life-size)

Uppermost,
well-developed human
foot

Middle, a
foot always
cramped by
boots

Bottom, a
bare foot,
never in
boots

Muskrat tracks,
(⅓ life-size)

game into dense cover, the trailer's first business was to make sure that it did not go out the other side. We went carefully around the pile; there were no tracks leading out.

"Now," I said, "if you will take the trouble to move that wood pile you will find in it the remains of the rabbit half devoured and the mink himself. At this moment he is no doubt curled up asleep."

As the pile was large and the conclusion more or less self-evident, my brother was content to accept my reading of the episode.

What About Winter Sleepers

Although so much is to be read in the wintry white, we cannot now make a full account of all the woodland four-foots, for there are some kinds that do not come out on the snow; they sleep more or less all winter.

Thus, one rarely sees the track of a chipmunk or woodchuck in truly wintry weather; and never, so far as I know, have the trails of jumping mouse or mud turtle been seen in the snow. These we can track only in the mud or dust.   Such trails cannot be followed as far as those in the snow, simply because the mud and dust do not cover the whole country, but they are usually as clear and in some respects more easy of record.

How to Make Pictures of Tracks

It is a most fascinating amusement to learn some creature's way of life by following its fresh track for hours in good snow. I never miss such a chance.   If I cannot find a fresh track, I take a stale one, knowing that, theoretically, it is fresher at every step, and from practical experience that it always brings one to some track that is fresh.

How often I have wished for a perfect means of transferring these wild life tales to paper or otherwise making a permanent collection.   My earliest attempts were in free-hand drawing, which answers, but has this great disadvantage — it is a translation, a record discolored by an intervening personality, and the value of the result is likely to be limited by one's own knowledge at the time.

Casting in plaster was another means attempted; but not one track in ten thousand is fit to cast.   Nearly all are blemished and imperfect in some way, and the most abundant — those in snow — cannot be cast at all.

Then I tried spreading plastic wax where the beasts would walk on it, in pathways or before dens.   How they did scoff! The simplest ground squirrel knew too much to venture on my waxen snare; around it, or if hemmed in, over it, with a mighty bound they went; but never a track did I so secure.

Photography naturally suggested itself, but the difficulties proved as great as unexpected, almost as great as in casting. Not one track in one thousand is fit to photograph; the essential details are almost always left out.   You must have open sunlight, and even when the weather is perfect there are practically but two times each day when it is possible — in mid-morning and mid-afternoon, when the sun is high enough for clear photographs and low enough to cast a shadow in the faint track.

The Coon that Showed Me How

Then a new method was suggested in an unexpected way. A friend of mine had a pet coon which he kept in a cage in his bachelor quarters up town.   One day, during my friend's absence the coon got loose and set about a series of long-deferred exploring expeditions, beginning with the bachelor's bedroom. The first promising object was a writing desk. Mounting by a chair the coon examined several uninteresting books and papers, and then noticed higher up a large stone bottle. He had several times found pleasurable stuff in bottles, so he went for it. The cork was lightly in and easily disposed of, but the smell was far from inviting, for it was merely a quart of ink. Determined to leave no stone unturned, however, the coon upset the ink to taste and try. Alas! it tasted even worse than it smelt; it was an utter failure as a beverage.

And the coon, pushing it contemptuously away, turned to a pile of fine hand-made, deckle-edge, heraldry note-paper — the pride of my friend's heart — and when he raised his inky little paws there were left on the paper some beautiful black prints. This was a new idea: the coon tried it again and again. But the ink held out longer than the paper, so that the fur-clad painter worked over sundry books, and the adjoining walls, while the ink, dribbling over everything, formed a great pool below the desk. Something attracted the artist's attention, causing him to jump down. He landed in the pool of ink, making it splash in all directions; some of the black splotches reached the white counterpane of the bachelor's bed. Another happy idea: the coon now leaped on the bed, racing around as long as the ink on his feet gave results. As he paused to rest, or perhaps to see if any places had been neglected, the door opened, and in came the landlady. The scene which followed was too painful for description; no one present enjoyed it. My friend was sent for to come and take his coon out of there forever. He came and took him away, I suppose "forever." He had only one other place for him — his office and there it was I made the animal's acquaintance and heard of his exploit — an ink and paper, if not a literary affair.

This gave me the hint at the Zoo I needed, a plan to make an authentic record of animal tracks. Armed with printer's ink and paper rolls I set about gathering a dictionary collection of imprints.

After many failures and much experiment, better methods were devised. A number of improvements were made by my wife; one was the substitution of black paint for printer's ink, as the latter dries too quickly; another was the padding of the paper, which should be light and soft for very light animals, and stronger and harder for the heavy. Printing from a mouse, for example, is much like printing a delicate etching; ink, paper, dampness, etc., must be exactly right, and furthermore, you have this handicap — you cannot regulate the pressure. This is, of course, strictly a Zoo method. All attempts to secure black prints from wild animals have been total failures. The paper, the smell of paint, etc., are enough to keep the wild things away.

In the Zoo we spread the black pad and the white paper in a narrow, temporary lane, and one by one drove, or tried to drive, the captives over them, securing a series of tracks that are life-size, properly spaced, absolutely authentic, and capable of yielding more facts as the observer learns more about the subject.

As related here, all this sounds quite easy. But no one has any idea how cross, crooked, and contrary a creature can be, until he wishes it to repeat for him some ordinary things that it has hitherto done hourly. Some of them balked at the paint, some at the paper, some made a leap to clear all, and thereby wrecked the entire apparatus. Some would begin very well, but rush back when half-way over, so as to destroy the print already made, and in most cases the calmest, steadiest, tamest of beasts became utterly wild, erratic, and unmanageable when approached with tracklogical intent.

Trying It on the Cat

Even domestic animals are difficult. A tame cat that was highly trained to do anything a cat could do, was selected as promising for a black track study, and her owner's two boys volunteered to get all the cat tracks I needed. They put down a long roll of paper in a hall, painted pussy's feet black, and proceeded to chase her up and down. Her docility banished under the strain. She raced madly about, leaving long, useless splashes of black; then, leaping to a fanlight, she escaped up stairs to take refuge among the snowy draperies. After which the boys' troubles began.

Drawing is Mostly Used

These, however, are mere by-accidents and illustrate the many practical difficulties. After these had been conquered with patience and ingenuity, there could be no doubt of the value of the prints. They are the best of records for size, spacing, and detail, but fail in giving incidents of wild life, or the landscape surroundings. The drawings, as already seen, are best for a long series and for faint features; in fact, the drawings alone can give everything you can perceive; but they fail in authentic size and detail.

Photography has this great advantage — it gives the surroundings, the essential landscape and setting, and, therefore, the local reason for any changes of action on the part of the animal; also the æsthetic beauties of its records are unique, and will help to keep the method in a high place.

Thus each of the three means may be successful in a different way, and the best, most nearly perfect alphabet of the woods, would include all three, and consist of a drawing, a pedoscript and a photograph of each track, and a trail; *i. e.*, a single footprint, and the long series of each animal.

My practice has been to use all whenever I could, but still I find free-hand drawing is the one of the most practical application. When I get a photograph I treasure it as an adjunct to the sketch.

A Story of the Trail

To illustrate the relative value as records, of sketch and photograph, I give a track that I drew from nature, but which could not at any place have been photographed. This was made in February 15, 1885, near Toronto. It is really a condensation of the facts, as the trail is shortened where uninteresting   Page 189, No. 2.

At *A*, I found a round place about 5 x 8 inches, where a cottontail had crouched during the light snowfall. At *B* he had leaped out and sat looking around; the small prints in front were made by his forefeet, the two long ones by his hind feet, and farther back is a little dimple made by the tail, showing that he was sitting on it. Something alarmed him, causing him to dart out at full speed toward *C* and *D*, and now a remarkable change is to be seen: the marks made by the front feet are behind the large marks made by the hind feet, because the rabbit overreaches each time; the hind feet track ahead of the front feet; the faster he goes, the farther ahead those hind feet get; and what would happen if he multiplied his speed by ten I really cannot imagine. This overreach of the hind feet takes place in most bounding animals.

Now the cottontail began a series of the most extraordinary leaps and dodgings (*D,E,F.*) as though trying to escape from some enemy. But what enemy? There were no other tracks. I began to think the rabbit was crazy — was flying from an imaginary foe — that possibly I was on the trail of a March hare. But at *G* I found for the first time some spots of blood.

This told me that the rabbit was in real danger but gave no clue to its source. I wondered if a weasel were clinging to its neck. A few yards farther, at *H*, I found more blood. Twenty yards more, at *I*, for the first time on each side of the rabbit trail, were the obvious marks of a pair of broad, strong wings. Oho! now I knew the mystery of the cottontail running from a foe that left no track. He was pursued by an eagle, a hawk,

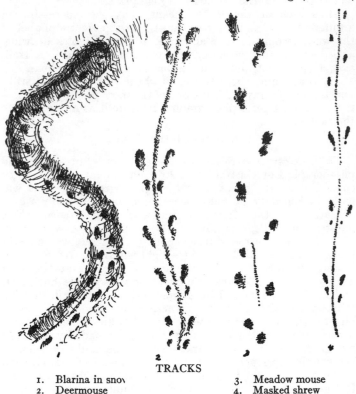

TRACKS

1. Blarina in snow
2. Deermouse
3. Meadow mouse
4. Masked shrew

or an owl. A few yards farther and I found the remains (*J*) of the cottontail partly devoured. This put the eagle out of the question; an eagle would have carried the rabbit off boldly. A hawk or an owl then was the assassin. I looked for something to decide which, and close by the remains found the peculiar two-paired track of an owl. A hawk's track would have been as *K*, while the owl nearly always sets its feet in the ground with two toes forward and two toes back. But which owl? There were at least three in the valley that might be blamed. I looked for more proof and got it on the near-by sapling — one small feather, downy, as are all owl feathers, and bearing three broad bars, telling me plainly that a barred owl had been there lately, and that, therefore, he was almost certainly the slayer of the cottontail.   As I busied myself making notes, what should come flying up the valley but the owl himself — back to the very place of the crime, intent on completing his meal no doubt.   He alighted on a branch ten feet above my head and just over the rabbit remains, and sat there muttering in his throat.

The proof in this case was purely circumstantial, but I think that we can come to only one conclusion; that the evidence of the track in the snow was complete and convincing.

Meadow Mouse

The meadow mouse autograph (page 189) illustrates the black-track method.   At first these dots look inconsequent and fortuitous, but a careful examination shows that the creature had four toes with claws on the forefeet, and five on the hind, which is evidence, though not conclusive, that it was a rodent; the absence of tail marks shows that the tail was short or wanting; the tubercules on each palm show to what group of mice the creature belongs.   The alternation of the track shows that it was a ground-animal, not a tree-climber; the spacing shows the shortness of the legs; their size determines the size of the creature.   Thus we come near to reconstructing the animal from its tracks, and see how by the help of these studies, we can get much light on the by-gone animals whose only monuments are tracks in the sedimentary rocks about us — rocks that, when they received these imprints, were the muddy margin of these long-gone creatures' haunts.

What the Trail Gives — The Secrets of the Woods

There is yet another feature of trail study that gives it exceptional value — it is an account of the creature pursuing its ordinary life.   If you succeeded in getting a glimpse of a fox or a hare in the woods, the chances are a hundred to one that it was aware of your presence first.   They are much cleverer than we are at this sort of thing, and if they do not actually sight or sense you, they observe, and are warned by the action of some other creature that did sense us, and so cease their occupations to steal away or hide.   But the snow story will

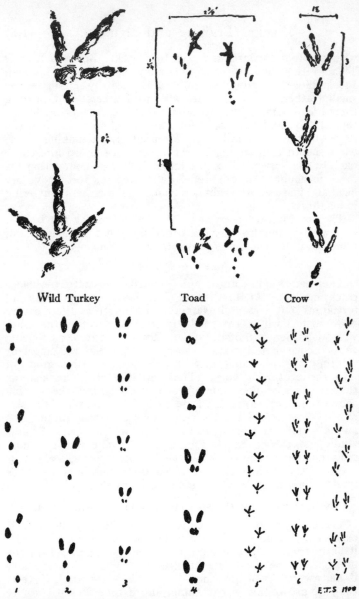

Wild Turkey   Toad   Crow

E.T.S 1900

1. Jackrabbit   2. Cottontail   3. Gray squirrel   4. Coon   5. Ground bird, such as quail   6. Tree-bird   7. A bird living partly in tree, partly on ground

tell of the life that the animal ordinarily leads — its method of searching for food, its kind of food, the help it gets from its friends, or sometimes from its rivals — and thus offers an insight into its home ways that is scarcely to be attained in any other

Horses' Tracks
N.B.—The large tracks represent the hind feet.

Walking

Trotting

Canter

O.F.   O.H   N.H   N.R.   O.F.
6' 6"   3' 10"   7' 6"   5' 0"
O.H.=Off Hind, etc.

Galloping

Lame Horse Walking : Which leg is he lame in ?

These are the tracks of two birds on the ground. One lives generally on the ground, the other in bushes and trees. Which track belongs to which bird ?

(From Sir Robert Baden Powell's book)

way. The trailer has the key to a new storehouse of Nature's secrets, another of the Sybilline books is opened to his view; his fairy godmother has, indeed, conferred on him a wonderful gift in opening his eyes to the foot-writing of the trail. It is like giving sight to the blind man, like the rolling away of fogs from a mountain view, and the trailer comes closer than others to the heart of the woods.

> Dowered with a precious power is he,
> He drinks where others sipped,
> And wild things write their lives for him
> In endless manuscript.

The American Morse Telegraph Alphabet

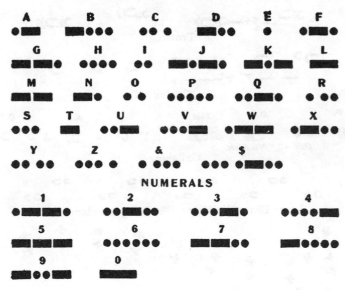

NUMERALS

Punctuation

Comma, ● ▬ ● ▬	Exclamation, ▬ ▬ ▬
Semicolon, Si	Parenthesis, Pn
Colon, Ko	Brackets, Bn
Period, ● ● ● ▬ ▬ ◡ ●	Dollar mark, Sx
Interrogation, ▬ ● ● ▬ ●	Dash, Dx
Quotation, Qn	Hyphen, Hx
Paragraph, ▬ ▬ ▬ ▬	Underline, Ux

Signals

4. Start me.
5. Have you anything for me?
9. Train order (or important military message) — give away.
13. Do you understand?

25. Busy.
30. Circuit closed (or closed station).
73. Accept compliments.
92. Deliver (ed).

Abbreviations

Ahr–Another.	G R–Government rate.
Ans–Answer.	N M–No more.
Ck–Check.	Min–Wait a moment
Col–Collect.	O B–Official business.
D H–Dead head.	O K–All right
G A–Go ahead.	Opr–Operator.
G E–Good evening.	Pd–Paid.
G M–Good morning.	Qk–Quick.
G N–Good night.	Sig–Signature.

Rememberable Morse or Re-Morse Alphabet

A

Nimble
Nig ———

Blunderbus Bang Bang Bang • • •

O

Couriers couring

Pussy's Prints • • • •

Dog & Ducts

Quails & toast

Eyelana •

R is Reverse of G

Frogs in France

Stones

Gay Goats

T

Hop Hop Hop Hop • • • •

U u u beast
• •

I's

V v-v-v-very
• • • —

J Jim; Jam;

Wolf & Waggons

Kids Kaherring

X x pen ; ;

Lance ———

Y Ya Ya

M ma ma

Z zoo ; !

&c is Z backward ● ●●●

By this method it is possible to learn the Morse alphabet in less than
an hour

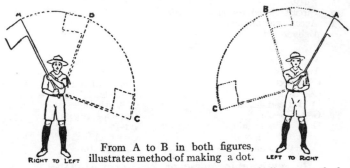

From A to B in both figures,
illustrates method of making a dot.

RIGHT TO LEFT　　　LEFT TO RIGHT

A complete swing from A to C in both figures indicates method of making a dash.

Wig-Wag or Myer Code

Instructions for Using the System

The whole number opposite each letter or numeral stands for that letter or numeral.

A.................22	J................1122	S.............212
B................2112	K...............2121	T..................2
C................121	L..............221	U.............112
D................222	M...............1221	V............1222
E.................12	N...............11	W............1121
F................2221	O................21	X............2122
G...............2211	P...............1212	Y.............111
H................122	Q...............1211	Z............2222
I..................1	R..............211	tion...........1112

Numerals

1..............1111	2..............2222
3..............1112	4..............2221
5..............1122	6..............2211
7..............1222	8..............2111
9..............1221	0..............2112

Conventional Signals

End of word....................3
End of sentence...............33
End of message 333
x x 3.......numerals follow (or) numerals end.
sig 3........signature follows.
Error....................12 12 3
Acknowledgment, or "I understand" 22 22 3
Cease signaling 22 22 22 333
Signal faster 2212 3

Wait a moment 1111 3
Repeat after (word)
　　121 121 3 22 3 (word).
Repeat last word ... 121 121 33
Repeat last message
　　121 121 121 333
Move a little to right
　　211 211 3
Move a little to left
　　221 221 3

Abbreviations

a	after	n	not	ur	your
b	before	r	are	w	word
c	can	t	the	wi	with
h	have	u	you	y	yes

Rememberable Myer Code

The elements — a thick and a thin, *i. e.* 2 and 1

A. 22 Angry Apes

N. 11. Ninepins

B. 2112, Beauty

O. 21, Owl & Onion

C. 121. Cooky Candles

P. 1212. Pots & Paddles

D. 222. Dree Donkeys

Q. 1211. Queer Quirks

E. 12 Emu & Elephant

R. 211 Ram Race

F. 2221 Funny Fruit

S. 212 Soup & Sausage

G. 2211 Girls & Goats

T. 2 Te- Two

H. 122 Happy Hooligans

U. 112 Uni- corn

I. 1

V. 1222 Viper & Venison

J. 1122 Jays & Jam

W. 1121 Wonderful Wind- mill

K. 2121 Kountry Kupples

X. 2122 Xtreme Xpress- ions

L. 221 Lambs & Lady

Y. 111. Yoemen

M. 1221 Maps & Monkeys

Z. 2222 Zoo Zoo Zoo Zoo or Two Two Two Two

To Signal with Flag or Torch Wig-Wag

There is but one position and three motions.

The first position is with the flag or other appliance held vertically, the signalman facing squarely toward the station with which it is desired to communicate.

The first motion ("one" or "1") is to the right of the sender and will embrace an arc of 90 degrees, starting with the vertical and returning to it, and will be made in a plane at right angle to the line connecting the two stations.

The second motion ("two" or "2") is a similar motion to the left of the sender.

The third motion ("front," "three" or "3") is downward, directly in front of the sender, and instantly returned upward to the first position.

Numbers which occur in the body of a message must be spelled out in full. Numerals may be used in signaling between stations having naval books, using the code calls.

To break or stop the signals from the sending station, make with the flag or other signal 12 12 12 continuously.

To Send a Message

To call a station signal its letter until acknowledged; if the call letter be not known, signal "E" until acknowledged. To acknowledge a call, signal "I understand," followed by the call letter of the acknowledging station.

Make a slight pause after each letter and also after "front." If the sender discovers that he has made an error he should make 3 followed by 12 12 3, after which he begins the word in which the error occurred.

The Semaphore Signal Code

The scout may learn the correct angles at which to hold the flags from the diagram. The easiest method of learning the alphabet is by grouping the various letters together as follows:

For all letters from A to G, one arm only is used, making a quarter of a circle for each letter in succession.

The letters from H to N (except J) — the right arm stands at A while the left moves round the circle for the other letters.

For O to S, the right arm stands at B — the left arm moves round as before.

For T, U, Y and the "annul," the right arm stands at C, the left moving to the next point of the circle successively.

The numerical sign J (or alphabetical sign) and V — the right arm stands at position for letter D the left arm only being moved.

W and X — the left arm stands at position for letter E, the right in this case moving down 45 degrees to show letter X.

For the letter Z, the left arm stands at the position G — the right arm crosses the breast taking the position F.

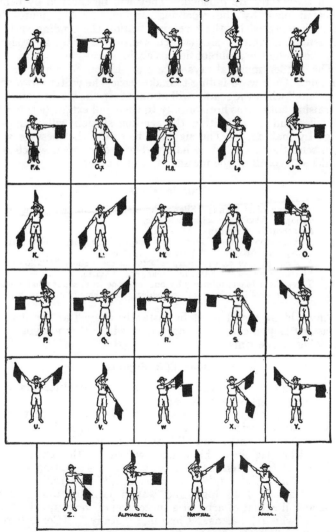

The letters A to I also stand for the figures 1 to 9 (K standing for O), if you make the numerical sign to show that you are going to send numbers followed by the alphabetical sign (J) when the figures are finished. They will be checked by being repeated back by the receiving station. Should figures be wrongly repeated by the receiving station the sending station will send the "annul" sign (which is answered by the same sign) and then send the group of figures again.

The sender must always face the station to which he is sending. On a word failing to make sense, the writer down will say, "no," when the reader will at once stop the sending station by raising both arms horizontally to their full extent (letter R). This demand for repetition the sending station will acknowledge by making J. The signaller receiving the message will then send the last word he has read correctly, upon which the sender will continue the message from that word.

Whistle Signs

1. One long blast means "Silence," "Alert," "Look out for my next signal." Also approaching a station.
2. Two short blasts means "All right."
3. A succession of long, slow blasts means "Go out," "Get farther away," or "Advance," "Extend," "Scatter."
4. A succession of short, sharp blasts means "Rally," "Close in," "Come together," "Fall in," "Danger," "Alarm."
5. Three short blasts followed by one long one from scout master calls up the patrol leaders — *i.e.*, "Leaders, come here."

Any whistle signal must be instantly obeyed at the double — as fast as you can run — no matter what other job you may be doing at the time.

Hand or Flag Signals

Hand signals, which can also be made by patrol leaders with their patrol flags when necessary:

Hand waved several times across the face from side to side or flag waved horizontally, from side to side opposite the face, means "No," "Never mind," "As you were."

Hand or flag held high, and waved as though pushing forward, at full extent of arm, or whistle a succession of slow blasts means "Extend," "Go farther out," "Scatter."

Hand or flag held high, and waved rapidly from side to side, at full extent of arm, or a succession of short, quick blasts on the whistle, means "Close in," "Rally," "Come here," "Danger," "Cattle on track."

Hand or flag pointing in any direction means "Go in that direction."

Clenched hand or flag jumped rapidly up and down several times means, "Hurry," "Run."

The movement, pushing or beckoning, indicates whether "Hurry here" or "Hurry there."

Hand (or flag) held straight up over head, palm forward, means "Stop," "Halt."

When a leader is shouting an order or message to a scout who is some way off, the scout, if he hears what is being said, should hold up his hand level with his head all the time. If he cannot hear, he should stand still, making no sign. The leader will then repeat louder, or beckon to the scout to come in nearer.

The following signals are made by a scout with his staff when he is sent out to reconnoitre within sight of his patrol, and they have the following meaning:

Staff held up horizontally, that is, level, with both hands above the head, means, "I have found."

The same, but with staff moved up and down slowly, means, "I have found, but a long way off."

The same, staff moved up and down rapidly, means, "I have found, and close by."

The staff held straight up over the head means, "Nothing in sight."

Indian Signs and Blazes

Shaking a blanket: I want to talk to you.

Hold up a tree-branch: I want to make peace.

Hold up a weapon, means war: I am ready to fight.

Hold up a pole horizontally, with hands on it: I have found something.

 This is good water.

 Good water not far in this direction.

 A long way to good water, go in direction of arrow.

 We camped here because one of us was sick.

War or trouble about.

Peace.

Road to be followed.

Letter hidden three paces from here in the direction of arrow.

This path not to be followed.

"I have gone home."

WIRELESS TELEGRAPHY

The Boy Scout Wireless Club
Y. M. C. A., Newark, N. J.

The following directions are given for an up-to-date wireless apparatus for stationary use in the home or at the meeting place of each patrol.

We will consider the receiving apparatus first:

The first thing to do is to build an aerial. First find out how long your location will allow you to build it, and how high. It ought to be at least 50 to 60 feet high and about 70 to 100 feet long. The main point in building an aerial is to have it

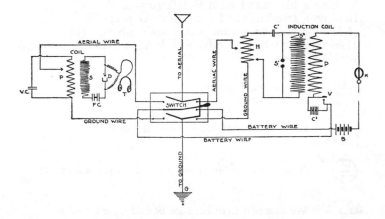

well insulated from the ground, and all connections in wire perfectly solid. It is advisable to solder every connection and to make your aerial strong as it has a great deal to do with the working qualities of the station.

After this is completed, the inside work on instruments should begin.

1. A pair of watch-case receivers having a resistance of 1,000 ohms each, manufactured by a reliable firm.
2. A loose coupler tuning coil of about 800 meters.
3. One of Mordock's metal detectors or one of similar design.
4. A variable condenser of about 5–10 plates.
5. A fixed condenser so arranged that its capacity can be changed if desired.

With these instruments the receiving set is complete, so we next take up the sending apparatus.

1. A two-inch induction coil.
2. A heavy spark gap (zinc preferable)
3. One wireless key with heavy contacts.
4. A plate condenser which can be easily made by any scout. Good glass is the main point.
5. A triple pole, double throw aerial switch. (Can be made by scouts.)

Now you have everything necessary to go ahead and assemble your station. The next thing is to connect them up

Above is a diagram which will make a good station for a scout. This station, if the aero is of the proper height, is capable of sending messages from 8 to 10 miles.

The Receiving Set

Perhaps the most fundamentally important part of a wireless telegraph station is the aerial. Its construction varies with each station, but a few general suggestions may be of use.

The builder should aim to get as high and as long an aerial as possible, height being the more important factor. In a stationary set the aerial may be fastened to a tree or pole or high building while in a field set a tree or an easily portable pole must be used.

The aerial itself should be made of copper wire and should be hung between spreaders as long as convenient and insulated from them by two cleat insulators in series at each end.

The experimenter should see that his leading-in wire is placed conveniently and comes in contact with the walls, etc., as little as possible. All points of contact must be well insulated with glass, porcelain, or hard rubber.

The tuning coil is very simple in construction. A cardboard tube, about three inches in diameter, is mounted between two square heads. This tube is wound with No. 24 insulated copper wire and very well shellaced to avoid loosening of the wire.

Two pieces of one quarter inch square brass rod, to be fastened between the heads, are secured, and a slider, as shown in drawing, is made. The rods are fastened on the heads and the insulation in the path of the slides is then well scraped off. Binding posts are then fastened to rods and coil ends.

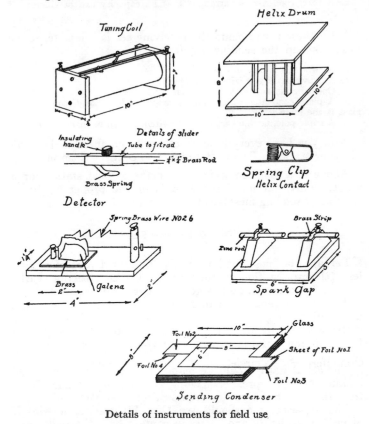

Details of instruments for field use.

The detector, although the most important of the instruments, is perhaps the simplest. It is constructed of a hardwood base with a small brass plate fastened on by means of a binding post. On the other end of the base is fastened a double binding post which holds a brass spring, as in the drawing. On the end of this spring is fastened a copper point made by winding a few inches of No. 36 or 40 wire on it and allowing about three sixteenths of an inch to project. This completes the detector but, for use in this instrument, lead sulphide or Galena crystals must be secured.

The condenser is made of two pieces of tin-foil, four by ten, and three pieces of waxed paper a little larger than the foil. A piece of wire is twisted into the end of each piece of foil, and then one sheet of foil is laid on a sheet of paper. This is then covered by another sheet of paper upon which is laid the second sheet of foil. On top of this is laid the third sheet of paper and the whole is folded into a convenient bundle. The sheets of foil must be well insulated from each other and the wires must project from the condenser.

The ground connection is made by soldering a wire to a cold-water pipe. In the case of a portable set the ground may be made by driving a metal rod into the ground or sinking metal netting into a body of water.

The telephone receivers cannot well be made and must therefore be bought. The type of 'phones used will therefore depend entirely on the builder's purse.

The Sending Set

The same aerial and ground are used for sending as were used for receiving, and for the experimenter, it will be far cheaper to buy a spark coil for his sending set than to attempt to make one.

For a field set there will be very little need of a sending helix, as close tuning will be hardly possible; but for the stationary set this is very useful.

The helix is made by building a drum with square heads fastened together by six or eight uprights, arranged on the circumference of a circle. On this then are wound ten or twelve turns of No. 10 or 12, brass or copper wire. Binding posts are fastened to the ends of the wire and variable contact made on the turns by means of metal spring clips.

The spark gap is made of a hard-wood base with two uprights to which are fastened strips of brass. Under these strips are placed two pieces of battery zincs so as to make the gap between their ends variable. Binding posts are fastened to the strips for contact.

The sending condenser is the same as the receiving in construction, but different in material. The dielectric is glass while the conducting surfaces are tin-foil, arranged in a pile of alternate sheets of glass and foil. The foil is shaped as in drawing and alternate sheets have their lugs projecting on opposite sides, all lugs on same side being connected together. For a one-inch coil but a few of these plates are needed, but for higher power a greater number are necessary.

All that now remains is the setting up of the instruments. They are arranged as in the drawing, a double-point,

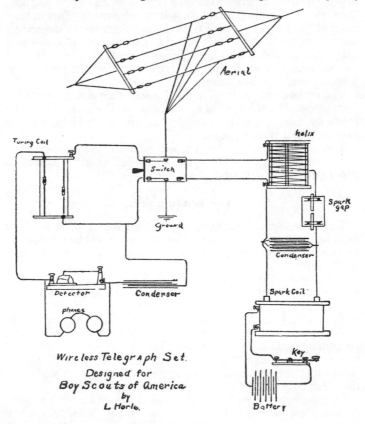

Wireless Telegraph Set.
Designed for
Boy Scouts of America
by
L. Horle.

double-throw switch being used to switch from sending to receiving.

After having connected up the receiving instruments, the receiver is placed at the ear and the point of the detector placed on the various parts of the mineral until the signals are heard clearly. Then the tuning coil is adjusted until the signals are loudest.

The sending apparatus is set up, the key and batteries having been bought or made, and used to call some other station. The clip is put on various twins of the helix until the other station signals that the signals are loudest. The station is then ready for actual operation.

NOTES

Notes

Notes

Notes

CHAPTER V

HEALTH AND ENDURANCE

George J. Fisher, M. D.

*Secretary, Physical Department International Committee Young Men's
Christian Association*

Fitness

Two things greatly affect the conditions under which a boy
lives in these days. One is that he lives in-doors for the greater
part of the time, and the other is that he must attend school,
which is pretty largely a matter of sitting still. Two things
therefore are needs of every boy: out-door experience and
physical activity.

To secure endurance, physical power, physical courage, and
skill, the first thing needful is to take stock of one's physical
make-up, put the body in the best possible condition for doing
its work and then keep it in good order.

Proper Carriage

Head up, chin in, chest out, and shoulders back is a good
slogan for a boy scout who desires an erect figure. One can
scarcely think of a round-shouldered scout. Yet there are
such among the boys who desire to be scouts.

There is no particular exercise that a boy can take to cure
round shoulders. The thing to remember is that all exercise
that is taken should be done in the erect position, then the
muscles will hold the body there.

An erect body means a deeper chest, room for the
important organs to work and thus affords them the best
chance to act.

A few setting-up exercises each day in the erect position will
help greatly to get this result.

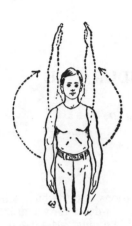
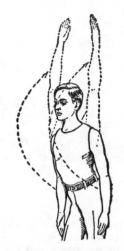

Exercise 1

Position: Heels together, arms down and at sides, palms in.

Movement: Swing arms, sideways, upward to vertical, and return.

Exercise 2

Same as Exercise 1, except that arms are swung forward, upward to vertical.

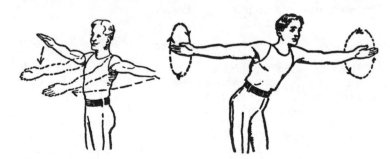

Exercise 3

Position: Arms extended to side horizontal.

Movement: Swing forward and return.

(Emphasis upon backward movement.)

Exercise 4

Position: Arms at side, horizontal, back slightly arched.

Movement: Circle arms backward.

Setting-up Exercises

Exercise 5

Position: Forearms flexed at side of chest.

Movement: Thrust arms forward and return.

Exercise 6

Position: Arms at front, horizontal, forearms flexed, fingers on shoulders.

Movement: Swing backward to side, horizontal in position.

Exercise 7

Position: Same as Exercise 6.

Movement: Swing downward, forward, bringing arms beyond sides of body. Rise on toes with end of backward swing.

Exercise 8a

Position: Arms at vertical, thumbs locked, head fixed between arms.

Exercise 8b

Movement: Bend forward as far as possible, without bending knees, and return.

Setting-up Exercises

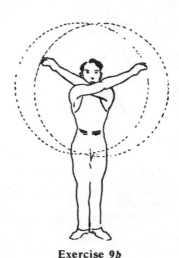

Exercise 9a

Position: Arms at vertical. Repeat exercise 8b

Exercise 9b

Movement: Arm circles, downward, inward, across chest. Reverse the movement.

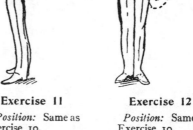

Exercise 10

Position: Arms on hips.
Movement: Forward bend.

Exercise 11

Position: Same as Exercise 10.
Movement: Backward bend.

Exercise 12

Position: Same as Exercise 10.
Movement: Sideward bend, right and left.

Setting-up Exercises

Exercise 13

Position: Same as Exercise 10.
Movement: Rotate body of waist.

Exercise 14

Position: Same as Exercise 10.
Movement: Raise high on toes. (Hold shoulders back firmly)

Setting-up Exercises

Exercise 15

Position: Same as Exercise 10.
Movement: Full knee bend.

Growth

The chief business of a boy is to grow. He may have other affairs, but this is his chief concern. He should, therefore, have a few simple rules for living and make them a part of his daily life.

Out-door Exercises

Each day should have its out-door exercises. Walking is a splendid form of exercise. Walk to school or business; don't ride unless absolutely necessary because of unusual distance. Walk with a good, swinging stride with chest well up and spine fairly straight. Slow running across country is great; it lacks strain and yet affords splendid stimulation to heart and lungs. Cross-country running and hiking should be favorite sport for scout patrols and troops. A boy ought to have at least two hours of sport daily in some good, vigorous game, such as baseball or tennis, and, if he can possibly afford it, at least two periods a week, of an hour each, in a gymnasium, where he can receive guidance in body building. Boys under sixteen should avoid exercise of strain, such as weight lifting, or sprint running over one hundred yards, or long distance racing. They should have careful guidance in all gymnastic work. Work on apparatus may prove harmful unless of the right sort. The horse and parallel bars should be used largely to jump over rather than perform upon. Exercises demanding a sustained support of the body with the arms are not helpful, but may be harmful. The chief activity should be of the legs, to strengthen heart and lungs. A boy should be careful not to overdo. In his excitement to win in a contest he is likely to do this unless cautioned. A boy should never try to reduce his weight. Now that there are weight classes in sports for boys there is a temptation to do this and it may prove very serious. Severe training for athletics should be avoided. All training should be in moderation.

Medical Examinations

Every boy ought to have, as he takes up his boy-scout work, a thorough medical examination. Some physician who is interested in boys will be willing to act as examiner for a patrol or troop. A boy should know the condition of his heart and lungs before entering any contest. If he has any defects in his breathing apparatus — nose, throat, or lungs, these should be attended to or they will seriously interfere with his endurance tests.

Baths

Beside exercises a boy should have simple, workable rules for living. A boy ought to take a good soap bath at least twice a week and always after he has played a hard game or performed work of a nature that has caused him to perspire freely.

Each morning a quick sponge bath should be the first order of the day, in water as cool as he can stand it, followed by a good rub with a coarse towel. If there is a feeling of warmth after the bath, it is helpful, if not, the water should be slightly warm or only a portion of the body should be bathed at a time.

Pain

One thing that should be regarded seriously is pain in any form in any part of the body. If there is a dull headache frequently, find out what causes it. Pain in the knee, the arch of the foot, or at any point, should be taken seriously. Pain means something wrong. It may be brave to bear it, but it is not wise. It may mean something serious. Remember that pain felt in one part of the body may be the result of something wrong in another part. See a wise doctor about it.

Eating

And now in reference to what one shall eat. The average boy ought to have and usually does have an appetite like an ostrich. Three points to remember are; don't eat too much, most healthy boys do; don't eat meat more than once a day; and, third, don't eat anything that you always taste for several hours after you have eaten it, even though you like it.

Digestion

The fact that you taste it is an indication that your stomach is having a wrestling match with the food. Some people can't digest onions, others thrive upon them. Some can't eat cucumbers, others can do so readily. The one must give them up; the other can continue to eat them. Each person has some peculiarity of diet and must observe it to be happy. Many a race has been lost through failure to obey this rule. A simple diet is best. Most boys eat too much of a mixed nature. They mix pickles, soda water, frankfurters, and chocolate without fear or favor. No wonder there is so much stomach ache. In boys' camps the chief trouble is indigestion caused by this riot of eating. Such boys are laying up for themselves for the future some beautiful headaches and bilious attacks, which, when they become chronic later, will cry out against them and seriously impair their value. Don't eat when very tired; lie down a while and get rested. Don't eat heavily before exercising, or, better, put it the other way around, don't exercise immediately after eating. Never eat when excited or angry and very lightly when worried or when expecting to study hard. We should learn to eat slowly and chew the food thoroughly remembering that all food before it can be taken up in the blood must be as thin as pea soup. Chewing well will help the digestive organs greatly. Always wash the hands before eating. Be careful about eating food that has been exposed to the dust unless it has been washed. Drink freely of clean water between meals. Never use a public drinking cup without thoroughly rinsing it. Don't touch your lips to the rim of the cup.

Boys who cook their own meals when in camp should be careful to have their food well done. Half-baked and soggy food proves indigestible.

Coffee and Tea

Should a boy drink coffee or tea? This is a question often asked by boys. Coffee and tea are the greatest stimulants known. But does a strong boy need a stimulant? What is a stimulant and what does it do? A stimulant is a whip, making the body do more at a given time than it ordinarily would. It doesn't add any fibre to the tissues, doesn't add any strength, isn't a food, but merely gets more out of the tissues or nervous system than they would ordinarily yield. Of course there is a reaction, because the tissues have had nothing to feed on. Herbert Fisher says that Peary's men, who drank lots of tea on their voyage north, during the most trying time of their trip showed it in their haggard faces and loss of tissue. Their own tissues had turned cannibal and fed on their own material. Stimulants are not foods. They add no strength to the body. They exact of the body what ought not to be exacted of it. There is always a reaction and one is always worse off as a result. Growing boys especially should have nothing to do with tea, coffee, or any stimulant.

Alcohol and Tobacco

Alcohol is not a stimulant, but is really a narcotic that is very depressing. It dulls rather than stimulates. The same is true of nicotine in tobacco. No growing boy should use either. The first athletes to drop out of a race are usually drinkers and all trainers know that smoking is bad for the wind.

Constipation

Those boys who find their digestion sluggish and are troubled with constipation may find the following plan helpful in overcoming the condition:

Drink a cool, copious draught of water upon arising. Then take some body-bending exercises. Follow this with the sponge bath. Then, if possible, take a walk around the block before breakfast. After school, play some favorite game for at least an hour. In the absence of this, take a good hike of three or four miles or a longer bicycle ride. At least twice a week, if possible, enter a gymnasium class and make special emphasis of body-bending exercises.

Have a regular time for going to stool. A good plan is to go just before retiring and immediately upon arising. Go even though you feel no desire to do so. A regular habit may be established by this method. Always respond quickly to any call of nature. Toasted bread and graham bread and the coarser foods and fruit will be found helpful.

The Teeth

Closely related to the matter of eating is the proper care of the teeth.

Perhaps — without care — the mouth is the filthiest cavity of the body. We spend a great deal of energy trying to keep food clean and water pure, but what is the use if we place them in a dirty cavity as they enter the body. Full 90 per cent. of the children examined in our schools have decayed and dirty teeth. These decayed teeth provide cavities in which food particles decay and germs grow, and through which poisons are absorbed. These conditions need not exist. Now just a few suggestions about the care of the teeth. Every boy should own his own tooth brush. The teeth should be scrubbed at least twice a day. At night they should receive most careful cleansing, using a good tooth paste or powder. Then again in the morning they should be rinsed at which time simply clean water is sufficient. Time should be taken in the cleansing of the teeth. The gums should be included in the scrubbing, as this acts as a good stimulant to the circulation of the blood to the teeth. Not only should the teeth be brushed with a backward and forward stroke, as we ordinarily do, but also upward and downward the length of the teeth. In addition to the scrubbing, particles of food which are lodged between the teeth should be removed after meals, or at least after the last meal of the day. This is most safely done by the use of a thread of a fair degree of thickness. Dentists and druggists furnish this thread in spools. Hard toothpicks often cause bleeding and detach fillings. A dentist should be visited once every six months so as to detect decay immediately. Never have a tooth pulled unless absolutely necessary.

Care of the Eyes

Most troubles with the eyes come from eye strain. Styes and red lids are usually due to this cause. See how foolish, therefore, it is to treat these conditions as causes, when really they are only the result of something else. Of course there are exceptions. Sometimes wild hairs and skin disease affect the eyes. Eye strain should be removed by wearing well-fitting glasses and then these other conditions will disappear. If constant headache is experienced or the eyes itch or become tired easily, there is possibly eye strain.

One way to test the eye is for vision. Place the following letters fifteen feet from you. If you cannot read them clearly with both eyes and with each eye separately, consult a first-class oculist.

C L V F O T

E A C F D L O T

D V C L A E O T F

Never buy eye-glasses unless fitted by an expert. Such glasses should be worn in proper relation to the eyes. They should not be permitted to slide forward on the nose or tilt. They may need to be changed often as the eyes grow better.

For reading, a good, steady light is needed. Never sit in front of a window facing it to read. Always have the light come from the rear and over the left shoulder preferably. The book should be held on a level with the face and not too close. Sit

erect. Reading when lying down or from the light of a fireplace is unwise.

Care of the Ears

Affections of the ears are exceedingly serious and may lead
to grave results. Any trouble with them should be given
very prompt attention and a good specialist consulted. Pain
in the ear, or ringing or hissing sounds, and particularly any
discharge from the ear, should not be neglected. Any sign of
deafness must be heeded. Sometimes deafness occurs in reference to some particular sounds while hearing is normal to
others. No matter what the degree of deafness may be do
not neglect to see a physician about it. Ordinarily the tick
of a watch can be heard at a distance of thirty inches. If you
cannot hear it at that distance and can hear it say at fifteen
inches then you are just one half from the normal in your
hearing. The test should be made with one ear closed.

Ear troubles are often caused by sticking foreign objects in
the ear, such as hair pins, pins, matches, oothpicks and lead
pencils. Never pick the ear with anything. Often the ear
drum is pierced in this way. The normal ear does not require
anything more than the usual cleansing with the wash rag over
the end of the finger.

If wax to any extent accumulates in the ear it should be
removed by syringing, but ought to be done by a physician.

In camp an insect might crawl into the ear and if alive
cause pain. Putting oil or other fluids in the ear to drown
it is unwise. If a foreign body should get in the ear it
should not cause great alarm unless attended with severe pain.
If a physician is not available at once such objects may remain for a day or two without serious results. Syringing
usually removes them, but it should be remembered that some
objects like peas or beans swell if made wet. In swimming
water is apt to get into the ear and cause annoyance. A rubber ear stop can be secured and placed in the ear at the time
of swimming, thus keeping the water out. Cotton should not
be stuffed into the ear to keep water out, as it may get inside.

One thing to keep in mind is that catarrh of the nose and
throat often extends into the ear passages through a tube
which reaches from the throat to the ear and that syringing
of the nose and throat frequently causes trouble in the ear.

Care of Nose and Throat

Always breathe through the nose. Air passing through the
nose is warmed and moistened and cleansed; thus it gets to

the lungs in a better condition. If you cannot breathe clearly through the nose, have it examined. There may be a growth present which needs to be removed. To become a good runner this is important. Adenoids, which are growths far back in the mouth, often interfere with nose breathing and are serious in other ways. Don't stick anything in the nose; and nose picking is not cleanly. If crusts form in the nose, use a little vaseline to soften them. Don't blow the nose too vigorously. It may cause trouble.

Frequent sore throat may be due to enlarged tonsils which either need treatment or removal. To one who has frequent colds in the head, the out-of-door life and morning sponge bath and moderate eating will be of help.

Care of the Feet

This is an important matter with scouts, as they will make frequent hikes and tramps. The first thing to do is to walk right. The straight foot is the normal foot. The normal foot is broad at the ball with space between the toes. How different from the awful feet we see with toes twisted upon each other and crowded together. Walk with feet pointing straight forward. The feet that turn outward are weak feet. Shoes therefore should be straight on the inner border, broad across the ball, and have a low, broad heel. The shoe adopted by the scout movement is a good design.

When a foot is normal, the inner border does not touch the floor. By wetting the foot one can see readily whether he is flat-footed by the imprint made. The following exercises are good to strengthen the arches of the foot if there is a tendency to flat feet: (1) Turn toes in, raise the heels, and come down slowly on the outer borders of the feet; (2) Walk with heels raised and toes pointing inward, or walk on the outer borders of the foot, inner borders turned up.

Shoes should fit the feet comfortably. Tight shoes, or shoes that fit loosely, will cause callouses or corns. The way to get rid of these is to remove the cause — namely, the badly-fitting shoes. Soft corns are due to pressure between the toes. The toes in such cases should be kept apart with cotton. Pointed shoes should be avoided. Patent-leather shoes are non-porous and hot. Ingrown toe nails are exceedingly painful. The pain comes from the nail piercing the soft parts. Allowing the nail to grow long and beyond the point of the tender spot will help;

and on the side of the nail and under it cotton should be inserted to protect the soft parts.

Hot foot baths will generally relieve tired feet. Boys should be very careful in trimming corns for fear of blood poisoning. Never buy plates at a store for flat feet. They may not be adapted to your needs. Always consult a foot specialist for treatment and buy plates if needed on his order. Only severe cases need plates.

Many boys are troubled with perspiring feet and are frequently annoyed by the odor resulting. Those who are thus troubled should wash the feet often and carefully, especially, between the toes. By dusting the feet with boric acid the odor will disappear. At first it may be necessary to change the stockings daily. In severe cases two pairs of shoes should be used, changing alternately.

Care of the Finger Nails

The chief thing in the care of the finger nails is to keep them clean. Each boy should possess and use a nail brush. Always wash the hands thoroughly before eating, and use the end of a nail file to remove the accumulation still remaining under the nails. Keep the nails properly trimmed. They should not be too long nor too short. If long they are liable to break and if short to be sensitive. Biting the nails is a filthy practice and mutilates the fingers dreadfully and makes them unsightly. It is a very hard habit to overcome ofttimes and will require persistent effort in order to succeed. By keeping the nails smooth the tendency to bite them will to some extent be overcome. A bitter application to the nails will often remind one of the habit, as often the biting is done unconsciously. The nails should never be pared with a knife; a curved pair of scissors is better as the cutting should be done in a curved direction; but the best method is to use a file. The skin overhanging the nails should be pressed back once a week to keep them shapely. Rubbing the nails with a nail buffer or cloth will keep them polished.

Sleep

One thing a growing boy wants to be long on is sleep, and yet he is most apt to be careless about it. It is during sleep that a boy grows most and catches up. During his waking hours he tears down and burns up more tissue than he builds. Good, sound and sufficient sleep is essential to growth, strength, and endurance. A boy scout should have at least nine or ten hours sleep out of every twenty-four. If you lose out on this amount on one day, make it up the next. Whenever unusually tired, or when you feel out of trim, stay in bed a few hours more if it is possible. A boy should wake up each morning feeling like a fighting cock. When he doesn't he ought to get to bed earlier that night. Sleep is a wonderful restorative and tonic. It helps to store up energy and conserve strength.

Sleeping Out of Doors

The conditions under which one sleeps are as important as the length of time one sleeps. Many people are finding it wonderfully helpful and invigorating to sleep out of doors. Often a back porch can be arranged, or, in summer, a tent can be pitched in the yard. But, by all means, the sleeping room should be well ventilated. Windows should be thrown wide open. Avoid drafts. If the bed is in such relation to the windows as to cause the wind to blow directly on it, a screen can be used to divert it or a sheet hung up as protection. Good, fresh, cool air is a splendid tonic. In winter open windows are a splendid preparation for camping out in summer.

Conservation

In this chapter much has been said of the active measures which a boy should take in order to become strong and well. We should be equally concerned in saving and storing up natural forces we already have. In the body of every boy, who has reached his teens, the Creator of the universe has sown a very important fluid. This fluid is the most wonderful material in all the physical world. Some parts of it find their way into the blood, and through the blood give tone to the muscles, power to the brain, and strength to the nerves. This fluid is the sex fluid. When this fluid appears in a boy's body, it works a wonderful change in him. His chest deepens, his shoulders broaden, his voice changes, his ideals are changed and enlarged. It gives him the capacity for deep feeling, for rich emotion. Pity the boy, therefore, who has wrong ideas of this important function, because they will lower his ideals of life. These organs actually secrete into the blood material that makes a boy manly, strong, and noble. Any habit which a boy has that causes this fluid to be discharged from the body tends to weaken his strength, to make him less able to resist disease, and often unfortunately fastens upon him habits which later in life he cannot break. Even several years before this fluid appears in the body such habits are harmful to a growing boy.

To become strong, therefore, one must be pure in thought and clean in habit. This power which I have spoken of must be conserved, because this sex function is so deep and strong that there will come times when temptation to wrong habits will be very powerful. But remember that to yield means to sacrifice strength and power and manliness.

For boys who desire to know more of this subject we would suggest a splendid book by Dr. Winfield S. Hall, entitled, "From Youth into Manhood." Every boy in his teens who wants to know the secret of strength, power, and endurance should read this book.

NOTES

Notes

Notes

Notes

CHAPTER VI

CHIVALRY

By John L. Alexander, Boy Scouts of America

Ancient Knighthood

A little over fifteen hundred years ago the great order of knighthood and chivalry was founded. The reason for this was the feeling on the part of the best men of that day that it was the duty of the stronger to help the weak. These were the days when might was right, and the man with the strongest arm did as he pleased, often oppressing the poor and riding rough shod without any regard over the feelings and affections of others. In revolt against this, there sprang up all over Europe a noble and useful order of men who called themselves knights. Among these great-hearted men were Arthur, Gareth, Lancelot, Bedivere, and Alfred the Great. The desire of these men was "To live pure, speak true, right wrong, follow the king." Of course in these days there also lived men who called themselves knights, but who had none of the desire for service that inspired Arthur and the others. These false knights, who cared for no one but themselves and their own pleasure, often brought great sorrow to the common people. Chivalry then was a revolt against their brutal acts and ignorance and a protest against the continuation of the idea that might was right.

Ancient knight

Nowhere in all the stories that have come down to us have the acts of chivalry been so well told as in the tales of the Round Table. Here it was that King Arthur gathered about him men like Sir Bors, Sir Gawaine, Sir Pellias, Sir Geraint, Sir Tristram, Sir Lancelot, and Sir Galahad. These men moved by the desire of giving themselves in service, cleared the forests of wild animals, suppressed the robber barons, punished the outlaws, bullies, and thieves of their day, and enforced wherever they went a proper respect for women. It was for this great service that they trained themselves, passing through the degrees of page, esquire, and knight with all the hard work that each of these meant in order that they might the better do their duty to their God and country.

Struggle for Freedom

Of course this struggle of right against wrong was not confined to the days in which chivalry was born. The founding of the order of knighthood was merely the beginning of the age-long struggle to make right the ruling thought of life. Long after knighthood had passed away, the struggle continued. In the birth of the modern nations, England, Germany, France, and others, there was the distinct feeling on the part of the best men of these nations that might should and must give way to right, and that tyranny must yield to the spirit of freedom. The great struggle of the English barons under King John and the wresting from the king of the Magna Charta, which became the basis of English liberty, was merely another development of the idea for which chivalry stood. The protest of the French Revolution, and the terrible doings of the common people in these days, although wicked and brutal in method, were symptoms of the same revolt against oppression.

Pilgrim father

The Pilgrim Fathers

When the Pilgrim Fathers founded the American colonies, the work of Arthur and Alfred and the other great men of ancient days was renewed and extended and fitted to the new conditions and times. With the English settlements of Raleigh and Captain John Smith we might almost say that a new race of men was born and a new kind of knight was developed. All over America an idea made itself felt that in the eyes of the law every man should be considered just as good as every other man, and that every man ought to have a fair and square chance at all the good things that were to be had in a land of plenty. It was this spirit that compelled the colonists to seek their independence and that found its way into our Declaration of Independence as follows:

> We hold these truths to be self-evident: that all men are created equal; that they are endowed by their Creator with certain inalienable rights; that among these are life, liberty and the pursuit of happiness.

The fight of the colonists was the old-time fight of the knights against the oppression and injustice and the might that dared to call itself right.

American Pioneers

No set of men, however, showed this spirit of chivalry more than our pioneers beyond the Alleghanies. In their work and service they paralleled very closely the knights of the Round Table, but whereas Arthur's knights were dressed in suits of armor, the American pioneers were dressed in buckskin. They did, however, the very same things which ancient chivalry had done, clearing the forests of wild animals, suppressing the outlaws and bullies and thieves of their day and enforcing a proper respect for women. Like the old knights they often were compelled to do their work amid scenes of great bloodshed, although they loved to live in peace. These American knight and pioneers were generally termed backwoodsmen and scouts, and were men of distinguished appearance, of athletic build, of high moral character and frequently of firm religious convictions. Such men as "Apple-seed Johnny," Daniel Boone, George Rogers Clark, Simon Kenton and John James Audubon, are the types of men these

Pioneer

pioneers were. They were noted for their staunch qualities of character. They hated dishonesty and were truthful and brave. They were polite to women and old people, ever ready to rescue a companion when in danger, and equally ready to risk their lives for a stranger. They were very hospitable, dividing their last crust with one another, or with the stranger whom they happened to meet. They were ever ready to do an act of kindness.

They were exceedingly simple in their dress and habits. They fought the Indians, not because they wished to, but because it was necessary to protect their wives and children from the raids of the savages. They knew all the things that scouts ought to know. They were acquainted with the woods and the fields; knew where the best fish were to be caught; understood the trees, the signs and blazes, the haunts of animals and how to track them; how to find their way by the stars; how to make themselves comfortable in the heart of the primeval forest; and such other things as are classed under the general term of woodcraft. And, with all this, they inherited the splendid ideas of chivalry that had been developed in the thousand years preceding them, and fitted these ideas to the conditions of their own day, standing solidly against evil and falsehood whenever they lifted their head among them. They were not perfect, but they did their best to be of service to those who came within their reach and worked conscientiously for their country.

Modern Knighthood

A hundred years have passed since then, and the conditions of life which existed west of the Alleghanies are no more. Just as the life of the pioneers was different from that of the knights of the Round Table, and as they each practised chivalry in keeping with their own surroundings, so the life of to-day is different from both, but the need of chivalry is very much the same. Might still tries to make right, and while there are now no robber barons or outlaws with swords and spears, their spirit is not unknown in business and commercial life. Vice and dishonesty lift their heads just as strongly to-day as in the past and there is just as much need of respect for women and girls as there ever was. So to-day there is a demand for a modern type of chivalry. It is for this reason that the Boy Scouts of America have come into being; for there is need of service in these days, and that is represented by the good turn done to somebody every day. Doing the good turn daily will help to form the habit of useful service. A boy scout, then, while living in modern times, must consider himself the heir of ancient chivalry

Modern knight

and of the pioneers, and he must for this reason give himself to ever renewed efforts to be true to the traditions which have been handed down to him by these great and good leaders of men.   The boy-scout movement is a call to American boys to-day to become in spirit members of the order of chivalry, and a challenge to them to make their lives count in the communities in which they live — for clean lives, clean speech, clean sport, clean habits, and clean relationships with others. It is also a challenge for them to stand for the right against the wrong, for truth against falsehood, to help the weak and oppressed, and to love and seek the best things of life.

Abraham Lincoln

Perhaps there is no better example of chivalry than the life and experience of Abraham Lincoln, the greatest of all our American men.   Every boy ought to read the story of his life and come to understand and appreciate what it means.

Lincoln was born in the backwoods of Kentucky. He was a tall, spare man of awkward build, and knew very little of the school room as a boy. He fought for his education. He borrowed books wherever he could. Many long nights were spent by him before the flickering lights of the log cabin, gleaning from his borrowed treasures the knowledge he longed to possess. He passed through all the experiences of life that other scouts and pioneers have experienced. He split rails for a livelihood, and fought his way upward by hard work, finally achieving for himself an education in the law, becoming an advocate in the courts of Illinois.   Wherever he went, he made a profound impression on the lives and minds of the people and won over his political opponents by his strength, sympathy.

and breadth of mind. At the period when storms threatened
to engulf our Ship of State, he became President of our country.
Although Lincoln was an untried pilot, he stood by the helm
like a veteran master. A man of earnest and intense con-
viction, he strove to maintain the glory of our flag and to
keep the Union un-
broken. Hundreds of
stories are told of his
great heart and al-
most boundless sym-
pathy for others.
The generals of the
Civil War were
deeply attached to
him, and the rank
and file of the sold-
iers who fought under
these generals loved
and revered him. He
was familiarly known
as "Honest Abe."
He could always be
relied upon to give
help and encourage-
ment. His smile
cheered the defenders

Using every opportunity

of the Union, and his wise counsel gave heart to the men who
were helping him to shape the destinies of the nation. At the
close of the war which saw the Union more firmly established
than ever, he fell by the hand of the assassin, mourned deeply
both by his own country and by the world at large.

The further we get from the scene of his life and work the
more firmly are we, his countrymen, convinced of his sincerity,
strength, wisdom, and bigness of heart. The two men who
stand out preëminently in history among great Americans are
Washington and Lincoln, the former as the founder of the Union
and the latter as the man who gave it unbreakable continuity
and preserved it, as we hope and believe, for all time.

Lincoln's life and career should be the study and inspiration
of every boy scout. He became familar with all of the things
for which the Boy Scouts of America stand. He was a lover of
the wild things in the woods, and loved and lived the life of
the out-of-doors. He had a high sense of honor and was
intensely chivalrous, as the many hundred stories told about

him testify. He did many times more than one good turn a day; he sincerely loved his country; he lived, fought, and worked for it; and finally he sealed his loyalty by giving his life. The path that he travelled from the log cabin to the White House clearly shows that an American boy who has well defined ideas of truth and right, and then dares to stand by them, can become great in the councils of the nation. The life, then, of Abraham Lincoln should be a steady inspiration to every boy who wishes to call himself a scout.

Challenge of the Present

Thus we see that chivalry is not a virtue that had its beginning long ago and merely lived a short time, becoming a mere story. Chivalry began in the far-distant past out of the desire to help others, and the knights of the olden days did this as best they could. Later the new race of men in America took up the burden of chivalry, and did the best they could. Now the privilege and responsibility comes to the boys of to-day, and the voices of the knight of the olden time and of the hardy pioneers of our own country are urging the boys of to-day to do the right thing, in a gentlemanly way, for the sake of those about them. All of those men, whether knights or pioneers, had an unwritten code, somewhat like our scout law, and their motto was very much like the motto of the boy scouts, *"Be Prepared."*

Politeness

Good Manners

The same thing that entered into the training of these men, knights, pioneers, and Lincoln, then, must enter into the training of the boy scouts of to-day. Just as they respected women and served them, so the tenderfoot and the scout must be polite and kind to women, not merely to well-dressed women, but to poorly-dressed women; not merely to young women, but to old women: to women wherever they may be found —

wherever they may be. To these a scout must always be courteous and helpful.

When a scout is walking with a lady or a child, he should always walk on the outside of the sidewalk, so that he can better protect them against the jostling crowds. This rule is only altered when crossing the street, when the scout should get between the lady and the traffic, so as to shield her from accident or mud. Also in meeting a woman or child, a scout, as a matter of course, should always make way for them even if he himself has to step off the sidewalk into the mud. When riding in a street car or train a scout should never allow a woman, an elderly person, or a child to stand, but will offer his seat; and when he does it he should do it cheerfully and with a smile.

When on the street, be continually on a quest, on the lookout to help others, and always refuse any reward for the effort. This kind of courtesy and good manners is essential to success. It was this unselfish desire to protect and help that made these men of olden time such splendid fellows.

Good manners attract and please, and should be cultivated by every boy who expects to win success and make his life interesting to others. In the home, on the street, in the school, in the workshop or the office, or wherever one may be, his relationship to others should be characterized as gentle, courteous, polite, considerate and thoughtful. These are virtues and graces that make life easier and pleasanter for all.

Cheerfulness

As has been said, whatever a scout does should be done with cheerfulness, and the duty of always being cheerful cannot be emphasized too much.

> Why don't you laugh, and make us all laugh too,
> And keep us mortals all from getting blue?
> A laugh will always win.
> If you can't laugh — just grin.
> Go on! Let's all join in!
> Why don't you laugh?

Benjamin Franklin said: "Money never yet made a man happy, and there is nothing in its nature to produce happiness, One's personal enjoyment is a very small thing, but one's personal usefulness is a very important thing." Those only are happy who have their minds fixed upon some object other and higher than their own happiness. Doctor Raffles once said,

"I have made it a rule never to be with a person ten minutes without trying to make him happier." A boy once said to his mother, "I couldn't make little sister happy, nohow I could fix it, but I made myself happy trying to make her happy."

There was once a king who had a tall, handsome son whom he loved with his whole heart, so he gave him everything that his heart desired — a pony to ride, beautiful rooms to live in, picture books, stories, and everything that money could buy. And yet, in spite of this, the young prince was unhappy and wore a wry face and a frown wherever he went, and was always wishing for something he did not have. By and by, a magician came to the court, and seeing a frown on the prince's face, said to the king, "I can make your boy happy and turn his frown into a smile, but you must pay me a very large price for the secret." "All right," said the king, "whatever you ask, I will do." So the magician took the boy into a private room, and with white liquid wrote something on a piece of paper; then he gave the boy a candle and told him to warm the paper and read what was written. The prince did as he was told. The white letters turned into letters of blue, and he read these words; "Do a kindness to some one every day." So the prince followed the magician's advice and became the happiest boy in all the king's realm.

Cheer up

To be a good scout one must remain cheerful under every circumstance, bearing both fortune and misfortune with a smile.

Character

If a scout is cheerful, follows the advice of the magician to the king's son, and does a good turn to some one every day, he will come into possession of a strong character such as the knights of the Round Table had; for, after all, character is the thing that distinguishes a good scout from a bad one. Character is not what men say about you. A great writer once said, "I can't hear what you say for what you are," and another one said, "Your life speaks louder than your words." It was not the words of the knights of old that told what they were. It was their strong life and fine character that gave power to their words and the thrust to their spears.

It is necessary that a boy should live right and possess such a character as will help him to do the hardest things of life. Every boy should remember that he is in reality just what he is when alone in the dark. The great quests of the knights were most often done singly and alone.

Will

Another thing that entered into the make-up of a knight was an iron will. He had staying powers because he willed to stick; and the way he trained his will to do the hard things was to keep himself doing the small things. Not long ago, there was a lad whom the boys nicknamed "Blockey" and "Wooden Man." When they played ball in the school play ground, Blockey never caught the ball. When they worked together in the gymnasium, Blockey was always left out of the game because he couldn't do things, and was slow and unwieldy in his motions. But one day, a great change came over Blockey and he began to train his will. He worked hard in the gymnasium: he learned to catch the ball, and, by sticking to it, was not only able to catch the ball but became proficient. Then there came a time when the first one chosen upon the team was Blockey; and it all came about because he had trained his will so that when he made up his mind to do a thing, *he did it*.

Thrift

Another thing which entered into the training of a knight was his readiness to seize his opportunities. The motto of the scout is "*Be Prepared*." He should be prepared for whatever opportunity presents itself. An interesting story is told by Orison Swett Marden. He says that a lad, who later became one of the millionaires of one of our great Western cities, began his earning career by taking advantage of an opportunity that came to him as he was passing an auction shop. He saw several boxes of a kind of soap which his mother was accustomed to buy from the family grocer. Hastening to the grocery store he asked the price of the soap. "Twelve cents a pound" was the reply. On being pressed for a lower figure the shopkeeper remarked in a bantering tone that he would buy all that the boy could bring to his store at nine cents a pound. The boy hurried back to the auction and bought the soap at six cents a pound. It was in this way that he made his first money in trade and laid the foundation of his fortune.

The knight never waited for opportunity to come to him. He went out looking for it, and wore his armor in order that he might be ready for it when it came. There is a story of a Greek god who had only one lock of hair upon his forehead. The remainder of his head was shining bald. In order to get this ancient god's attention, it was necessary to grip him by his fore-lock, for when he had passed, nothing could check his speed. So it is with opportunity, and the hour of opportunity. A good scout is ready for both and always grips "time by the forelock."

Individuality

If the foregoing qualities enter into a scout's training, an individuality will be developed in him, which will make itself known and felt.

Every scout should read over the following list of scout vir-tues, and should strive at all times to keep them before him in his training, thus making them a part of his life:

Unselfishness: The art of thinking of others first and one's self afterward.

Self Sacrifice: The giving up of one's comfort, desires, and pleasures for the benefit of some one else.

Kindness: The habit of thinking well of others and doing good to them.

Friendliness: The disposition to make every one you meet feel at ease, and to be of service to him if possible.

Honesty: The desire to give to every one a square deal and the same fair chance that you yourself wish to enjoy. It means also respect for the property and rights of others, the ability to face the truth, and to call your own faults by their right name.

Fair Play: Scorning to take unfair advantage of a rival and readiness even to give up an advantage to him.

Loyalty: The quality of remaining true and faithful not only to your principles but also to your parents and friends.

Obedience: Compliance with the wishes of parents or those in places of authority.

Discipline: That self-restraint and self-control that keep a boy steady, and help him in team work.

Endurance: A manly moderation which keeps a boy fit and strong and in good condition.

Self Improvement: The ambition to get on in life by all fair means.

Humility: That fine quality which keeps a scout from boasting, and which generally reveals a boy of courage and achievement.

Honor: That great thing which is more sacred than anything else to scouts and gentlemen; the disdain of telling or implying an untruth; absolute trustworthiness and faithfulness.

Duty to God: That greatest of all things, which keeps a boy faithful to his principles and true to his friends and comrades;

Scout protecting child from mad dog

that gives him a belief in things that are high and noble, and which makes him prove his belief by doing his good turn to some one every day.

This list of virtues a scout must have, and if there are any that stand out more prominently than the others, they are the following:

Courage

It is horrible to be a coward. It is weak to yield to fear and heroic to face danger without flinching. The old Indian who had been mortally wounded faced death with a grim smile on his lips and sang his own death song. The soldier of the

Roman legions laughed in the face of death, and died often with a "Hail, Imperator!" for the Roman Cæsar upon his lips.

One of the stories connected with the battle of Agincourt tells us that four fair ladies had sent their knightly lovers into battle. One of these was killed. Another was made prisoner. The third was lost in the battle and never heard of afterward. The fourth was safe, but owed his safety to shameful flight. "Ah! woe is me," said the lady of this base knight, "for having placed my affections on a coward. He would have been dear to me dead. But alive he is my reproach."

A scout must be as courageous as any knight of old or any Roman soldier or any dying Indian.

Loyalty

Loyalty is another scout virtue which must stand out prominently, because it is that which makes him true to his home, his parents, and his country. Charles VIII, at the Battle of Foronovo, picked out nine of his bravest officers and gave to each of them a complete suit of armor, which was a counterpart of his own. By this device he outwitted a group of his enemies who had leagued themselves to kill him during the fight. They sought him through all the ranks, and every time they met one of these officers they thought they had come face to face with the king. The fact that these officers hailed such a dangerous honor with delight and devotion is a striking illustration of their loyalty.

The scout should be no less loyal to his parents, home, and country.

Duty to God

No scout can ever hope to amount to much until he has learned a reverence for religion. The scout should believe in God and God's word. In the olden days, knighthood, when it was bestowed, was a religious ceremony, and a knight not only considered himself a servant of the king, but also a servant of God. The entire night preceding the day upon which the young esquire was made knight was spent by him on his knees in prayer, in a fast and vigil.

There are many kinds of religion in the world. One important point, however, about them is that they all involve the worship of the same God. There is but one leader, although many ways of following Him. If a scout meets one of another religion, he should remember that he, too, is striving for the best

A scout should respect the convictions of others in matters of custom and religion.

A Boy Scout's Religion

The Boy Scouts of America maintain that no boy can grow into the best kind of citizenship without recognizing his obligation to God. The first part of the boy scout's oath or pledge is therefore: "I promise on my honor to do my best to honor my God and my country." The recognition of God as the ruling and leading power in the universe, and the grate-

ful acknowledgement of His favors and blessings is necessary to the best type of citizenship and is a wholesome thing in the education of the growing boy. No matter what the boy may be — Catholic, or Protestant, or Jew — this fundamental need of good citizenship should be kept before him. The Boy Scouts of America therefore recognize the religious element in the training of a boy, but it is absolutely non-sectarian in its attitude toward that religious training. Its policy is that the organization or institution with which the boy scout is connected shall give definite

Scout helping old lady across street

attention to his religious life. If he be a Catholic boy scout, the Catholic Church of which he is a member is the best channel for his training. If he be a Hebrew boy, then the Synagogue will train him in the faith of his fathers. If he be a Protestant, no matter to what denomination of Protestantism he may belong, the church of which he is an adherent or a member should be the proper organization to give him an education in the things that pertain to his allegiance to God. The Boy Scouts of America, then, while recognizing the fact that the boy should be taught the things that pertain to religion, insists upon the boy's religious life being stimulated and fostered by the institution with which he is connected. Of course, it is a fundamental principle of the Boy Scouts of America to insist on clean, capable leadership in its scout masters, and the influence of the leader on the boy scout should be of a distinctly helpful character.

Work, Not Luck

Life, after all, is just this: Some go through life trusting to luck. They are not worthy to be scouts. Others go through life trusting to hard work and clear thinking. These are they who have cleared the wilderness and planted wheat where forests once grew, who have driven back the savage, and have fostered civilization in the uncultivated places of the earth. The good scout is always at work — working to improve himself and to improve the daily lot of others.

The thing that is to be noticed in all of these men, those of the Round Table, and those of American pioneer days, is the fact that they were ever ready to do a good turn to some one. The knights of the Round Table did theirs by clash of arms, by the jousts and the tourney, and by the fierce hand-to-hand fights that were their delight in open battle. The old scouts, our own pioneers, very often had to use the rifle and the hatchet and the implements of war. However, those days have passed, and we are living in a non-military and peace-loving age; and the glory of it is that, whereas these men took their lives in their hands and by dint of rifle and sword did their part in helping others, our modern civilization gives the Boy Scouts of America an opportunity to go out and do their good turn daily for others in the thousand ways that will benefit our American life the most. Sometimes they will have to risk their lives, but it will be in case of fire or accident or catastrophe. At other times they will be given the privilege of showing simple deeds of chivalry by their courteous treatment of their elders, cripples, and children, by giving up their seats in street cars, or by carrying the bundles of those who are not as physically strong as themselves. And in it all will come the satisfying feeling that they are doing just as much and perhaps a great deal more than the iron-clad men or the buckskin clothed scouts in making their country a little safer and a little better place to live in. Chivalry and courtesy and being a gentleman mean just as much now as they ever did, and there is a greater demand in these days to live pure, to speak true, and to help others by a good turn daily than ever before in the world's history.

NOTES

Notes

Notes

CHAPTER VII

FIRST AID AND LIFE SAVING

Major Charles Lynch, Medical Corps, U. S. A. Acting for the American Red Cross

PREVENTION OF ACCIDENTS

General

Considerably over a million persons are seriously injured in the United States each year. The enormous loss of life and the great suffering involved certainly demand that every boy scout do what he can to improve conditions in this respect. Some accidents happen under all circumstances, but, on the other hand a great many accidents are avoidable and probably quite one half of the injuries which occur in the United States yearly could be prevented if common care were exercised.

Panics and Their Prevention

In case of a panic, at an in-door assembly, scouts, if they live up to their motto, "*Be Prepared*," will be able to save hundreds of lives. There is usually plenty of time for people to get out of a building if the exits are not blocked by too many crowding them at once. One should, if possible, try to arrange to have the performance go on, and the others could reassure the people and get them to go out quietly through the exits provided. Almost all scouts know how quickly and safely our school buildings are cleared by means of the fire drill.

Fires

Fires constitute a danger as great as panics, and scouts should be equally well informed what to do in case of fire. It is the duty of a scout to know how to prevent fires. Many fires are caused by carelessness. Never throw away a lighted match, for it may fall on inflammable material and start a fire. Reading in bed by the light of a lamp or candle is dangerous, for if the reader goes to sleep the bed clothing is likely to catch fire.

A scout may often have to dry his clothes before a fire and if so, they should be carefully watched. Hot ashes in wooden boxes, or in barrels, are responsible for many fires. In camp, dry grass should be cut away from the locality of the camp fire; and not to put out a camp fire on leaving a camp is criminal. Many of the great fires in our forests have been due to carelessness in this respect. Fires also result frequently from explosions of gas or gunpowder. A room in which the odor of gas is apparent should never be entered with a light, and in handling gunpowder a scout should have no matches loose in his pockets.

How To Put Out Burning Clothing

If your own clothing should catch fire do not run for help as this will fan the flames. Lie down and roll up as tightly as possible in an overcoat, blanket, or rug. If nothing can be obtained in which to wrap up, lie down and roll over slowly at the same time beating out the fire with the hands. If another person's clothing catches fire, throw him to the ground and smother the fire with a coat, blanket, or rug.

What To Do in Case of Fire

A fire can usually be put out very easily when it starts, and here is an occasion when a scout can show his presence of mind and coolness. At first a few buckets of water or blankets or woollen clothing thrown upon a fire will smother it. Sand, ashes, or dirt, or even flour, will have the same effect.

If a scout discovers a building to be on fire, *he should sound the alarm for the fire department at once.* If possible he should send some one else, as the scout will probably know better what to do before the fire-engine arrives. All doors should be kept closed so as to prevent draughts. If you enter the burning building, close the window or door after you, if possible, and leave some responsible person to guard it so it will not be opened and cause a draught. In searching for people, go to the top floor and walk down, examining each room as carefully as possible. If necessary to get air while making the search, close the door of the room, open a window, and stick the head out until a few breaths can be obtained. Afterward close the window to prevent a draught. If doors are found locked and you suspect people are asleep inside, knock and pound on doors to arouse them. If this produces no results, you will have to try to break down the door. While searching through a burning building it will be best to tie a wet handkerchief or cloth over the nose and mouth.   You will get a little air from the water.

Remember the air within six inches of the floor is free from smoke, so when you have difficulty in breathing, crawl along the floor, with the head low, dragging any one you have rescued behind you.

If you tie the hands of an insensible person together with a handkerchief and put them over your head, you will find it fairly easy to crawl along the floor dragging him with you.

Learning by doing

Never jump from a window unless the flames are so close to you that this is the only means of escape.

If you are outside a buildling, put bedding in a pile to break the jumper's fall, or get a strong carpet or rug to catch him, and have it firmly held by as many men and boys as can secure hand holds.

In country districts, scouts should organize a bucket brigade which consists of two lines from the nearest water supply to the fire.   Scouts in one line pass buckets, pitchers, or anything else that will hold water from one to another till the last scout throws the water on the fire. The buckets are returned by the other line.

Drowning

Drowning accidents are very common. Every scout should know how to swim and to swim well, but this is not all that is necessary. He should also know how to prevent accidents that may result in drowning. In summer, boating and bathing accidents are common. Remember a light boat is not intended for heavy seas; do not change seats except in a wide and steady boat; and above all things do not put yourself in the class of idiots who rock a boat.

At the sea-shore, unless you are a strong swimmer, do not go outside the life line, and if the undertow is strong be careful not to walk out where the water is so deep it will carry you off your feet. Very cold water and very long swims are likely to exhaust even a strong swimmer and are therefore hazardous unless a boat accompanies the swimmer.

Rescue of the Drowning
(See pages 279 to 285)

Ice Rescue

To rescue a person who has broken through the ice you should first tie a rope around your body and have the other end tied, or held, on shore. Then secure a long board or a ladder or limb of a tree, crawl out on this, or push it out, so that the person in the water may reach it. If nothing can be found on which you can support your weight do not attempt to walk out toward the person to be rescued, but lie down flat on your face and crawl out, as by doing this much less weight bears at any one point on the ice than in walking. If you yourself break through the ice remember that if you try to crawl up on the broken edge it will very likely break again with you. If rescuers are near, it would be much better to support yourself on the edge of the ice and wait for them to come to you.

Restoring the Drowning and Artificial Respiration
(See pages 286 to 288)

Electric Accidents

For his own benefit and that of his comrades, the scout should know how to avoid accidents from electricity. The third rail is always dangerous, so do not touch it. Swinging wires of any kind may somewhere in their course be in contact with live wires, so they should not be touched.

A person in contact with a wire or rail carrying an electric current will transfer the current to the rescuer. Therefore he must not touch the unfortunate victim unless his own body is thoroughly insulated. The rescuer must act very promptly, for the danger to the person in contact is much increased the longer the electric current is allowed to pass through his body. If possible, the rescuer should insulate himself by covering his hands with a mackintosh, rubber sheeting, several thicknesses of silk, or even dry cloth. In addition he should, if possible, complete his insulation by standing on a dry board, a thick piece of paper, or even on a dry coat. Rubber gloves and rubber shoes or boots are still safer, but they cannot usually be procured quickly.

If a live wire is under a person and the ground is dry, it will be perfectly safe to stand on the ground and pull him off the wire with the bare hands, care being taken to touch only his clothing, and this must not be wet.

A live wire lying on a patient may be flipped off with safety with a dry board or stick. In removing the live wire from the person, or the person from the wire, do this with one motion, as rocking him to and fro on the wire will increase shock and burn.

A live wire may be safely cut by an axe or hatchet with dry, wooden handle. The electric current may be short circuited by dropping a crow-bar or poker on the wire. These must be dropped on the side from which the current is coming and not on the farther side, as the latter will not short circuit the current before it is passed through the body of the person in contact. Drop the metal bar; do not place it on the wire or you will then be made a part of the short circuit and receive the current of electricity through your body.

What To Do for Electric Shocks

Always send for a doctor, but do not wait for him. Treatment should be given even if the man appears to be dead. Loosen the clothing around neck and body. Proceed to restore breathing by artificial respiration as in drowning. (See pages 286, 287.)

Gas Accidents

The commonest gas encountered is the ordinary illuminating gas. To prevent such gas from escaping in dangerous quantities, leaks in gas pipes should be promptly repaired. Be careful in turning off gas to make sure that gas is actually shut off. It is dangerous to leave a gas jet burning faintly when you go to sleep, as it may go out if pressure in the gas pipe becomes less, and if pressure is afterward increased gas may escape into the room.

Coal gas will escape through red-hot cast-iron, and very big fires in such stoves are dangerous, especially in sleeping rooms. Charcoal burned in open vessels in tight rooms is especially dangerous. In underground sewers and wells other dangerous gases are found. If a lighted candle or torch will not burn in such a place, it is very certain the air will be deadly for any person who enters.

To rescue an unconscious person in a place filled with gas, move quickly and carry him out without breathing yourself. Take a few deep breaths before entering and if possible hold breath while in the place. Frequently less gas will be found near the floor of a building, so one may be able to crawl where it would be dangerous to walk.

What To Do for Gas Poisoning

Proceed to restore breathing by artificial respiration as in drowning. (See pages 286, 287.)

Runaway Horses

The method for checking a horse running away is not to run out and wave your arm in front of him, as this will only cause him to dodge to one side and to run faster, but to try to run alongside the vehicle with one hand on the shaft to prevent yourself from falling, seizing the reins with the other hand and dragging the horse's head toward you. If when he has somewhat slowed down by this method, you can turn him toward a wall or a house he will probably stop.

Mad Dog

The first thing to do is to kill the mad dog at once. Wrap a handkerchief around the hand to prevent the dog's teeth from entering the flesh and grasp a club of some kind. If you can stop the dog with a stick you should hit him hard over the head with it, or kick him under the jaw. A handkerchief held in front of you in your outstretched hands will generally cause the dog to stop to paw it before he attempts to bite you. This will give you an opportunity to kick him under the lower jaw.

Another way suggested is to wrap a coat around the left arm and let the dog bite it; then with the other hand seize the dog's throat and choke him.

FIRST AID FOR INJURIES

General Directions

Keep cool. There is no cause for excitement or hurry. In not one case in a thousand are the few moments necessary to find out what is the matter with an injured man going to result in any harm to him, and of course in order to treat him intelligently you must first know what is the matter. Common-sense will tell the scout that he must waste no time, however, when there is severe bleeding, or in case of poisoning.

If possible, always send for a doctor, unless the injury is a trivial one. Don't wait until he arrives, however, to do something for the injured person. A crowd should always be kept back and tight clothing should be loosened. If the patient's face is pale, place him on his back with his head low. If his face is flushed, fold your coat and put it under his head so as to raise it slightly.

In case of vomiting, place the patient on his side. Do not give an unconscious person a stimulant, as he cannot swallow, and it will run down his windpipe and choke him.

If the injury is covered by clothing, remove it by cutting or tearing, but never remove more clothing than necessary, as one of the results of injury is for a person to feel cold. Shoes and boots should be cut in severe injuries about the feet.

Shock

For example, a scout is riding on a trolley-car. The car runs into a loaded wagon. The wagon is overturned and the driver thrown to the pavement. Part of the load falls upon his body and when you reach him he is unconscious. So far as you can find out, nothing else is the matter with him. This is called shock. It accompanies all serious injuries and is itself serious, as a person may die without ever recovering from shock. Of course, there are different degrees of shock. In severe shock the person is completely unconscious or he may be only slightly confused and feel weak and uncertain of what has happened.

In shock always send for a doctor when you can. Before he comes, warm and stimulate the patient in every possible way. Place him on his back with his head low and cover him with your coat or a blanket. Rub his arms and legs toward his body but do not uncover him to do this. If you have ammonia or smelling salts, place them before the patient's nose so he may breathe them.

This is all you can do when unconsciousness is complete. When the patient begins to recover a little, however, and as soon as he can swallow, give him hot tea or coffee, or a half teaspoonful of aromatic spirits of ammonia in a quarter glass of water.

Warning: Remember always that a person with shock may have some other serious injuries. These you should always look for and treat if necessary.

Injuries in Which the Skin is Not Broken—Fractures

A fracture is the same thing as a broken bone. When the bone pierces or breaks through the skin, it is called a compound fracture, and when it does *not*, a simple fracture.

A scout is in the country with a comrade. The latter mounts a stone wall to cross it. The wall falls with him and he calls out for help. When the other scout reaches him, he finds the injured scout lying flat on the ground with both legs stretched out. One of these does not look quite natural, and the scout

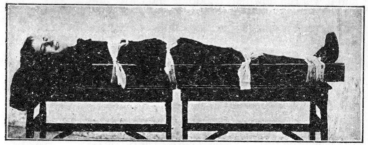

Splints for broken thigh

complains of a great deal of pain at the middle of the thigh and thinks he felt something break when he fell. He cannot raise the injured leg. Carefully rip the trousers and the underclothing at the seam to above the painful point. When you have done this the deformity will indicate the location of the fracture. You must be very gentle now or you will do harm, but if one hand is put above where you think the break occurred and the other below it and it is lifted gently you will find that there is movement at the broken point.

Send for a doctor first, if you can, and, if you expect him to arrive very soon, let your comrade lie where he is, putting his injured leg in the same position as the sound one and holding it there by coats or other articles piled around the leg. But if the doctor cannot be expected for some time, draw the injured limb into position like the sound one and hold it there by splints. Splints can be made of anything that is stiff and rigid. Something flat like a board is better than a pole or staff; limbs broken off a tree will do if nothing else can be found. Shingles make excellent splints. In applying splints remember that they should extend beyond the next joint above and the next joint below; otherwise, movements of the joint will cause movement at the broken point. With a fracture of the thigh, such as that described, the outer splint should be a very long one, extending below the feet from the arm pit. A short one extending just below the knee will do for the inner

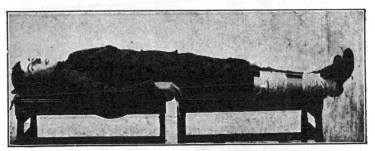

Splints for broken leg

splint. Splints may be tied on with handkerchiefs, pieces of cloth torn from the clothing, or the like. Tie firmly but not tight enough to cause severe pain. In a fracture of the thigh it will also be well to bind the injured leg to the sound one by two or three pieces of cloth around both. The clothing put back in place will serve as padding under the splint, but with thin summer clothing it is better to use straw, hay, or leaves in addition. Fractures of the lower leg and of the upper and lower arm are treated in the same way with a splint on the inner and outer sides of the broken bone. A sling will be required for a fracture of the arm. This may be made of the triangular bandage, or of a triangular piece of cloth, torn from your shirt.

The Red Cross First Aid Outfit is very convenient to use in fractures as well as in other injuries. The gauze bandage may be used for the strips to tie on the splints and the triangular bandage for an arm sling; or, if a sling is not needed, for strips to fix the splints firmly in place.

Compound Fractures

The edges of a broken bone are very sharp and may cut through the skin at the time of an injury, but more often after-

Splints and sling for fracture of upper arm

ward, if the injured person moves about or if the splints are not well applied so as to prevent movement at the point where the bone is broken. If a compound fracture has occurred, the wound produced by the sharp bone must always be treated first. The treatment is the same for any other wound.

Warning: You will not always be able to tell whether or not a fracture has occurred. In this case do not pull and haul the limb about to make sure, but treat as a fracture. There will always be a considerable amount of shock with fracture and this must also be treated.

Bruises

Everybody has suffered from a bruise at some time in his life and knows just what it is. A slight bruise needs no treatment. For a severe one, apply very hot or very cold water to prevent pain and swelling.

Sprains

A scout slips and twists his ankle and immediately suffers severe pain, and in a little while the ankle begins to swell

The sprained joint should be put in an elevated position and cloths wrung out in very hot or very cold water should be wrapped around it and changed very frequently. Movement of any sprained joint is likely to increase the injury, so this ought not to be permitted. Walking with a sprained ankle is not only exceedingly painful but it generally increases the hurt.

Dislocation

A dislocation is an injury where the head of a bone has slipped out of its socket at a joint. A scout is playing foot-ball. He suddenly feels as though his shoulder has been twisted out of place. Comparison with the other side will show that the injured shoulder does not look like the other one, being longer, or shorter, and contrary to the case with fracture there will not be increased movement at the point of injury but a lessened movement. Do not attempt to get a dislocated joint back in place. Cover the joint with cloths wrung out in very hot or very cold water, and get the patient into the hands of a doctor as soon as possible.

Triangular sling for arm

Injuries in Which the Skin is Broken

Such injuries are called wounds. There is one very important fact which must be remembered in connection with such injuries. Any injury in which the skin is unbroken is much less dangerous, as the skin prevents germs from reaching the injured part. The principle to be followed in treating a wound is to apply something to prevent germs from reaching the injury.

All wounds unless protected from germs are very liable to become infected with matter, or pus. Blood poisoning and even death may result from infection. To prevent infection of wounds, the scout should cover them promptly with what is called a sterilized dressing. This is a surgical dressing which has been so treated that it is free from germs. A number of dressings are on the market and can be procured in drug stores. In using them, be very careful not to touch the surface of the dressing which is to be placed in contact with the wound. The Red Cross First Aid Dressing is so made that this accident is almost impossible.

Head bandage

In taking care of a wound, do not handle it or do anything else to it. Every one's hands, though they may appear to be perfectly clean, are not so in the sense of being free from germs; nor is water, so a wound should never be washed.

It will be a good thing for a scout always to carry a Red Cross First Aid Outfit, or some similar outfit, for with this he is ready to take care of almost any injury; without it he will find it very difficult to improvise anything to cover a wound with safety to the injured person. If no prepared dressing is procurable, boil a towel if possible for fifteen minutes, squeeze the water out of it without touching the inner surface, and apply that to the wound. The next best dressing, if you cannot prepare this, will be a towel or handkerchief which has been recently washed and has not been used. These should be held in place on the wound with a bandage. Do not be afraid to leave a wound exposed to the air; germs do not float around in the air and such exposure is much safer than water or any dressing which is not free from germs. Of course you can bind up a wound with a towel not boiled or piece of cotton torn from your shirt, but you cannot do so without the liability of a great deal of harm to the injured person.

Snake Bites

While snake bites are wounds, the wounds caused by venomous snakes are not important as such but because the venom is quickly absorbed and by its action on the brain may cause speedy death. The rattlesnake and the moccasin are the most dangerous snakes in the United States.

In order to prevent absorption of the poison, immediately tie a string, handkerchief, or bandage above the bite. This can only be done in the extremities, but nearly all bites are received on the arms or legs. Then soak the wound in hot water and squeeze or suck it to extract the poison. Sucking a wound is not dangerous unless one has cuts or scrapes in the mouth. Then burn the wound with strong ammonia. This is not aromatic spirits of ammonia, but what is commonly known as strong ammonia in any drug store. Aromatic spirits of ammonia should also be given as a stimulant.

If you have nothing but a string to tie off the wound, be sure to do that and to get out as much poison as you can by squeezing or sucking the wound. A doctor should of course always be sent for when practicable in any injury as severe as a snake bite. Leave your string or bandage in place for an hour. A longer period is unsafe, as cutting off the circulation may cause mortification. Loosen the string or bandage after an hour's time, so that a little poison escapes into the body. If the bitten person does not seem to be much affected, repeat at the end of a few moments, and keep this up until the band has been entirely removed. If, however, the bitten person seems to be seriously affected by the poison you have allowed to escape into his body, you must not loosen the bandage again, but leave it in place and take the chance of mortification.

Wounds Without Severe Bleeding

These constitute the majority of all wounds. Use the Red Cross Outfit as described in the slip contained in the outfit. The pressure of a bandage will stop ordinary bleeding if firmly bound into place.

Wounds With Severe Bleeding

A scout must be prepared to check severe bleeding at once, and he should then dress the wound. Bleeding from an artery is by far the most dangerous. Blood coming from a cut artery is bright red in color and flows rapidly in spurts or jets. As the course of the blood in an artery is away from the heart, pressure must be applied on the heart side just as a rubber pipe which is cut must be compressed on the side from which the water is coming in order to prevent leakage at a cut beyond. The scout must also know the course of the larger arteries in order that he may know where to press on them. In the arm the course of the large artery is down the inner side of

the big muscle in the upper arm about in line with the seam of the coat. The artery in the leg runs down from the centre of a line from the point of the hip to the middle of the crotch, and is about in line with the inseam of the trousers. Pressure should be applied about three inches below the crotch. In making pressure on either of these arteries, use the fingers and press back against the bone. You can often feel the artery beat under your fingers, and the bleeding below will stop when you have your pressure properly made. Of course you cannot keep up the pressure with

How to apply first aid dressing

your fingers indefinitely in this way as they will soon become tired and cramped. Therefore, while you are doing this have some other scout prepare a tourniquet. The simplest form of tourniquet is a handkerchief tied loosely about the limb. In this handkerchief a smooth stone or a cork should be placed just above your fingers on the artery. When this is in place put a stick about a foot long under the handkerchief at the outer side of the limb and twist around till the stone makes pressure on the artery in the same way that your

fingers have.   Tie the stick in position so it will not
untwist.

Warning: When using a tourniquet remember that cutting
off the circulation for a long time is dangerous.   It is much
safer not to keep on a tourniquet more than an hour.   Loosen
it, but be ready to tighten it again quickly if bleeding
re-commences.

Another method to stop bleeding from an artery when the
wound is below the knee or elbow is to place a pad in the bend
of the joint and double
the limb back over it
holding t h e p a d in
tightly.   Tie the arm
or leg in this position.
If these means do not
check the bleeding put
a pad into the wound
and press on it there.
If you have no dress-
ing and blood is being
lost very rapidly, make
pressure in the wound
w i t h y o u r fingers.
Remember,   however,
that this should only
be resorted to in the
case of absolute necessity as it will infect the
wound.

Blood   from   veins
flows in a steady stream
back toward the heart
and is dark in color.   How to apply tourniquet to upper arm
From most veins a pad
firmly bandaged on the bleeding point will stop the bleeding.
If a vein in the neck is wounded, blood will be lost so rapidly
that the injured person is in danger of immediate death, so you
must disregard the danger of infection and jam your hand
tightly against the bleeding point.

Keep the patent quiet in all cases of severe bleeding, for even
if it is checked it may start up again.   Do not give any stimulants until the bleeding has been checked unless the patient
is very weak.   The best stimulant is aromatic spirits of ammonia, one teaspoonful in half a glass of water.

Unconsciousness and Poisoning

Unconsciousness, of course, means lack of consciousness, or, in other words, one who is unconscious knows nothing of his surroundings or of what is happening. A person may, however, be partially, as well as wholly, unconscious.

Unconsciousness may be due to so many causes that, in order to give the best treatment, the scout should first know the cause. Always try to find this out if you can. If you cannot do this, however, you should at least determine whether unconsciousness is due to poison, to bleeding, to sunstroke, or to freezing; for each of these demand immediate, special treatment. If it is not due to one of these causes, and the patient is pale and weak, have him placed with his head low, and warm and stimulate him in every possible way. If the face is red and the pulse is bounding and strong, that patient should have his head raised on a folded coat. No stimulants should be given him and cold water should be sprinkled on his face and chest.

The common causes of unconsciousness are shock, electric shock, fainting, apoplexy and injury to the brain, sunstroke and heat exhaustion, freezing, suffocation, and poisoning. The first two have already been described and the treatment of any form of suffocation in artificial respiration.

Fainting

Fainting usually occurs in overheated, crowded places. The patient is very pale and partially or completely unconscious. The pupils of the eye are natural, the pulse is weak and rapid. The patient should be placed in a lying-down position with the head lower than the rest of the body so that the brain will receive more blood. Loosen the clothing, especially about the neck. Keep the crowd back and open the windows if in-doors so that the patient may get plenty of fresh air. Sprinkle the face and chest with cold water. Apply smelling salts or ammonia to the nose, rub the limbs toward the body. A stimulant may be given when the patient is so far recovered that he is able to swallow.

Apoplexy and Injury to the Brain

Apoplexy and unconsciousness from injury to the brain are due to the pressure of blood on the brain so that they may be described together. Apoplexy is of course much harder to distinguish than injury to the brain as in the latter the scout can always see that the head has been hurt. With both, unconsciousness will usually be complete. Pupils are large and frequently unequal in size, breathing is snoring, and the pulse is usually full and slow. One side of the body will be paralyzed. Test this by raising arm or leg; if paralyzed, it will drop absolutely helpless. Send for a doctor at once. Keep patient quiet and in a dark room if possible. Put in lying-down position with head raised by pillows. Apply ice or cold cloths to head. No stimulants. Drunkenness is sometimes mistaken for apoplexy. If there is any doubt on this point always treat for apoplexy.

Sunstroke and Heat Exhaustion

Any one is liable to sunstroke or heat exhaustion if exposed to excessive heat. A scout should remember not to expose himself too much to the sun nor should he wear too heavy clothing in the summer. Leaves in the hat will do much to prevent sunstroke. If the scout becomes dizzy and exhausted through exposure to the sun he should find a cool place, lie down, and bathe the face, hands, and chest in cold water and drink freely of cold water.

Sunstroke and heat exhaustion, though due to the same cause, are quite different and require different treatment. In sunstroke unconsciousness is complete. The face is red, pupils large, the skin is very hot and dry with no perspiration. The patient sighs and the pulse is full and slow. The treatment for sunstroke consists in reducing the temperature of the body. A doctor should be summoned whenever possible. The patient should be removed to a cool place and his clothing loosened, or better the greater part of it removed. Cold water, or ice, should be rubbed over the face, neck, chest, and in arm pits. When consciousness returns give cold water freely.

Heat exhaustion is simply exhaustion or collapse due to heat. The patient is greatly depressed and weak but not usually unconscious. Face is pale and covered with clammy sweat, breathing and pulse are weak and rigid. While this condition is not nearly as dangerous as sunstroke, a doctor should be summoned if possible. Remove the patient to a cool place and have him lie down with his clothing loosened. Don't use anything cold externally, but permit him to take small sips of cold water. Stimulants should be given just as in fainting.

Freezing

The patient should be taken into a cold room and the body should be rubbed with rough cloths wet in cold water. The temperature of the room should be increased if possible. This should be done gradually and the cloths should be wet in warmer and warmer water. As soon as the patient can swallow give him stimulants. It will be dangerous to place him before an open fire or in a hot bath until he begins to recover. You will know this by his skin becoming warmer, by his better color, and by his generally improved appearance.

Frost-Bite

Remember that you are in danger of frost-bite if you do not wear sufficient clothing in cold weather, and that rubbing any part of the body which becomes very cold helps to prevent frost-bite, because it brings more warm blood to the surface. The danger is when, after being cold, the part suddenly has no feeling.

The object of the treatment is gradually to restore warmth to the frozen part. To do this the part should be rubbed first with snow or cold water; the water should be warmed gradually. The use of hot water at once would be likely to cause mortification of the frozen part.

Poisoning

For all poisons give an emetic. Send for a doctor at once and if possible have the messenger tell what poison has been taken so that the doctor may bring the proper antidote. Do not wait for him to arrive, but give an emetic to rid the stomach of the poison. Good emetics are mustard and water, salt water, or lukewarm water alone in large quantities. Never mind the exact dose and if vomiting is not profuse repeat the dose.

Fits

A person in a fit first has convulsive movements of the body, then he usually becomes unconscious. A scout should have no difficulty in making out what is the matter with a person in a fit.

Put the sufferer on the floor or the ground where he can not hurt himself by striking anything. Loosen tight clothing and do not try to restrain the convulsive movements. A wad of cloth thrust in the mouth will prevent biting the tongue. When he becomes quiet do not disturb him.

INJURIES DUE TO HEAT AND COLD

Burns and Scalds

For slight burns in order to relieve the pain some dressing to exclude the air is needed. Very good substances of this character are pastes made with water and baking soda, starch, or flour. Carbolized vaseline, olive or castor oil, and fresh lard or cream are all good. One of these substances should be smeared over a thin piece of cloth and placed on the burned part. A bandage should be put on over this to hold the dressing in place and for additional protection.

Severe burns and scalds are very serious injuries which require treatment from a physician. Pending his arrival the scout should remember to treat the sufferer for shock as well as to dress the wound.

Burns from electricity should be treated exactly like other burns.

Do not attempt to remove clothing which sticks to a burn; cut the cloth around the part which sticks and leave it on the burn.

FIRST AID FOR EMERGENCIES

Besides the accidents which have been mentioned, certain emergencies may demand treatment by a scout.

The commonest of these are described here.

Something in the Eye

No little thing causes more pain and discomfort than something in the eye. Do not rub to remove a foreign body from the eye, as this is likely to injure the delicate covering of the eyeball. First, close the eye so the tears will accumulate, these may wash the foreign body into plain view so that it may be easily removed. If this fails, pull the upper lid over the lower two or three times, close the nostril on the opposite side and have the patient blow his nose hard. If the foreign body still remains in the eye, examine first under the lower and then the upper lid. For the former have the patient look up, press lower lid down, and if the foreign body is seen lift it out gently with the corner of a clean handkerchief. It is not so easy to see the upper lid.   Seat the patient in a chair with his head bent backward.   Stand behind him and place a match or thin pencil across the upper lid one half an inch from its edge,

Eye bandage

turn the upper lid back over the match, and lift the foreign body off as before. A drop of castor oil in the eye after removing the foreign body will soothe it.

Sunburn

This is simply an inflammation of the skin due to action of the sun. It may be prevented by hardening the skin gradually. Any toilet powder or boracic acid will protect the skin to a considerable extent. The treatment consists of soothing applications such as ordinary or carbolized vaseline.

Ivy Poisoning

Poison ivy causes a very intense inflammation of the skin. Better avoid, even though it has not harmed you before. Baking soda made in a thick paste with water or carbolized vaseline are good remedies.   In severe cases a doctor should be consulted.

Bites and Stings

Ammonia should be immediately applied.   Wet salt and wet earth are also good applications.

Nosebleed

Slight nosebleed does not require treatment as no harm will result from it.   When more severe the collar should be loosened. Do not blow the nose. Apply cold to the back of the neck by means of a key or cloth wrung out in cold water.

Position of hands   Chair carry

A roll of paper under the upper lip, between it and the gum, will also help. When the bleeding still continues shove a cotton or gauze plug into the nostrils, leaving it there until the bleeding stops.

Earache

This is likely to result seriously and a doctor should be consulted in order to prevent bad results with possible loss of hearing.   Hot cloths, a bag of heated salt, or a hot bottle applied to the ear will often cure earache.   A few drops of alcohol on a hot cloth so placed that the alcohol fumes enter the ear will often succeed.   If neither is effective, heat a few drops of sweet oil as hot as you can stand, put a few drops in the ear and plug with cotton.   Be careful that it is not too hot.

Toothache

Remember that toothache indicates something seriously wrong with the teeth which can only be permanently corrected by a dentist. In toothache if you can find a cavity, clean it out with a small piece of cotton or a toothpick. Then plug it with cotton, on which a drop of oil of cloves has been put if you have it. If no cavity is found, soak a piece of cotton in camphor and apply it to the outside of the gum. Hot cloths and hot bottles or bags will help in toothache, just as they do in earache.

Inflammation of the Eye

Cover with a cloth wrung out in cold water and change cloths from time to time when they get warm. See a doctor in order to safeguard your sight.

Cramp or Stomachache

This is usually due to the irritation produced by undigested food. A hot bottle applied to the stomach or rubbing will often give relief. A little peppermint in hot water and ginger tea are both excellent remedies. The undigested matter should be gotten rid of by vomiting or a cathartic.

Remember this kind of pain is sometimes due to something serious and if it is very severe or continues for some time, it is much safer to send for a doctor.

Arm carry

Hiccough

This is due to indigestion. Holding the breath will often cure, as will also drinking a full glass of water in small sips without taking a breath. If these fail vomiting is an almost certain remedy.

Chills

In order to stop a chill drink hot milk or hot lemonade and get into bed. Plenty of covers should be used, and hot water bottles or hot milk or lemonade help to warm one quickly.

Carrying Injured

A severely injured person is always best carried on a stretcher. The easiest stretcher for a scout to improvise is the coat stretcher. For this two coats and a pair of poles are needed. The sleeves of the coat are first turned inside out. The coats are then placed on the ground with their lower sides touching each

Improvised stretcher

other. The poles are passed through the sleeves on each side, the coats are buttoned up with the button side down. A piece of carpet, a blanket, or sacking can be used in much the same way as the coats, rolling in a portion at each side. Shutters and doors make fair stretchers. In order not to jounce the patient in carrying him the bearers should break step. The bearer in front steps off with the left foot and the one in the rear with the right. A number of different methods for carrying a patient by two bearers are practised. The four-handed

seat is a very good one.   To make this each bearer grasps his
left wrist in his right hand, and the other bearer's right wrist
in his left hand with the backs of the hands uppermost.   The

First position

Fireman's lift

bearers then stoop and place the chair under the sitting patient
who steadies himself by placing his arms around their necks.

It will sometimes be necessary for one scout to carry an injured
comrade. The scout should first turn the patient on his face;
he then steps astride his body, facing toward the patient's
head, and, with hands under his arm-pits, lifts him to his
knees; then, clasping hands over the abdomen, lifts him to his
feet; he then, with his left hand, seizes the patient by the left
wrist and draws his left arm around his (the bearer's) neck
and holds it against his left chest, the patient's left side resting against his body, and supports him with his right arm about
the waist. The scout, with his left hand, seizes the right
wrist of the patient and draws the arm over his head and down
upon his shoulder, then, shifting himself in front, stoops and
clasps the right thigh with his right arm passed between the
legs, his right hand seizing the patient's right wrist; lastly, the
scout, with his left hand, grasps the patient's left hand, and
steadies it against his side when he arises.

WATER ACCIDENTS

Wilbert E. Longfellow, United States Volunteer Life Saving Corps

The scout's motto, "*Be Prepared*," is more than usually
applicable to the work of caring for accidents which
happen in the water.

To save lives, the scout must know first how to swim, to care
for himself, and then to learn to carry another and to break
the clutch, the "death grip," which we read so much about
in the newspaper accounts of drowning accidents. By constant
training, a boy, even though not a good swimmer, can be
perfectly at home in the water, fully dressed, undressed, or
carrying a boy of his own size or larger. In fact two boys of
twelve or fourteen years can save a man.

Swimming

For physical development the breast stroke is useful, for it
is one that is used in carrying a tired swimmer and is used to
go to the bottom for lost articles and to search for a person
who has sunk before help has reached him. It is possible, you
know, to go to the bottom and bring a body to the surface and
swim with it to shore before life is extinct and to restore consciousness by well-directed efforts. The body of an unconscious
person weighs little when wholly or partially submerged, and

in salt water weighs less than in fresh water, and is consequently more readily carried. Training makes a small boy the equal or superior of an untrained boy much larger and of greater strength, and the way to learn to carry a drowning person is to carry a boy who is not drowning to get used to handling the weights. A little struggle now and then lends realism

Breast stroke for tired swimmer

Under-arm carry

to the work and increases the skill of the scout candidate for a life saver's rating. Speed swimming for itself alone is a very selfish sport so that the scout should develop his ability to make it generally useful to others.

Floating

After the breast stroke is learned, floating on the back for rest and swimming on the back, using feet only for propulsion, leaving the hands free to hold a drowning person, should be learned. This can be readily acquired with a little practice, carrying the hands on the surface of the water, arms half bent, with the elbows close to the sides at the waist line. To carry a man this way the hands are placed at either side of the drowning man's head and he is towed floating on his back, the rescuer swimming on his back, keeping the other away. It is well to remember to go with the tide or current, and do not wear your strength away opposing it. Other ways

Swimming on back without hands

of carrying are to place the hands beneath the arms of the drowning man, or to grasp him firmly by the biceps from beneath, at the same time using the knee in the middle of his back to get him into a floating position, the feet acting as propellers.

Head carry—swim on back

Methods which enable the rescuer's use of one arm in addition to the feet are known as the "German army" and the "cross shoulder." In the first, the swimmer approaches the drowning person from the back, passes the left arm under the other's left arm, across in front of the chest, and firmly grasps the right arm, either by the biceps or below the elbow, giving him control. This leaves the right arm to swim with. The other one-arm hold mentioned is one in which the rescuer passes an arm over the shoulder of the one to be carried, approaching from the back as before, and getting a hold under the other's arm, which makes the drowning man helpless. The breast stroke carry previously mentioned is used only for helping a tired swimmer, and one in possession of his faculties who will not try to grasp the rescuer. The tired swimmer lies on the back and, extending his arms fully in front, rests a hand on either shoulder of the swimmer who rests facing him in the regular breast position allowing the feet of the other to drop between his own. Quite good speed can be made in this way, and all of these methods are practical as a trial will show. A little practice will enable the beginner to see which he can do most readily and then he can perfect himself in it for instant use.

Breaking "Death Grips"

If one uses care in approaching a frightened or drowning person in the water, there will be no use for the release methods;

Break for wrist hold   Breaking back strangle hold

but the best of swimmers get careless at times and all swimmers need to know how to get clear when gripped.

Wrist Grip

Of these the simplest is the one where the wrists of the swimmer have been grasped by the drowning man in his struggles. The swimmer throws both hands above his head which forces both low in the water and then turns the leverage of his arms against the other's thumbs, breaking the hold easily.

Break for front strangle hold

It should be borne in mind that a drowning man grasps what he can see above the surface of the water, so he will not attempt to grasp his rescuer below the points of the shoulders. Remember also that a tall man and a short man would have about the same amount of their body projecting above the surface of the water.

Neck Grip

For the grip around the swimmer's neck from the front, for both arms around the shoulders, and for a grip in which the drowning man had the other over one shoulder and under the other arm, the break is much the same. As soon as the rescuer feels the hold, he covers the other's mouth with the palm of his hand, clasping the nostrils tightly between his first two fingers, at the same time pulling the drowning man to him with the left hand in the small of the back, treading water in the meantime. Then, taking a full breath, he applies his knee in the other's stomach, forcing him to expel the air in his lungs and at the same time preventing him from getting more by pressure on the nostrils and mouth. Should the pressure of the grip around the body be too great to allow freedom of the arms, the preliminary move in that case would be to bring both arms to the level of the shoulder, thus sliding the other's arms to the neck, leaving the rescuer's arms to cover the nose.

Back Strangle

The back strangle hold is an awkward one to break and one which must be broken without an instant's delay, or the would-be rescuer himself will be in great need of help. In practice it will be found that, by grasping the encircling arms at the wrists and pushing back with the buttocks against the other's abdomen, room to slip out can be obtained. In a life and death struggle, sharper measures are needed, and if the rescuer throws his head suddenly back against the nose of the drowning man, he will secure his freedom very readily and have him under control by the time he has recovered from his dazed condition.

Rescue From Shore or Boat

It is not always necessary to go into the water to attempt a rescue, and in many cases, when some one has fallen off a bridge or dock, a line or buoy or boat can be used to advantage without placing more lives in danger than the one in the water. Discretion in such matters is worthy of recognition rather than too much recklessness in swimming out. *Use a boat when possible*. Practice in throwing a life buoy should be indulged in where possible, and a good scout should always leave the line coiled over pegs and the buoy hanging on top to bind it in place for instant use in an emergency.

Diving From the Surface

When a bather or victim from a boating accident sinks to the bottom of a river or pond of from seven to twenty feet in depth, prompt rescue methods may bring him to the surface, and resuscitation methods, promptly applied, will restore breath. If there is no current in the pond or lake, bubbles from the body will indicate its whereabouts directly beneath the place where it sank. Should there be tide or currents, the bubbles are carried at an angle with the streams and the searcher must go from the spot where the person disappeared and look along the bottom going with the current. When a drowning man gives up his struggle and goes down, his body sinks a little way and is brought up again by the buoyancy within it and the air is expelled. It sinks again and next rises less high and air is again expelled. This happens several times until enough water is taken into the stomach and air passages to offset the floating capacity. The floating capacity is barely overcome,

Throwing feet for dive from surface

so the body weighs but little. It is very simple, as almost any youthful swimmer knows, to go to the bottom if one can dive from a float, pier, or boat, but to be able to dive down ten feet from the surface requires practice. In most cases to go deeper would require a weight after the manner of the Southern sponge and pearl fishers. Grasp a ten or fifteen pound stone and dive in; to come up the swimmer lets go and rises to the top.

Diving For Lost Objects

In covering a considerable area in search for bodies or lost objects, several ropes can be anchored with grapnels or rocks in squares and a systematic search thus maintained by divers. Going down from the surface is not so simple and the knack is attained by practice, especially by athletic lads. The secret is to swim to a point where a sounding is to be made, and to plunge the head and shoulders under, elevating the hips above the surface to drive the shoulders deep and give chance for a few strokes — breast stroke preferred — until the whole body in a vertical position is headed for the bottom. The elevation of the feet and lower legs in the air gives the body additional impetus downward, and when the object is attained a push-off from the bottom with both feet sends the swimmer to the surface in quick order. To carry any weight ashore, it is necessary to carry it low on the body, hugged close to the waist line, allowing one hand and both feet for swimming, or if on the back, hold by both hands using the feet as propellers.

Restoring Breathing

Knowledge of resuscitation of the apparently drowned is an important part of the equipment of a first-class scout, and a

Artificial respiration (*a*)

Artificial respiration (*b*)

great many lives could have been saved had it been more general. To be effective no time must be lost in getting the apparently drowned person out of the water and getting the water out of him. The Schaefer or prone method requires but one operator at a time and no waste of time in preliminaries.

When taken from the water the patient is laid on the ground face downward, arms extended above the head, face a little to one side, so as not to prevent the free passage of air. The operator kneels astride or beside the prone figure and lets his hands fall into the spaces between the short ribs. By letting the weight of the upper body fall upon his hands resting on the prone man, the air is forced out of the lungs; by relaxing the pressure, the chest cavity enlarges and air is drawn in to take the place of that forced out. By effecting this change of air — pressing and relaxing, twelve to fifteen times a minute (time it by watch at first, and then count) artificial breathing is performed. Sometimes it is necessary to work an hour or two before the flicker of an eyelid or a gasp from the patient rewards the life saver's efforts, and then he must carefully "piece in" the breathing until natural breathing is resumed. When breathing starts, then promote circulation by rubbing the legs and body toward the heart. Do not attempt to stimulate by the throat until the patient can swallow. Give a teaspoonful of aromatic spirits of ammonia, in half a glass of water.

Remember that by laying the patient face downward fluids in the air passages will run or be forced out and the tongue will drop forward, and require no holding, always an awkward task.

Treatment After Respiration Begins

The after treatment is important. Put the patient to bed, keep quiet and warm. Always get the services of a physician as soon as possible, but do not wait for him to come. Start work instantly. The patient needs oxygen, so keep spectators away. They are robbing the man of the life-giving properties of the air. For this reason, in all but the most severe weather, it is well to work on the patient in the open.

Life Buoys

If one is to place a life buoy for instant use in emergencies it should be hung upon four pegs driven into holes in two pieces of wood nailed together in the form of the diameter of a two-foot square or three pegs in strips of wood arranged in the form of a T, about eighteen or twenty inches high, the two pegs at either side of the top bar of the T and the other one on the upright near the bottom. Most life buoys used on shore have fifty or seventy-five feet of light line attached to draw the rescued person ashore or to recover the buoy after a faulty throw. Commencing at the free end of the line, where a small wooden float is often attached, the rope should first be coiled on the pegs, hanging the buoy outside the coil to bind it in place

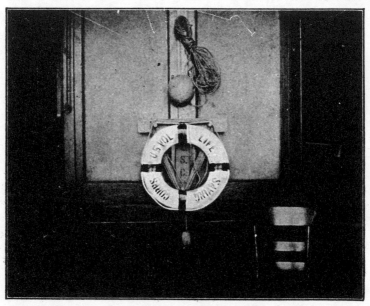

Life buoy and ice ball

so wind or jars will not loosen it. Then, when the buoy is needed, the ring is grasped by the throwing hand which clasps the buoy itself, and the coil is clasped in the free hand, the end of the rope being secured ashore by standing upon it with one foot. After each use or practice the buoy line should be restored to its pegs for instant use.

Notes

Notes

CHAPTER VIII

GAMES AND ATHLETIC STANDARDS

THE GAMES

By Ernest Thompson Seton, Chief Scout

Deer Hunting

The deer hunt has proved one of our most successful games.

The deer is a dummy, best made with a wire frame, on which soft hay is wrapped till it is of proper size and shape, then all is covered with open burlap. A few touches of white and black make it very realistic.

If time does not admit of a well-finished deer, one can be made of a sack stuffed with hay, decorated at one end with a smaller sack for head and neck, and set on four thin sticks.

The side of the deer is marked with a large oval, and over the heart is a smaller one.

Bows and arrows only are used to shoot this deer.

A pocketful of corn, peas, or other large grain is now needed for scent. The boy who is the deer for the first hunt takes the dummy under his arm and runs off, getting ten minutes' start, or until he comes back and shouts "ready!" He leaves a trail of corn, dropping two or three grains for every yard and making the trail as crooked as he likes, playing such tricks as a deer would do to baffle his pursuers. Then he hides the deer in any place he fancies, but not among

Wooden legged Deer

rocks or on the top of a ridge, because in one case many arrows would be broken, and in the other, lost.

The hunters now hunt for this deer just as for a real deer, either following the trail or watching the woods ahead; the best hunters combine the two. If at any time the trail is quite lost the one in charge shouts: "*Lost Trail!*" After that the one who finds the trail scores *two*. Any one giving a false alarm by shouting "*Deer*" is fined *five*.

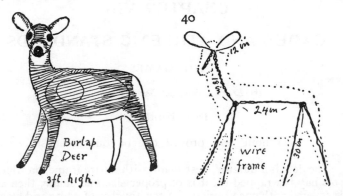

Burlap Deer
3ft. high.

40

wire frame

Thus they go till some one finds the deer. He shouts: "*Deer!*" and scores *ten* for finding it. The others shout: "*Second*," "*Third*," etc., in order of seeing it, but they do not score.

The finder must shoot at the deer with his bow and arrow from the very spot whence he saw it. If he misses, the second hunter may step up five paces, and have his shot. If *he* misses, the third one goes five, and so on till some one hits the deer, or until the ten-yard limit is reached. If the finder is within ten yards on sighting the deer, and misses his shot, the other hunters go back to the ten-yard limit. Once the deer is hit, all the shooting must be from the exact spot whence the successful shot was fired.

A shot in the big oval is a *body wound;* that scores *five*. A shot outside that is a *scratch;* that scores *two*. A shot in the small oval or heart is a *heart wound;* it scores *ten*, and ends the hunt. Arrows which do not stick do not count, unless it can be proved that they passed right through, in which case they take the highest score that they pierced.

If all the arrows are used, and none in the heart, the deer escapes, and the boy who was deer scores *twenty-five*.

The one who found the dummy is deer for the next hunt. A clever deer can add greatly to the excitement of the game.

Originally we used paper for scent, but found it bad. It littered the woods; yesterday's trail was confused with that of to-day, etc. Corn proved better, because the birds and the squirrels kept it cleaned up from day to day, and thus the ground was always ready for a fresh start. But the best of all is the hoof mark for the shoe. These iron hoof marks are fast to a pair of shoes, and leave a trail much like a real deer. This has several advantages. It gives the hunter a chance to tell where the trail doubled, and which way the deer was going. It is more realistic, and the boy who can follow this skilfully can follow a living deer. In actual practice it is found well to use a little corn with this on the hard places, a plan quite consistent with realism, as every hunter will recall.

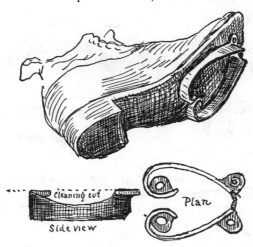

It is strictly forbidden to any hunter to stand in front of the firing line; all must be back of the line on which the shooter stands.

There is no limit to the situations and curious combinations in this hunt. The deer may be left standing or lying. There is no law why it should not be hidden behind a solid tree trunk. The game develops as one follows it. After it has been played for some time with the iron hoof mark as above, the boys grow so skilful on the trail that we can dispense with even the corn. The iron mark like a deer hoof leaves a very realistic "slot" or track, which the more skilful boys readily follow through the woods. A hunt is usually for three, five, or more deer, according to agreement and the result is reckoned by points on the whole chase.

The Bear Hunt

This is played by half a dozen or more boys. Each has a club about the size and shape of a baseball club, but made of *straw*

tied around two or three switches and tightly sewn up in burlap.
—One big fellow is selected for the bear. He has a school bag
tightly strapped on his back, and in that a toy balloon fully
blown up. This is his heart. On his neck is a bear-claw
necklace of wooden beads and claws. (See cut.)

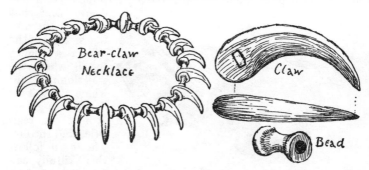

He has three dens about one hundred yards apart in a triangle. While in his den the bear is safe. If the den is a tree
or rock, he is safe while touching it. He is obliged to come out
when the chief hunter counts one hundred, and must go the
rounds of the three till the hunt is settled.

The object of the hunters is to break the balloon or heart;
that is, to kill the bear. He must drop dead when the heart
bursts. The hunter who kills him claims the necklace.

But the bear also has a club for defence. Each hunter must
wear a hat, and once the bear knocks a hunter's hat off, *that
one is dead* and out of this hunt. He must drop where his
hat falls.

Tackling of any kind is forbidden.

The bear wins by killing or putting to flight all the hunters.
In this case he keeps the necklace.

The savageness of these big bears is indescribable. Many
lives are lost in each hunt, and it has several times happened
that the whole party of hunters has been exterminated by some
monster of unusual ferocity.

This game has also been developed into a play.

Spearing the Great Sturgeon

This water game is exceedingly popular and is especially good for public exhibition, being spectacular and full of amusement and excitement.

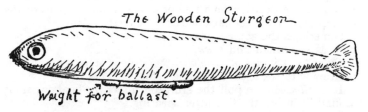

The Wooden Sturgeon

Weight for ballast.

The outfit needed is:

(1) A sturgeon roughly formed of soft wood; it should be about three feet long and nearly a foot thick at the head. It may be made realistic, or a small log pointed at both ends will serve.

(2) Two spears with six-inch steel heads and wooden handles (about three feet long). The points should be sharp, but not the barbs. Sometimes the barbs are omitted altogether. Each head should have an eye to which is attached twenty feet of one-quarter inch rope. On each rope, six feet from the spearhead, is a fathom mark made by tying on a rag or cord.

(3) Two boats with crews. Each crew consists of a spearman, who is captain, and one or two oarsmen or paddlers, of whom the after one is the pilot. All should be expert swimmers or else wear life-belts during the game.

The Game. — Each boat has a base or harbor; this is usually part of the shore opposite that of the enemy; or it obviates all danger of collision if the boats start from the same side. The sturgeon is left by the referee's canoe at a point midway between the bases. At the word "Go!" each boat leaves its

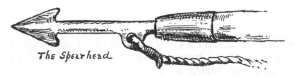

The Spearhead

base and, making for the sturgeon, tries to spear it, then drag it by the line to his base. When both get their spears into it the contest becomes a tug of war until one of the spears pulls out.

The sturgeon is landed when the prow of the boat that has it in tow touches its proper base, even though the spear of the enemy is then in the fish: or it is landed when the fish itself touches base. The boats change bases after each heat.

Matches are usually for one, three, or five sturgeon. Points are counted only for the landing of the fish, but the referee may give the decision on a foul or a succession of fouls, or the delinquent may be set back one or more boat lengths.

Sometimes the game is played in canoes or boats, with one man as spearman and crew.

Rules. — It is *not allowable* to push the sturgeon into a new position with the spear or paddle before striking.

It *is allowable* to pull the sturgeon under the boat or pass it around by using the line after spearing.

It *is allowable* to lay hands on the other boat to prevent a collision, but otherwise it is forbidden to touch the other boat or crew or paddle or spear or line, or to lay hands on the fish, or to touch it with the paddle or oar, or touch your own spear while it is in the fish, or to tie the line around the fish except so far as this may be accidentally done in spearing.

It *is allowable* to dislodge the enemy's spear by throwing your own over it. The purpose of the barbs is to assist in this.

It *is allowable to run on to* the sturgeon with the boat.

It *is absolutely forbidden to throw the spear over the other boat or over the heads of your crew.*

In towing the sturgeon the fathom mark must be over the gunwale — at least six feet of line should be out when the fish is in tow. It is not a foul to have less, but the spearman must at once let it out if the umpire or the other crew cries "fathom!"

The spearman is allowed to drop the spear and use the paddle or oar at will, but not to resign his spear to another of the crew. The spearman must be in his boat when the spear is thrown.

If the boat is upset the referee's canoe helps them to right. Each crew must accept the backset of its accidents.

Tilting in The Water

For this we usually have two boats or war canoes manned by four men each. These are a spearman, who is also a captain, a pilot, and two oarsmen.

The spearman is armed with a light pole or bamboo eight or ten feet long, with a soft pad on the end. Sometimes this is further provided with a hook. This is a forked branch with limbs a foot long; one is lashed to the bamboo, the other projecting out a foot, and slightly backward. The end of the

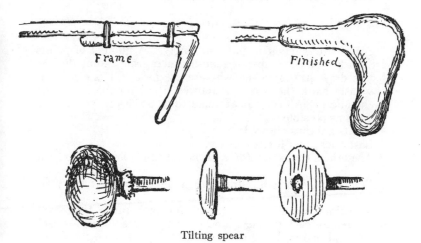

Tilting spear

spear and the fork are now thoroughly padded with burlap to the shape of a duck's head and bill. And it must be cased in waterproof, to keep it from getting wet and heavy. The object of the hook is to change suddenly from pushing, and to pull the enemy by hooking round his neck. Each boat should have a quarter-deck or raised platform at one end, on which the spearman stands.

The battle is fought in rounds and by points.

To put your opponent back into the canoe with one foot counts you five; two feet, ten. If he loses his spear you count five (excepting when he is put overboard). If you put him down on one knee on the fighting deck, you count five; two knees, ten. If you put him overboard it counts twenty-five. One hundred points is a round.

A battle is for one or more rounds, as agreed on.

It is forbidden to hook or strike below the belt.

The umpire may dock for fouls.

Canoe Tag

Any number of canoes or boats may engage in this. A rubber cushion, a hot-water bag full of air, any rubber football, or a cotton bag with a lot of corks in it is needed.   The game is to tag the other canoe by throwing this *into* it.

The rules are as in ordinary cross-tag.

Scouting

Scouts are sent out in pairs or singly.   A number of points are marked on the map at equal distances from camp, and the scouts draw straws to see where each goes.   If one place is obviously hard, the scout is allowed a fair number of points as handicap.   All set out at same time, go direct, and return as soon as possible.

Points are thus allowed:

Last back, *zero* for travelling.

The others count one for each minute they are ahead of the last.

Points up to one hundred are allowed for their story on return.

Sometimes we allow ten points for each turtle they have seen; ten for each owl seen and properly named; five for each hawk, and one each for other wild birds; also two for a cat one for a dog.

No information is given the scout; he is told to go to such a point and do so and so, but is fined points if he hesitates or asks how or why, etc.

The Game of Quicksight

Make two boards about a foot square, divide each into twenty-five squares; get ten nuts and ten pebbles.   Give to one player one board, five nuts, and five pebbles.   He places

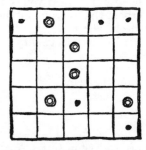

Quicksight Game

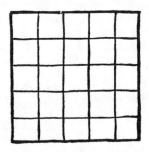

counters

these on the squares in any pattern he fancies, and when ready the other player is allowed to see it for five seconds. Then it is covered up, and from the memory of what he saw the second player must reproduce the pattern on his own board. He counts one for each that was right, and takes off one for each that was wrong. They take turn and turn about.

This game is a wonderful developer of the power to see and memorize quickly.

Farsight, or Spot the Rabbit

Take two six-inch squares of stiff white pasteboard or whitened wood. On each of these draw an outline rabbit, one an exact duplicate of the other. Make twenty round black wafers

6 inches sq

or spots, each half an inch across. Let one player stick a few of these on one rabbit-board and set it up in full light. The other, beginning at one hundred yards, draws near till he can see the spots well enough to reproduce the pattern on the other which he carries. If he can do it at seventy-five yards he has wonderful eyes. Down even to seventy (done three times out of five), he counts high honor; from seventy to sixty counts honor. Below that does not count at all.

Pole-star

Each competitor is given a long straight stick in daytime, and told to lay it due north and south. In doing this he may guide himself by sun, moss, or anything he can find in nature—anything, indeed, except a compass.

The direction is checked by a good compass corrected for the locality. The one who comes nearest wins.

It is optional with the judges whether the use of a timepiece is to be allowed.

Rabbit Hunt

The game of rabbit hunting is suited for two hunters in limited grounds.

Three little sacks of brown burlap, each about eight inches by twelve, are stuffed with hay.

At any given place in the woods the two hunters stand in a ten-foot circle with their bows and arrows. One boy is blindfolded; the other, without leaving the circle, throws the rabbits into good hiding places on the ground. Then the second hunter has to find the rabbits and shoot them without leaving the circle. The lowest number of points wins, as in golf. If the hunter has to leave the circle he gets one point for every step he takes outside. After he sees the rabbit he must keep to that spot and shoot till it is hit once. One shot kills it, no matter where struck. For every shot he misses he gets five points.

After his first shot at each rabbit the hider takes alternate shots with him.

If it is the hider who kills the rabbit, the hunter adds ten points to his score. If the hunter hits it, he takes ten off his score.

If the hunter fails to find all the rabbits, he scores twenty-five for each one he gives up.

The hider cannot score at all. He can only help his friend into trouble. Next time the two change places.

A match is usually for two brace of rabbits.

Hostile Spy

Hanging from the totem pole is a red or yellow horse-tail. This is the grand medicine scalp of the band. The hostile spy has to steal it. The leader goes around on the morning of the day and whispers to the various braves, "Look out — there's a spy in camp." At length he gets secretly near the one he has selected for spy and whispers, "Look out, there's a spy in camp, and *you are it.*" He gives him at the same time some bright-coloured badge, that he must wear as soon as he has secured the medicine scalp. He must not hide the scalp on his person, but keep it in view. He has all day till sunset to get away with it. If he gets across the river or other limit, with warriors in close pursuit, they give him ten arrow heads (two and one half cents each), or other ransom agreed on. If he gets away safely and hides it, he can come back and claim fifteen arrow heads from the council as ransom for the scalp. If he is caught, he pays his captor ten arrow heads ransom for his life.

The Man-Hunt

This is played with a scout and ten or more hostiles, or hounds, according to the country, more when it is rough or wooded.

The scout is given a letter addressed to the "Military Commandant"* of any given place a mile or two away.   He is told to take the letter to any one of three given houses, and get it endorsed, with the hour when he arrived, then return to the starting-point within a certain time.

The hostiles are sent to a point half-way, and let go by a starter at the *same time* as the scout leaves the camp.   They are to intercept him.

If they catch him before he delivers the letter he must ransom his life by paying each two arrow heads (or other forfeit) and his captor keeps the letter as a trophy.   If he gets through, but is caught on the road back, he pays half as much for his life. If he gets through, but is over time, it is a draw.   If he gets through successfully on time he claims three arrow heads from each hostile and keeps the letter as a trophy.

They may not follow him into the house (that is, the fort), but may surround it at one hundred yards distance.   They do not know which three houses he is free to enter, but they do know that these are within certain limits.

The scout should wear a conspicuous badge (hat, shirt, coat, or feather), and may ride a wheel or go in a wagon, etc., as long as his badge is clearly visible.

To "tag" the scout is not to capture.   "The blockade to be binding must be effectual."

Hunt the Coon

This is an in-door game, founded on the familiar "Hunt the Thimble."

We use a little dummy coon; either make it or turn a ready-made toy rabbit into one by adding tail and black mask, and cropping the ears.

---

*The "Military Commandant" is usually the lady of the house that he gets to.

All the players but one go out of the room. That one places the coon anywhere in sight, high or low, but in plain view; all come in and seek. The first to find it, sits down silently, and scores one. Each sits down, on seeing it, giving no clue to the others.

The first to score three coons is winner, usually. Sometimes we play till every one but one has a coon; that one is the booby. The others are first, second, etc.

Sometimes each is given his number in order of finding it. Then, after seven or eight coons, these numbers are added up, and the *lowest* is winner. If no coon is available use a thimble.

Spear Fights

This is an in-door game with out-door weapons. The soft-headed, eight foot spears of the tilting-match are used. The contestants stand on barrels eight feet apart. Each tries to put the other off his barrel. It is well to have a catcher behind each player to save him if he falls.

Games are for seven, eleven, or thirteen points.

Navajo Feather Dance

An eagle feather hung on a horse-hair, so as to stand upright, is worked by a hidden operator, so as to dance and caper. The dancer has to imitate all its motions. A marionette may be used. It is a great fun-maker.

Feather Football or Feather Blow

This is an in-door, wet-weather game.

The players hold a blanket on the knees or on the table. A soft feather is put in the middle. As many may play as can get near. They may be in sides, two or four or each for himself. At the signal, "Go!" each tries to blow the feather off the blanket at the enemy's side, and so count one for himself.

A game is usually best out of seven, eleven, or thirteen.

Cock-Fighting

Get two stout sticks, each two feet long (broomsticks will do). Pad each of these on the end with a ball of rag. These are the spurs. Make an eight-foot ring. The two rivals are on their hunkers, each with a stick through behind his knees, his hands clasped in front of the knees, and the arms under the ends of the spurs.

Now they close; each aiming to upset the other, to make him lose his spurs, or to put him out of the ring, any of which ends that round and scores one for the victor.   If both fall, or lose a spur, or go out together, it is a draw.   Battle is for seven, eleven, or thirteen rounds.

Hand-Wrestling

This is a jiujitsu game, introduced by Dr. L. H. Gulick.

The two contestants stand right toe to right toe, each right hand clasped, left feet braced, left hand free.   At the word, "Go!" each tries to unbalance the other: that is, make him lift or move one of his feet.   A lift or a shift ends the round.

Battles are for best out of five, seven, eleven, or thirteen rounds.

Badger-Pulling

The two contestants, on hands and knees, face each other. A strong belt or strap is buckled into one great loop that passes round the head of each: that is, crosses his nape.   Half-way between them is a dead line.   The one who pulls the other over this line is winner.

The contestant can at any time end the bout by lowering his head so the strap slips off; but this counts one against him.

Game is best out of five, seven, eleven, or thirteen points.

Poison

This is an ancient game.   A circle about three feet across is drawn on the ground.   The players, holding hands, make a ring around this, and try to make one of the number step into the poison circle.   He can evade it by side-stepping, by jumping over, or by dragging another fellow into it.

First to make the misstep is "it" for the time or for next game.

Hat-Ball

When I was among the Chepewyan Indians of Great Slave Lake, in 1907, I made myself popular with the young men, as well as boys, by teaching them the old game of hat-ball.

The players (about a dozen) put their hats in a row near a house, fence, or log (hollows up).   A dead line is drawn ten feet from the hats; all must stand outside of that.   The one who is "it" begins by throwing a soft ball into one of the hats. If he misses the hat, a chip is put into his own, and he tries over.   As soon as he drops the ball into a hat, the owner runs to get the ball; all the rest run away. The owner must not follow beyond the dead line, but must throw the ball at some one. If he hits him, a chip goes into that person's hat; if not, a chip goes into his own.

As soon as some one has five chips, he wins the booby prize: that is, he must hold his hand out steady against the wall, and each player has five shots at it with the ball, as he stands on the dead line.

Duck-on-a-Rock

This is a good old grandfather game.

Each player has a large, smooth, roundish stone, about five or six inches through. This is his duck. He keeps it permanently.

The rock is any low bowlder, block, stump, bump, or hillock on level ground. A dead line is drawn through the rock, and another parallel, fifteen feet away, for a firing line.

The fellow who is "it," or "keeper," perches his duck on the rock. The others stand at the firing line and throw their ducks at his. They must not pick them up or touch them with their hands when they are beyond the dead line. If one does, then the keeper can tag him (unless he reaches the firing line), and send him to do duty as keeper at the rock.

But they can coax their ducks with their feet, up to the dead line, not beyond, then watch for a chance to dodge back to the firing line, where they are safe at all times.

If the duck is knocked off by any one in fair firing, the keeper is powerless till he has replaced it. Meantime, most of the players have secured their ducks and got back safely to the firing line.

Road-side Cribbage

This is a game we often play in the train, to pass the time pleasantly.

Sometimes one party takes the right side of the road, with the windows there, and the other the left. Sometimes all players sit on the same side.

The game is, whoever is first to see certain things agreed on scores so many points. Thus:

A crow or a cow counts	1
A cat	2
A hawk	3
An owl	4
A sheep	5
A goat	6
A horse	7

The winner is the one who first gets twenty-five or fifty points, as agreed.

When afoot, one naturally takes other things for points, as certain trees, flowers, etc.

Lion Hunting*

A lion is represented by one scout, who goes out with tracking irons on his feet, and a pocketful of corn or peas, and six lawn-tennis balls or rag balls. He is allowed half an hour's start, and then the patrol go after him, following his spoor, each armed with one tennis ball with which to shoot him when they find him. The lion may hide or creep about or run, just as he feels inclined, but whenever the ground is hard or very greasy he must drop a few grains of corn every few yards to show the trail.

If the hunters fail to come up to him neither wins the game. When they come near to his lair the lion fires at them with his tennis balls, and the moment a hunter is hit he must fall out dead and cannot throw his tennis ball. If the lion gets hit by a hunter's tennis ball he is wounded, and if he gets wounded three times he is killed.

Tennis balls may only be fired once; they cannot be picked up and fired again in the same fight.

Each scout must collect and hand in his tennis balls after the game. In winter, if there is snow, this game can be played without tracking irons, and using snowballs instead of tennis balls.

Plant Race

Start off your scouts, either cycling or on foot, to go in any direction they like, to get a specimen of any ordered plant, say a sprig of yew, a shoot of ilex, a horseshoe mark from a chestnut tree, a briar rose, or something of that kind, whichever you may order, such as will tax their knowledge of plants and will test their memory as to where they noticed one of the kind required and will also make them quick in getting there and back.

Throwing the Assegai

Target, a thin sack, lightly stuffed with straw, or a sheet of card-board, or canvas stretched on a frame.

Assegais to be made of wands, with weighted ends sharpened or with iron arrow heads on them.

*The games from Lion Hunting to Hare and Hounds are from General Baden-Powell.

Flag Raiding

Two or more patrols on each side.

Each side will form an outpost within a given tract of country to protect three flags (or at night three lanterns two feet above ground), planted not less than two hundred yards (one hundred yards at night) from it. The protecting outpost will be posted in concealment either all together or spread out in pairs. It will then send out scouts to discover the enemy's position. When these have found out where the outpost is, they try to creep round out of sight till they can get to the flags and bring them away to their own line. One scout may not take away more than one flag.

This is the general position of a patrol on such an outpost:

Pair of Scouts   Pair of Scouts   Pair of Scouts

Patrol Leader

P. P. P.
Flags

Any scout coming within fifty yards of a stronger party will be put out of action if seen by the enemy; if he can creep by without being seen it is all right.

Scouts posted to watch as outposts cannot move from their ground, but their strength counts as double, and they may send single messages to their neighbors or to their own scouting party.

An umpire should be with each outpost and with each scouting patrol.

At a given hour operations will cease, and all will assemble at the given spot to hand in their reports. The following points might be awarded:

For each flag or lamp captured and brought in.................... 5
For each report or sketch of the position of the enemy's outposts up
   to five 5
For each report of movement of enemy's scouting patrols 2

The side which makes the biggest total wins.

The same game may be played to test the scouts in stepping lightly — the umpire being blindfolded. The practice should preferably be carried out where there are dry twigs lying about, and gravel, etc. The scout may start to stalk the blind enemy at one hundred yards' distance, and he must do it fairly fast — say, in one minute and a half — to touch the blind man before he hears him.

Stalking and Reporting

The umpire places himself out in the open and sends each scout or pair of scouts away in different directions about half a mile off. When he waves a flag, which is the signal to begin, they all hide, and then proceed to stalk him, creeping up and watching all he does. When he waves the flag again, they rise, come in, and report each in turn all that he did, either by handing in a written report or verbally, as may be ordered. The umpire meantime has kept a lookout in each direction, and, every time he sees a scout he takes two points off that scout's score. He, on his part, performs small actions, such as sitting down, kneeling, looking through glasses, using handkerchief, taking hat off for a bit, walking round in a circle a few times, to give scouts something to note and report about him. Scouts are given three points for each act reported correctly. It saves time if the umpire makes out a scoring card beforehand, giving the name of each scout, and a number of columns showing each act of his, and what mark that scout wins, also a column of deducted marks for exposing themselves.

Spider and Fly

A bit of country or section of the town about a mile square is selected as the web, and its boundaries described, and an hour fixed at which operations are to cease.

One patrol (or half-patrol) is the "spider," which goes out and selects a place to hide itself.

The other patrol (or half-patrol) go a quarter of an hour later as the "fly" to look for the "spider." They can spread themselves about as they like, but must tell their leader anything that they discover.

An umpire goes with each party.

If within the given time (say, about two hours) the fly has not discovered the spider, the spider wins. The spiders write down the names of any of the fly patrol that they may see.

Stalking

Instructor acts as a deer — not hiding, but standing, moving a little now and then if he likes.

Scouts go out to find, and each in his own way tries to get up to him unseen.

Directly the instructor sees a scout, he directs him to stand up as having failed. After a certain time the instructor calls "time," all stand up at the spot which they have reached, and the nearest wins.

Demonstrate the value of adapting color of clothes to background by sending out one boy about five hundred yards to stand against different backgrounds in turn, till he gets one similar in color to his own clothes.

The rest of the patrol to watch and to notice how invisible he becomes when he gets a suitable background. E. g., a boy in a gray suit standing in front of dark bushes, etc., is quite visible — but becomes less so if he stands in front of a gray rock or house; a boy in a dark suit is very visible in a green field, but not when he stands in an open door-way against dark interior shadow.

Scout Hunting

One scout is given time to go out and hide himself, the remainder then start to find him; he wins if he is not found, or if he can get back to the starting point within a given time without being touched.

Relay Race

One patrol pitted against another to see who can get a message sent a long distance in shortest time by means of relays of runners (or cyclists). The patrol is ordered out to send in three successive notes or tokens (such as sprigs of certain plants), from a point, say, two miles distant or more. The leader in taking his patrol out to the spot drops scouts at convenient distances, who will then act as runners from one post to the next and back. If relays are posted in pairs, messages can be passed both ways.

Track Memory

Make a patrol sit with their feet up, so that other scouts can study them. Give the scouts, say, three minutes to study the boots. Then leaving the scouts in a room or out of sight, let one of the patrol make some footmarks in a good bit of ground. Call up the scouts one by one and let them see the track and say who made it.

Spot the Thief

Get a stranger to make a track unseen by the scouts. The scouts study his track so as to know it again.

Then put the stranger among eight or ten others and let them all make their tracks for the boys to see, going by in rotation. Each scout then in turn whispers to the umpire which man, made the original track — describing him by his number in filing past. The scout who answers correctly wins; if more than one answers correctly, the one who then draws the best diagram, from memory, of the footprint wins.

Smugglers Over the Border

The "border" is a certain line of country about four hundred yards long, preferably a road or wide path or bit of sand, on which foot tracks can easily be seen.   One patrol watches the border with sentries posted along this road, with a reserve posted farther inland.   This latter about half-way between the "border" and the "town"; the "town" would be a base marked by a tree, building, or flags, etc., about half a mile distant from the border.   A hostile patrol of smugglers assemble about half a mile on the other side of the border.   They will all cross the border, in any formation they please, either singly or together or scattered, and make for the town, either walking or running, or at scouts' pace.   Only one among them is supposed to be smuggling, and he wears tracking irons, so that the sentries walk up and down their beat (they may not run till after the "alarm"), waiting for the tracks of the smuggler.   Directly a sentry sees the track, he gives the alarm signal to the reserve and starts himself to follow up the track as fast as he can.   The reserves thereupon coöperate with him and try to catch the smuggler before he can reach the town. Once within the boundary of the town he is safe and wins the game.

Shop Window Out-doors in Town

Umpire takes a patrol down a street past six shops, gives them half a minute at each shop, then, after moving them off to some distance, he gives each boy a pencil and card, and tells him to write from memory, or himself takes down, what they noticed in, say, the third and fifth shops.   The one who sets down most articles correctly wins.   It is useful practice to match one boy against another in heats — the loser competing again, till you arrive at the worst.   This gives the worst scouts the most practice.

Similar Game In-doors

Send each scout in turn into a room for half a minute; when he comes out take down a list of furniture and articles which he notices.   The boy who notices most wins.

The simplest way of scoring is to make a list of the articles in the room on your scoring paper with a column for marks for each scout against them, which can then easily be totalled up at foot.

Follow the Trail

Send out a "hare," either walking or cycling, with a pocketful of corn, nutshells, confetti paper, or buttons, etc., and drop a few here and there to give a trail for the patrol to follow.

Or go out with a piece of chalk and draw the patrol sign on walls, gate posts, pavements, lamp posts, trees, etc., every here and there, and let the patrol hunt you by these marks. Patrols should wipe out all these marks as they pass them for tidiness, and so as not to mislead them for another day's practice.

The other road signs should also be used, such as closing up certain roads as not used, and hiding a letter at some point, giving directions as to the next turn.

Scout's Nose In-doors

Prepare a number of paper bags, all alike, and put in each a different smelling article, such as chopped onion in one, tan in another, rose leaves, leather, anise-seed, violet powder, orange peel, etc. Put these packets in a row a couple of feet apart, and let each competitor walk down the line and have five seconds sniff at each. At the end he has one minute in which to write down or to state to the umpire the names of the different objects smelled, from memory, in their correct order.

Scout Meets Scout in Town or Country

Single scouts, or complete patrols or pairs of scouts, to be taken out about two miles apart, and made to work toward each other, either alongside a road, or by giving each side a landmark to work to, such as a steep hill or big tree, which is directly behind the other party, and will thus insure their coming together. The patrol which first sees the other wins. This is signified by the patrol leader holding up his patrol flag for the umpire to see, and sounding his whistle. A patrol need not keep together, but that patrol wins which first holds out its flag, so it is well for the scouts to be in touch with their patrol leaders by signal, voice, or message.

Scouts may employ any ruse they like, such as climbing into trees, hiding in carts, etc., but they must not dress up in disguise.

This may also be practised at night.

Shoot Out

Two patrols compete. Targets: bottles or bricks set up on end to represent the opposing patrol. Both patrols are drawn up in line at about twenty to twenty-five yards from the targets. At the word "fire," they throw stones at the targets. Directly a target falls, the umpire directs the corresponding man of the other patrol to sit down — killed. The game goes on, if there are plenty of stones, till the whole of one patrol is killed. Or a certain number of stones can be given to each patrol, or a certain time limit, say one minute.

Kim's Game

Place about twenty or thirty small articles on a tray, or on the table or floor, such as two or three different kinds of buttons, pencils, corks, rags, nuts, stones, knives, string, photos — anything you can find — and cover them over with a cloth or coat.

Make a list of these, and make a column opposite the list for each boy's replies.

Then uncover the articles for one minute by your watch, or while you count sixty at the rate of "quick march." Then cover them over again.

Take each boy separately and let him whisper to you each of the articles that he can remember, and mark it off on your scoring sheet.

The boy who remembers the greatest number wins the game.

Morgan's Game

Scouts are ordered to run to a certain boarding, where an umpire is already posted to time them. They are each allowed to look at this for one minute, and then to run back to headquarters and report to the instructor all that was on the boarding in the way of advertisements.

Snow Fort

The snow fort may be built by one patrol according to their own ideas of fortification, with loopholes, etc., for looking out. When finished, it will be attacked by hostile patrols, using snowballs as ammunition. Every scout struck by a snowball is counted dead. The attackers should, as a rule, number at least twice the strength of the defenders.

Siberian Man Hunt

One scout as fugitive runs away across the snow in any direction he may please until he finds a good hiding place, and there conceals himself. The remainder, after giving him twenty minutes' start or more, proceed to follow him by his tracks. As they approach his hiding place, he shoots at them with snowballs, and every one that is struck must fall out dead. The fugitive must be struck three times before he is counted dead.

Hare and Hounds

Two or more persons representing the hares, and provided with a large quantity of corn, are given a start of several minutes and run a certain length of time, then return by another route to the starting point, all the time scattering corn in their path. After the lapse of the number of minutes' handicap given the hares, those representing the hounds start in pursuit, following by the corn and trying to catch the hares before they reach the starting-point in returning.

The handicap given the hares should be small, depending on the running abilities of the hares and hounds. The fastest runners are usually picked for the hounds.

Chalk the Arrow

This is usually played in the city streets, one player running and trying to keep out of sight of the others who follow. The runner is given time to disappear around the first corner before the others start after him, and at every corner he turns he marks (with chalk) an arrow pointing in the direction he takes. Those pursuing follow by the arrow, the first one seeing him being the runner for the next time.

This may also be played by having any number run and only one follow, the first becoming "it" for the next time.

Dodge Ball

Of any number of players, half of that number form a circle, while the other half stand inside of the ring (centre) facing outward. Now, the game for those in the centre is to dodge the ball which is thrown by any of those forming the circle with the intention of striking the centre ones out.   Every time a member is struck he is dead, and takes his place among those of the circle.   Now he has a chance to throw at those remaining in the centre.   This arrangement keeps all taking part busy.   Only one is out at a time.   This being kept up until finally only one is left.   He is hailed the king.   For next round, players exchange places, *i. e.*, those who were in the centre now form the circle.

Note: If the touch is preceded by a bound of the ball it does not count.

Prisoner's Base

Goals are marked off at both ends of the playground, the players divided into two equal divisions, occupying the two goals.   About ten paces to the right of each goal is a prison. A player advances toward the opposite goal, when one from that goal starts out to catch him.   He retreats, and one from his side runs to his rescue by trying to catch the pursuer — who in turn is succored by one from his side, and so on. Every player may catch any one from the opposite side who has been out of goal longer than he has.   Any player caught is conducted to the prison by his captor and must remain there until rescued by some one from his side, who touches him with the hand.   The one who does this is subject to being caught like any other player.

Throwing the Spear

The game is an old Greek and Persian pastime.   "Throw the spear and speak the truth," was a national maxim of the Persians that we may copy with advantage.

The apparatus required is some light spears and an archery target.   The spears should vary from five to six feet in length; the point should be shod with a steel tip, having a socket into which the wooden handle is fitted, and made fast by small screws passing through holes in the sides of the metal, and then into the wood itself.   The wood, for about.a foot above the barb, should be about three quarters of an inch in diameter, and from thence gradually taper to about a quarter of an inch in thickness, until the end of the spear is reached.

Some spears are fitted with feathers, like an arrow, but these are not necessary to obtain a good throw, and soon get dismantled in continually falling upon the ground.   Any ordinary target will serve.   It may be an archery target, a. sack full of straw, or a sod bank.

The object of the contest is to hit the target from a given mark, the firing line. Whoever throws nearest to the centre of the target the greatest number of times out of six shots is hailed the winner.

The best form for throwing is with the left foot forward, the leg perfectly straight, body well back, its weight resting on the right leg. Now extend the left arm forward, in a line with the shoulder, and over the left leg; poise the spear horizontally in the right hand, holding at the centre of gravity by the forefinger and thumb. Bring the right arm backward until the hand is behind the right shoulder.

Now, inclining the point of the spear slightly upward, make your cast, bringing the right arm forward, followed by the right side of the body, the right leg forward and the left arm backward. Count yourself fortunate if you even hit the target in the first few attempts, but practice will make a wonderful difference. The distance should be mutually agreed upon, but fifty feet for a boy of fifteen and one hundred feet for an adult will be found about right.

To "throw the javelin" is another phase of this pastime. The javelin is four to five feet in length, three quarters of an inch in thickness, and fitted with a barbed end, slightly heavier than the spear end. The "object of the game" is to throw the javelin as far as possible but not at a target; instead, the javelin must stick into the ground.

In throwing the javelin, hold it in the right hand, the left leg and hand being advanced; the barb and arm at this point should be at the rear. Then, describing a semicircle with the arm over the right shoulder, and leaning well to the rear, hurl the weapon as far as possible forward.

Arctic Expedition

Each patrol make a bob sleigh with ropes, harness, for two of their number to pull or for dogs if they have them and can train them to do the work. Two scouts or so go a mile or two ahead, the remainder with the sleigh follow, finding the way by means of the spoor, and by such signs as the leading scouts may draw in the snow. All other drawings seen on the way are to be examined, noted, and their meaning read. The sleigh carries rations and cooking pots, etc.

Build snow huts. These must be made narrow, according to the length of the sticks available for forming the roof, which can be made with brushwood and covered with snow.

Dragging Race

A line of patients from one patrol is laid out fifty feet distant from the start. Another patrol, each carrying a rope, run out, tie ropes to the patients, and drag them in. Time taken of last in. Patrols change places. The one which completes in the shortest time wins. Knots must be carefully tied, and patients' coats laid out under their heads.

Far and Near

Umpire goes along a given road or line of country with a patrol in patrol formation. He carries a scoring card with the name of each scout on it.

Each scout looks out for the details required, and directly he notices one he runs to the umpire and informs him or hands in the article, if it is an article he finds. The umpire enters a mark accordingly against his name. The scout who gains the most marks in the walk wins.

Details like the following should be chosen to develop the scout's observation and to encourage him to look far and near, up and down, etc.

The details should be varied every time the game is played; and about eight or ten should be given at a time.

Every match found	1 point
Every button found	1 point
Bird tracks	2 points
Patch noticed on stranger's clothing or boots	2 points
Gray horse seen	2 points
Pigeon flying	2 points
Sparrow sitting	2 points
Ash tree	2 points
Broken chimney-pot	2 points
Broken window	1 point

Fire-lighting Race

To collect material, build, and light a fire till the log given by umpire is alight.

Follow My Leader

With a large number of boys this can be made a very effective display, and is easy to do at a jog trot, and occasional "knee-up" with musical accompaniment. It also can be done at night, each boy carrying a Chinese lantern on top of his staff. If in a building all lights, of course, would be turned down. A usual fault is that the exercise is kept on too long, till it wearies both audience and performers.

Games in Path-finding

Instructor takes a patrol in patrolling formation into a strange town or into an intricate piece of strange country, with a cycling map. He then gives instructions as to where he wants to go, makes each scout in turn lead the patrol, say, for seven minutes if cycling, fifteen minutes if walking. This scout is to find the way entirely by the map, and points are given for ability in reading.

Mountain Scouting

This has been played by tourists' clubs in the lake district, and is very similar to the "Spider and Fly" game. Three hares are sent out at daybreak to hide themselves about in the mountains: after breakfast a party of hounds go out to find them before a certain hour, say 4 o'clock P.M. If they find them even with field-glasses, it counts, provided that the finder can say definitely who it was he spotted. Certain limits of ground must be given, beyond which any one would be out of bounds, and therefore disqualified.

Knight Errantry

Scouts go out singly, or in pairs, or as a patrol. If in a town, to find women or children in want of help, and to return and report, on their honor, what they have done. If in the country, call at any farms or cottages and ask to do odd jobs — for nothing. The same can be made into a race called a "Good Turn" race.

Unprepared Plays

Give the plot of a short, simple, play and assign to each player his part, with an outline of what he has to do and say, and then let them act it, making up the required conversation as they go along.

This develops the power of imagination and expression on points kept in the mind, and is a valuable means of education.

It is well before starting to act a play in this way to be a little less ambitious, and to make two or three players merely carry out a conversation on given topics leading up to a given point, using their own words and imaginations in doing so.

The Treasure Hunt

The treasure hunt needs observation and skill in tracking, and practically any number can take part in it.

Several ways of playing the game are given below.

1. The treasure is hidden and the scouts know what the treasure is; they are given the first clew, and from this all the others can be traced. Such clews might be (a) written on a gate post: "Go west and examine third gate on north side of stream"; (b) on that gate, scout's sign pointing to notice board on which is written, "Strike south by south-east telegraph post, No. 28," and so on. The clews should be so worded as to need some skill to understand, and the various points should be difficult of access from one another. This method might be used as a patrol competition, starting off patrols at ten-minute intervals, and at one particular clew there might be different orders for each patrol, to prevent the patrols behind from following the first.

2. The clews may be bits of colored wood tied to gates, hedges, etc., at about three-yard intervals, leading in a certain direction, and when these clews come to the end it should be known that the treasure is hidden within so many feet. To prevent this degenerating into a mere game of follow my leader, several tracks might be laid working up to the same point, and false tracks could be laid, which only lead back again to the original.

3. Each competitor or patrol might be given a description of the way — each perhaps of a slightly different way; the description should make it necessary to go to each spot in turn; and prevent any "cutting" in the following way: "Go to the tallest tree in a certain field, from there go one hundred yards north, and then walk straight toward a church tower which will be on your left," etc. All the descriptions should lead by an equal journey to a certain spot where the treasure is hidden. The first to arrive at that spot should not let the others know it is the spot, but should search for the treasure in as casual a manner as possible.

Will-o'-the-Wisp

This game should take place across country at night. Two scouts set off in a given direction with a lighted bull's-eye lantern. After two minutes have passed the patrol or troop starts in pursuit.

The lantern bearer must show his light at least every minute concealing it for the rest of the time. The two scouts take turns in carrying the light, and so may relieve each other in difficulties, but either may be captured. The scout without the light can often mingle with the pursuers without being recognized and relieve his friend when he is being hard pressed. They should arrange certain calls or signals between themselves.

Treasure Island

A treasure is known to be hidden upon a certain island or bit of shore marked off, and the man who hid it leaves a map with clews for finding it (compass, directions, tide marks, etc.). This map is hidden somewhere near the landing-place; the patrols come in turn to look for it — they have to row from a certain distance, land, find the map, and finally discover the treasure. They should be careful to leave no foot tracks, etc., near the treasure, because then the patrols that follow them will easily find it. The map and treasure are to be hidden afresh for the next patrol when they have been found. The patrol wins which returns to the starting place with the treasure in the shortest time. (This can be played on the river, the patrols having to row across the river to find the treasure.)

Horse and Rider Tourney

In playing this game it is necessary to have a soft, velvety piece of grass, or if in doors, in the gymnasium, cover the floor with regular gymnasium mats. It requires four boys to play the game, two being horses and the other two riders. The riders mount their horses and dash at each other with great caution, striving to get a good hold of each other in such a way as to compel the opponent to dismount. This can be done either by dragging him from his mount or by making the horse and rider lose their balance so as to throw them off their feet. A great deal of sport can be gotten out of this game, and boys become very skilful after a little practice.

Mumbly Peg*

First: Hold the right fist with the back to the ground and with the jack-knife, with blade pointing to the right, resting

---

* From Daniel Carter Beard, National Scout Commissioner.

on top of the closed fingers.   The hand is swung to the right, up and over, describing a semicircle, so that the knife falls point downward and sticks, or should stick, upright in the ground.   If there is room to slip two fingers, one above the other, beneath the handle of the knife, and if the point of the knife is hidden in the ground, it counts as a fair stick or throw.

Second: The next motion is the same as the one just described, but is performed with the left.

Third: Take the point of the blade between the first and second fingers of the right hand, and fillip it with a jerk so that the knife turns once around in the air and strikes the point into the ground.

Fourth: Do the same with the left hand.

Fifth: Hold the knife as in the third and fourth positions, and bring the arm across the chest so that the knife handle touches the left ear.   Take hold of the right ear with the left hand and fillip the knife so that it turns once or twice in the air and strikes on its point in the earth.

Sixth: Do the same with the left hand.

Seventh: Still holding the knife in the same manner, bring the handle up to the nose and fillip it over through the air, so that it will stick in the ground.

Eighth: Do the same with the handle at the right eye.

Ninth: Repeat with the handle at the left eye.

Tenth: Place the point of the blade on the top of the head. Hold it in place with the forefinger, and with a downward push send it whirling down to earth, where it must stick with the point of blade in the earth.

Eleventh to Fifteenth: Hold the left hand with the fingers pointing upward and, beginning with the thumb, place the point of the knife on each finger as described above, and the forefinger of the right hand on the end of the knife handle.   By a downward motion, throw the knife revolving through the air, so that it will alight with the point of the blade in the sod.

Sixteenth to Twentieth: Repeat, with the right hand up and the forefinger of the left hand on the knife handle.

Twenty-first, twenty-second: Do the same from each knee.

Twenty-third: Hold the point of the blade between the first and second fingers, and, placing the hand on the forehead, fillip the knife back over the head, so that it will stick in the ground behind the person ready for the next motion.

Twenty-fourth: After twenty-three the knife is left in the ground.   Then with the palm of the hand strike the knife handle a smart blow that will send it revolving over the ground for a yard, more or less, and cause it to stick in the ground where it stops. This is called "ploughing the field."

When a miss is made the next player takes his turn, and when the first player's turn comes again he must try the feat over that he failed to perform last. A good player will sometimes go through almost all the twenty-four motions without failing to make a "two finger," that is, a fair stick, each time; but it is very unusual for any one to run the game out in one inning. This is the game in twenty-four motions; many boys play it double that number.

Outdoor Athletic Standards

The athletic standards given below are those which most boys ought to be able to attain. They are the result of the experience of several physical directors who have made a special study of athletics and physical work among boys.

The rules governing the events are found in the official handbook of the Athletic League of North America. These rules must be strictly adhered to.

	Events	Under 90 Lbs.	Under 110 Lbs.	Under 125 Lbs.	Under 140 Lbs.	Over 140 Lbs.
(1)	Running Broad Jump	12 ft.	13 ft.	14 ft.	15 ft.	16 ft.
(2)	Running High Jump	3 ft. 11 in.	4 ft. 1 in.	4 ft. 4 in.	4 ft. 7 in.	4 ft. 10 in.
(3)	Standing Broad Jump	6 ft. 6 in.	7 ft.	7 ft. 6 in.	8 ft.	8 ft. 6 in.
(4)	Standing High Jump	3 ft. 2 in.	3 ft. 4 in.	3 ft. 6 in.	3 ft. 8 in.	3 ft. 10 in.
(5)	Pull-Up	5 times	7 times	9 times	11 times	13 times
(6)	20-Yard Swim	20 sec.	18 sec.	16 sec.	14 sec.	12 sec.
(7)	40-Yard Swim	40 sec.	39 sec.	38 sec.	37 sec.	36 sec.
(8)	50-Yard Dash	7 4-5 sec.	7 2-5 sec.	7 sec.	6 3-5 sec.	6 1-5 sec.
(9)	Eight-Potato Race	45 sec.	43 sec.	41 sec.	39 sec.	37 sec.
(10)	8 lb-Shot Put	*	25 ft.	30 ft.	35 ft.	40 ft.
(11)	Push-Up from Floor	*	11 times	13 times	15 times	17 times
(12)	Rope Climb	*	14 sec.	12 sec.	10 sec.	8 sec.
(13)	100-Yard Dash	*	*	13 sec.	12 3-5 sec.	12 1-5 sec.

*Should not attempt this event

For merit badge a boy under ninety pounds must qualify in seven of the first nine events; a boy under one hundred and ten pounds must qualify in ten of the first twelve events; all others must qualify in their proper class in eleven of the thirteen events.

Notes

Notes

CHAPTER IX

PATRIOTISM AND CITIZENSHIP

By Waldo H. Sherman, Author of "Civics — Studies in American Citizenship"

OUR COUNTRY

America is the home of social, religious, and political liberty — "the land of the free and the home of the brave."

As a nation, we have always been rich in land, and for this reason millions of people have sought our shores. We have come into possession of our territory through treaty, purchase, and annexation. In speaking of our territorial area we usually speak of the "original territory" and "additions" to same. When we speak of "original territory" we mean that part of the United States which was ceded to us by Great Britain in the peace treaty of 1783, at the close of the War of the Revolution. This territory, in brief, is described as follows: East to the Atlantic Ocean, west to the Mississippi River, north to the Great Lakes and Canada, and as far south as the northern line of Florida. We sometimes hear it spoken of as the territory of the "Thirteen Original States," meaning the states that formed the Government of the Constitution in 1789. However if we look at the map we shall see that the original territory includes not only the territory of the thirteen original states, but comprises also land out of which twelve other states have been formed. Looking at this area to-day, however, it seems a small part of our country compared with our present limits.

Additions

Louisiana Purchase: What is known as the Louisiana Purchase we bought from France in 1803. It consisted of 875,025 square miles, for which we paid $15,000,000. It is described as follows: west of the Mississippi River to the Rocky Mountains, north to Canada, and south to the Gulf of Mexico, exclusive of Texas. This is a territory greater than the present combined areas of Spain, Portugal, Italy, Hungary, and the Balkan states.

Florida Purchase: In 1819, we purchased Florida from Spain at a cost of over $5,000,000, and this single state is larger in territorial area than the combined territory of Denmark, Netherlands, Belgium, and Switzerland.

Texas: In 1845, Texas came to us by annexation, but the outcome of this annexation later on was our war with Mexico. In territorial area this is an empire in itself — larger than the whole German Empire.

Oregon Territory: In 1846, by treaty with Great Britain, we acquired what is known as the Oregon Territory. This includes the states of Oregon, Washington, and Idaho.

Mexican Cession and Purchase from Texas: As an outcome of the Mexican War, we obtained from Mexico, in 1848, the territory of California, Nevada, Utah, Arizona, and a part of New Mexico at a cost of $15,000,000; and in 1850, we purchased from Texas the remaining part of New Mexico and that part of Colorado not included in the Louisiana Purchase, at a cost of $10,000,000.

Gadsden Purchase: In 1853, we made what is known as the Gadsden Purchase, acquiring thus from Mexico a needed tract of land on the boundary between Mexico, Arizona, and New Mexico, paying for this tract $10,000,000.

Alaska: In 1867, we paid Russia $7,000,000, and added Alaska to our possessions. This purchase is spoken of in history as "Seward's Folly," because the transaction, made while he was secretary of state, was not generally considered a good bargain. Nevertheless it has proved one of our most valuable possessions.

Hawaii: In 1898, we reached out into the Pacific waters and annexed the beautiful Hawaiian or Sandwich Islands.

Porto Rico, Pine Islands, Guam, Philippine Islands: In 1898, the island of Porto Rico with an area of 3600 square miles came into our possession as an outcome of the Spanish-American War; likewise the Pine Islands with their 882 square miles; Guam with 175 square miles; and the Philippine Islands with a territorial area of 143,000 square miles. But for these latter in settlement of a number of private claims, and to gain peaceable possession of various public lands, we paid Spain $20,000,000.

Samoan Islands: In 1899, we acquired the Samoan Islands, with an area of 73 square miles; and, in 1901, some additional islands in the Philippines.

Land Settlements

The first permanent English settlements in America were made at Jamestown, Va., in 1607, and at Plymouth, Mass., in 1620; and from these two settlements we may trace in large part the growth, character, and development of our national life. The story of the "Pilgrim Fathers" in Massachusetts has been told for generations in literature and in song, and can never cease to be of romantic and thrilling interest.

The story of the settlement and dispersal of other nationalities in America — the Swedes in Delaware, the Dutch in New York, the Spanish and French in Florida and along the banks of the Mississippi and Ohio Rivers — all this is summed up in what is known as "colonial history."

In 1763, at the close of the French and Indian wars, England had come into possession of practically all the territory east of the Mississippi — that territory which was ceded in 1783 as the original territory of the United States.

You will sometimes hear it said that thirteen is an unlucky number. Indeed you may have known people so superstitious that they refuse to sit down at a table when the number is thirteen. Again you may know it to be a fact that some hotels do not have a room numbered thirteen, and that many steamboats likewise follow the same custom in state room arrangement. Strange superstition for Americans! It took thirteen states to make our Union; we have made thirteen additions to our territory; when George Washington was inaugurated as president, a salute of thirteen guns was fired; and, finally, the foundation of the flag of our country bears thirteen stripes.

The American Revolution

The story of the American Revolution (1775–1783) — Declaration of Independence (1776), the adoption of the Articles of Confederation (1781), and, finally, the making and adoption of the Constitution of the United States in 1789 — all is summed up in a period of fourteen years, and may be told and written in the life of George Washington, who was indeed the "Father of His Country."

The cause of the American Revolution was England's oppression of her American colonists; and the injustice of taxation without representation, with other injustices, finally brought about rebellion. The war began in Massachusetts with the battles of Lexington and Concord, April 19, 1775, and ended at Yorktown, Va., October 19, 1781. The treaty of peace was signed at Paris, France, September 3, 1783, and November 25 of that year, known in history as "Evacuation Day," the British took their departure down the bay of New York harbor and America was free.

Now do we find ourselves at the fireside of American patriotism. Here is Washington. He is a Virginian, and the American people know him at this time as Colonel Washington. It is the 13th day of June, 1775, and the second Continental Congress is in session at Philadelphia. John Adams of Massachusetts has the floor. He is to show himself at this time the master statesman. Justly has he been called the "Colossus of the Revolution." On his way to Independence Hall this morning he meets his cousin, Samuel Adams, and tells him what he is going to do. "We must," he says, "act on this matter at once. We must make Congress declare for or against something. I'll tell you what I am going to do. I am determined this very morning to make a direct motion that Congress shall adopt the army before Boston, and appoint the Virginian, Colonel Washington, commander of it."

Adams is now stating to the Congress the gravity of the situation; he points out the necessity of immediate action — the colonies must be united, the army must be brought together, disciplined, and trained for service, and, under Congress, a fitting commander appointed. "Such a gentleman," he said, "I have in mind. I mention no names, but every gentleman here knows him at once as a brave soldier and a man of affairs. He is a gentleman from Virginia, one of this body, and well known to all of us. He is a gentleman of skill and excellent universal character and would command the approbation of all the colonies better than any other person in the Union."

George Washington is in the hall. The eyes of all Congress have turned toward him. He is surprised, confused, and embarrassed, leaves his seat and hurries into the library.

Congress spent two days considering Adams's motion, for there were other men who had hoped for the appointment; but finally, on the 15th of June, 1775, a ballot was taken, and Washington was unanimously elected commander-in-chief of the Continental Army.

On July 2, 1775, he took command of the army at Cambridge, Mass., and March 17, 1776, the British were expelled from Boston.

We now come to the Declaration of Independence, July 4, 1776. It was written by Thomas Jefferson, at that time a young man of thirty-three. The committee of the General Congress appointed to draft it, consisted of the following: Thomas Jefferson, John Adams, Benjamin Franklin, Roger Sherman, and Robert R. Livingston.

The strong feeling of Thomas Jefferson as he wrote the Declaration is indicated by his statement that, "Rather than submit to the right of legislating for us assumed by the British Parliament, I would lend my hand to sink the whole island in the ocean." Here also we get a glimpse of one of the most interesting and delightful characters in the history of this period — Benjamin Franklin. History records that while Thomas Jefferson wrote the Declaration of Independence, a few verbal suggestions were made by Doctor Franklin, as the following conversation reported to have taken place between them would indicate: "Well, Brother Jefferson," said Franklin, "is the fair copy made?" "All ready, doctor," replied Jefferson. "Will you hear it through once more?" "As many times as you wish," responded the smiling doctor, with a merry twinkle in his eyes. "One can't get too much of a good thing, you know." Jefferson then read to Franklin the Declaration of Independence, which has been pronounced one of the world's greatest papers. "That's good, Thomas! That's right to the point! That will make King George wince. I wish I had done it myself." It is said Franklin would "have put a joke into the Declaration of Independence, if it had fallen to his lot to write that immortal document."

The Declaration of Independence went forth to the world signed by one man, John Hancock — which explains the expression you sometimes hear, "Put your John Hancock there." It was, however, signed later by all the members of that Congress — fifty-four in number. This immortal document has been carefully preserved and the original may be seen at Washington.

The Declaration was a notice to Great Britain and to all the world that the American colonists would no longer be subject to Great Britain; that henceforth they were to be a free and independent people, holding Great Britain as they held the rest of mankind, "enemies in war — in peace friends." This Declaration marks the birth of our nation.

Our government fathers fully realized the step they were taking. They knew it meant a final breaking with the home government of England, but — "with a firm reliance on the protection of Divine Providence," in support of this Declaration, they pledged to each other "their lives, their fortunes and their sacred honor."

Following the expulsion of the British from Boston, the battle field of the Revolution changes to New York, moving to Harlem Heights and White Plains; then to New Jersey; Trenton, and Princeton; then to Pennsylvania; Brandywine, Westchester, Germantown, Valley Forge, and on to Monmouth.

But here let us pause. It has been a terrible winter at Valley Forge. While the British at Philadelphia, twenty miles away, have been living in luxury, our Washington and his men have suffered bitterly with hunger and cold; and out of a list of eleven thousand men, three thousand at Valley Forge lay sick at one time. But at last the spring has come and Washington has now been nearly three years in service. Listen! The order has gone forth! At 10:30 o'clock comes the signal, and the firing of a cannon sees all men under arms! At 11:30 o'clock the second signal is given and the march begins. It is May 7, 1778, and Washington is assembling his men. Great news has come and it is fitting to return thanks to Divine Providence — so reads his proclamation.

Now comes the third signal, the firing of thirteen cannon! Another signal! and the whole army breaks into a loud huzza — "Long live the King of France!" followed by a running fire of guns.

On this same day in the afternoon, Washington gives a banquet to his officers, aides, and guests, to which they march arm-in-arm, thirteen abreast. What does it mean? It means that Benjamin Franklin has been heard from, and that an alliance with France, England's bitterest enemy, has been made. Some day when you are in Washington, you may see directly in front of the White House, Lafayette Park, and, knowing the story of the Revolution, you understand why it is there. You also understand why Washington's army on that May morning shouted, "Long live the King of France."

But it is not our purpose here to tell the whole story: we can only touch the high points. Again the army moves to White Plains and on to Middlebrook and New Windsor; and Washington spends the winter (1781) at Morristown, N. J. The end is approaching. He joins Lafayette at Yorktown, Va., and on October 19th, Cornwallis, the British general, surrenders to George Washington, commander-in-chief of the American Army. Thus the conflict begun in one English settlement is ended in the other. Massachusetts marks the beginning and Virginia the ending of the War of the Revolution.

The War of 1812 - 1815

The War of 1812 was a naval war. It was a battle for rights — the rights of our sailors, the rights of our commerce. American ships and cargoes were being confiscated. France and England and the Barbary pirates were engaged in a profitable war on our commerce, and last but not least twenty thousand American seamen had been pressed into service and were slaves on ships that were foreign, England especially claiming the right to search American ships and press into service all men found on board who were English by birth, though American by choice and adoption.

"Once a subject always a subject," said Great Britain, but our answer in 1812 was as it is now: any foreigner after five years' residence within our territory, who has complied with our naturalization laws and taken the oath of allegiance to our flag, becomes one of our citizens as completely as if he were native born.

This war is sometimes spoken of as a "leaderless war," but great leaders came out of it. The names of Hull, Perry, and Lawrence are memorable in its history; it was the war which made Andrew Jackson, known as "Old Hickory," President of the United States in 1828. You will read the story of his great victory in the Battle of New Orleans.

Some day you will read the life story of David Glasgow Farragut of whom it is said that, with the exception of Nelson, the great English admiral, "he was as great an admiral as ever sailed the broad or narrow seas." Although the great work of Farragut was in the Civil War, the story of his life began in the War of 1812 when he was but ten years old. Admiral Farragut is reported as giving this explanation, in the late years of his life, of his success in the service of his country

"It was all owing to a resolution that I formed when I was ten years old. My father was sent to New Orleans with the little navy we had, to look after the treason of Burr. I accompanied him as cabin-boy. I had some qualities that I thought made a man of me. I could swear like an old salt, could drink as stiff a glass of grog as if I had doubled Cape Horn, and could smoke like a locomotive. I was great at cards, and was fond of gambling in every shape. At the close of dinner one day, my father turned everybody out of the cabin, locked the door, and said to me:

"'David, what do you mean to be?'

"'I mean to follow the sea,' I said.

"'Follow the sea!' exclaimed my father; 'yes, be a poor, miserable, drunken sailor before the mast, kicked and cuffed about the world, and die in some fever hospital in a foreign clime?'

"'No, father,' I replied, 'I will tread the quarter-deck, and command as you do!'

"'No, David; no boy ever trod the quarter-deck with such principles as you have, and such habits as you exhibit. You will have to change your whole course of life if you ever become a man.'

"My father left me and went on deck. I was stunned by the rebuke, and overwhelmed with mortification. 'A poor, miserable, drunken sailor before the mast, kicked and cuffed about the world, and die in some fever hospital!' That's my fate is it? I'll change my life, and I will change it at once. I will never utter another oath, never drink another drop of intoxicating liquor, never gamble, and as God is my witness I have kept these three vows to this hour."

The Star Spangled Banner

The sun is slowly sinking in the west. The men of the army and navy are drawn up at attention. At every fort, army post, and navy yard, and on every American battle-ship at home or abroad, the flag of our country is flying at full mast. The sunset gun will soon be fired, and night will follow the day as darkness follows the light. All is ready, the signal is given, the men salute, and the flag to the band's accompaniment of "The Star Spangled Banner" slowly descends for the night to be folded and kept for the morning's hoisting.

"And the Star Spangled Banner in triumph shall wave
While the land of the free is the home of the brave."

In the cemetery of Mt. Olivet, near Frederick, Md., there is a spot where the flag of our country is never lowered. It is keeping watch by night as by day over the grave of Francis Scott Key, author of "The Star Spangled Banner." He was born in Frederick County, Md., August 1, 1779, and died in Baltimore, January 11, 1843.

The Congress of the United States has never formally adopted "The Star Spangled Banner" as a national anthem, but it has become such through the recognition given to it by the army and navy. It is played on all state occasions at home or abroad and is the response of our bands at all international gatherings. In the theatre, at a public meeting, or at a banquet — whenever it is played, the people rise and remain standing to the end as a tribute to the flag of our country.

The poem itself is descriptive of what the author saw and felt on the night of September 13, 1814, as he watched the bombardment of Fort McHenry by the British during the War of 1812. The city of Washington had been sacked, bombarded, and burned by the British, and now in their march of destruction, they were bombarding the fort to gain entrance to Baltimore's harbor, in which city they had purposed to spend the winter. We can well imagine the joy of Key's heart, the son of a Revolutionary patriot, held in custody on a British battle-ship, to see in the morning "that our flag was still there," and to know, therefore, that there was still hope for our country.

> "Then conquer we must, when our cause it is just,
> And this be our motto, 'In God is our Trust'."

The Birth of New States

The history of the fifty-six years between 1789 and 1845 is marked by the development of new states formed out of the territorial settlement of the wilderness. The people of our country have always been pioneering, going ahead of civilization, so to speak, but always taking it with them. Scouts they have been in every sense of the word. Following the rivers, clearing the forests, fording the streams, braving the dangers, living the wild life — brave men and women!

The first state to come into the Union of the thirteen original states was Vermont, the "Green Mountain" state (1791); next came Kentucky (1792), the "Blue Grass" state, the home of Daniel Boone, the great hunter and pioneer. Four years later, (1796) came Tennessee, the "Volunteer" state, receiving this name because of its large number of volunteer soldiers for the Seminole war and the War of 1812; next comes Ohio (1803), the "Buckeye," so called because of the large number of buckeye trees, the nut of which bears some resemblance to a buck's eye. This is the first state to be formed out of the public domain, known at this time as the "Northwest Territory." The land ordinance bill of 1785 and the homestead act of 1862 relate to the development and settlement of the public domain, the first being a plan of survey applied to all public lands owned by the United States government; the other being a law by which the possession of these lands was made possible to settlers.

Following Ohio into the Union came Louisiana(1812), the "Creole" state whose people were descendants of the original French and Spanish settlers. This was the first state to be formed west of the Mississippi, and New Orleans, its chief city, known as the "Crescent City," is one of the oldest in our country and full of historic interest.

After the War of 1812 the new states began to come in rapidly. The admission of Indiana (1816), "The Hoosier"; Mississippi (1817), the "Bayou"; Illinois, the "Prairie" (1818); Alabama (1819), the "Cotton," show that the pioneer settlements of our people had been closing in along the banks of the Ohio and the Mississippi Rivers.

We now go back to the far East, for the state of Maine, our "Pine Tree" state, has now been developed, and its admission (1820) completes the coast line of states as far south as Georgia. The next state admitted is Missouri (1821), the "Iron," followed by Arkansas, the "Bear" (1836), to be followed in turn by Michigan (1836), the "Lake" or "Wolverine" state, the thirteenth state to be admitted; and the stars in our flag are now doubled.

The first census of the United States was taken in 1790, and the Constitution provided that it must be taken every ten years thereafter. In that year, the order of states in rank of population was as follows: Virginia first, Pennsylvania second, North Carolina third, Massachusetts fourth, and New York fifth.

The census of 1820 makes a decided change, we find, in the order of population, and New York comes first, Virginia second, Pennsylvania third, North Carolina fourth, Ohio fifth, Kentucky sixth, and Massachusetts seventh.

The states of Florida and Texas came into the Union in the same year — the one March 3 and the other December 29, 1845; and thereby hangs a tale. It had been claimed by our government that Texas was included in the Louisiana Purchase of 1803; but the Mexicans claimed it also, and, in 1819, in order to close the deal for the purchase of Florida, our government was obliged to relinquish its claim to Texas. At this time the possession of Florida was more desirable and necessary to the peace of our country than the possession of Texas; it was under Spanish rule, overrun with outlaws and a most undesirable neighbor, besides being very necessary to the rounding out of our coast territory.

The Mexican War

The annexation and admission of Texas into the Union in 1845 came about through the pioneering and settlement of our people in her territory; where at first welcomed and encouraged by the Mexicans, they were later deluged in blood. The spirit of Americanism grew rampant under the barbaric and military despotism of the Mexican government, and in 1835 there was an uprising of the settlers led by a pioneer, an ex-governor of Tennessee, Gen. Samuel Houston, the man for whom the city of Houston, Texas, was named. At this time there were about ten thousand Americans in Texas, and on March 2, 1836, through their representatives in convention assembled, these Americans in true Revolutionary spirit declared Texas an independent republic. The Mexican government tried to put down this rebellion, but met with a crushing defeat, and Texas, the "Lone Star" state, remained an independent republic up to the time of her annexation and admission as a state of the Union.

The cause of the war with Mexico, then, was her resentment because Texas began to move for annexation to the United States. The fact that Texas had been for many years an independent republic and been so recognized by the United States, Great Britain, France, and some smaller countries, gave Texas the right on her part to ask for annexation, and the United States the right to annex her. But in order to bring Texas into the Union and save her people from the Mexicans, the United States was obliged to declare war against Mexico. This she did May 13, 1845, although Texas was not admitted as a state until December 29th of that year. The war lasted nearly three years, peace being declared February 2, 1848. As an outcome of the war the peaceful possession of Texas was secured, and also possession of the territory of California, Nevada, Utah, Arizona, and a part of Colorado and New Mexico, for which territory, however, our government in final settlement paid Mexico, $15,000,000.

New States — 1845 - 1861

During the Mexican War, Iowa (1846), the "Hawkeye" state, came into the Union, followed by the state of Wisconsin (1848).

the "Badger." Next comes the story of the "Forty-niners," and California (1850), the "Golden State," enters the Union; and then comes Minnesota (1858), the "North Star" State, and the Great Lakes are walled in, this state completing the circuit. Oregon,(1859),the "Beaver" follows,then the "Garden of the West," Kansas (1861), and the Civil War is upon us. Of course, we do not mean to say that Kansas was the cause of the Civil War, although it had much to do with it.

The Civil War — 1861 - 1865

The Civil War was a war between states, in the government of the United States — between states that were slave and states that were free.

The rights of property ownership are involved in state rights, and slaves held as property in slave-holding states were not recognized as such in states that were free. Therefore, the principle of slavery became involved not alone in the individual ownership of slaves, but also in the rights of a state, and the relationship of states to each other in the government of the United States.

At the close of the Revolutionary War, one of the first things to be settled was the boundaries as between states of the land comprising the thirteen original states; and as an outcome of this settlement, there came into possession of the United States all of that territory ceded by Great Britain in 1783, which was not included in the boundaries of those states. This territory, in brief, may be described as the territory east of the Mississippi, and north and south of the Ohio River; and out of this territory and that west of the Mississippi added later (1803) through the Louisiana Purchase, most of the new states were formed that came into the Union before the Civil War. And this was the beginning of what is known as the "public domain" — that is, land owned by the Federal Government.

In 1785, Congress passed a law which has become general in its application to all public lands of the United States. It is a law for the uniform survey of public lands into townships six miles square, subdivided into sections containing 640 acres, and quarter sections containing 160 acres. The purpose of the government in making this survey was to make public lands in the territories of the government easy of settlement, and as the townships became settled, to develop in them the local township form of government.

The territory north of the Ohio River was designated the "Northwest Territory." As soon as the public lands in this territory were thrown open to settlers, they began to pour in. Indeed, in many instances, they went ahead of the survey.

The next step taken by Congress was to pass a law, in 1787, for the government and protection of those settlers in this Northwest Territory, and in this law Congress made provision that slavery should be prohibited. Therefore, states formed in this territory had to come into the Union as free states. This was a restriction of slavery, however, which did not apply to the territory south of the Ohio, nor west of the Mississippi; so that when a new state came into the Union, formed out of either one of these territories, it became a great political factor in our government either for or against slavery.

In the passing of the years, many changes were taking place in our government, but there came a time when the people began to realize that slavery was spreading and that our government was politically divided between states that were slave and states that were free — or, in other words, that in the principle of slavery the peace and preservation of the Union were involved.

And thus it happened that the slave-holding states, not being able to live at peace in the Union, decided to go out of it, and live by themselves. The right of a state to leave the Union was called "the right of secession" — a right which the North held did not exist under the Constitution.

Nevertheless, one by one, under the leadership of South Carolina, December 20, 1860, the slave-holding states announced their secession, either by act of state legislature or in convention assembled; and on February 4, 1861, there had been formed in our government a Southern confederency. At this time the whole number of states in the Union was thirty-two, and of this number eleven entered the Southern confederacy.

The first shot was fired by the Southern confederacy on April 12, 1861, against Fort Sumter, a fortification of the Federal Government over which floated the stars and stripes. The war lasted four years, ending on April 9, 1865, when Robert E. Lee, commander-in-chief of the army of the Southern confederacy, surrendered to Ulysses S. Grant, commander-in-chief of the Federal army.

Abraham Lincoln

The central figure in the Civil War is Abraham Lincoln — in heart, brain, and character, not only one of our greatest Americans, but one of the world's greatest men.

Lincoln was born February 12, 1809, in Hardin County, Kentucky. His parents had come to this then pioneer state from Virginia, and his grandfather, whose Christian name he bore, moved there as early as 1781, where, a few years later, he was killed by the Indians while trying to make a home in the forest. When Lincoln was eight years old, his people moved to the new state of Indiana about the time it came into the Union, and there he lived until he was twenty-one, when he went to Illinois, from which state, eventually, he was elected President.

In 1859, when he was beginning to gain some recognition as a national figure, he was asked to write a little sketch of his life, and in the letter enclosing it he said: "There is not much of it, for the reason, I suppose, there is not much of me." In this sketch, which is indeed brief, he tells us he was raised to farm work until he was twenty-two; that up to that time he had had little education; and when he became of age he did not know much beyond reading, writing, and ciphering to the "rule of three." He clerked for one year in a store and was elected and served as captain of the volunteers in the Black Hawk War; later on he ran for the state legislature (1832) and was defeated, though successful in the three succeeding elections. While in the state legislature, he studied law and later went to Springfield to practise it. The only other public office he makes note of is his election to the lower house of Congress for one term (1846). He returned to Springfield and took up more earnestly the study and practice of law; he entered with spirit into the political campaigns, and constantly was growing in public esteem. His public debates with Douglas (1858) made him a familiar figure throughout the state of Illinois, and his profound knowledge and masterful handling of questions debated, his convincing and unanswerable arguments, his clear grasp of the political situation, began to gain the attention of Eastern politicians, convincing them and the country at large that they had a mighty force to reckon with in the prairie state of Illinois.

Although he lost the election to the United States Senate, and Douglas won, the campaign had pushed him to the front as a national figure, and paved the way for his presidential nomination.

In 1860, at the Republican convention assembled in Chicago, Abraham Lincoln was nominated for President. In November he was elected and March 4, 1861, he was inaugurated. His address at this time was an earnest plea for peace and friendship between the North and the South: "We are not enemies but friends. We must not be enemies. Though passion may have strained, it must not break our bond of affection."

But the war tide was rising and could not be stemmed; four years of bitter conflict ensued. Lincoln's emancipation of the slaves was made only after he had convinced himself it could not be longer deferred and preserve the Union. "My paramount duty," he said, "is to save the Union, and not either to destroy or save slavery. What I do about slavery and the colored race, I do because I believe it helps to save the Union; and what I forbear, I forbear because I do not believe it would save the Union." His Emancipation Proclamation, officially freeing the slaves, was finally issued in September, 1862, to take effect Jan, 1st of the following year.

Lincoln was elected to the Presidency for the second term and inaugurated March 4, 1865, while the war was still on. His second inaugural address closes with these words with which every boy should be familiar, voicing as they do the exalted spirit of a great and good man:

With malice toward none, with charity for all, with firmness in the right, as God gives us to see the right, let us strive on to finish the work we are in; to bind up the nation's wounds; to care for him who shall have borne the battle, and for his widow and for his orphan; to do all which may achieve and cherish a just and lasting peace among ourselves, and with all nations.

The war ended on April 9th of this same year, and on April 14th, the President, weary with the cares of state, but with the burden of the war clouds lifted, had gone to Ford's Theatre in Washington for an evening's entertainment and pleasure, accompanied by Mrs. Lincoln. The box which the President occupied had been most elaborately decorated with the flag of the country. His coming had been heralded abroad and the audience that had assembled in his honor was large, brilliant, and joyously happy over the assured preservation of the Union. In the midst of the play, the assassin, J. Wilkes Booth, entered the box and fired the fatal shot. The body of the bleeding President was taken to a house across the street where the next morning at 7:20 o'clock he died. Thus the emancipator of the slave, the friend of the whole people and the savior of our country died, a martyr to the cause of freedom.

Washington has been called "the aristocrat," and Lincoln "the man of the people." The one had culture, wealth, and social position; the other lacked all of these in his early years. Lincoln's early life was cradled in the woods, and all of life out of doors had been his in the new and pioneer states of the wilderness. He grew up not knowing many people, but somehow in his up-coming there was developed in his life a great heart full of tenderness and kindly feeling. Doubtless it was the very hardships of life that made him what he was. At any rate, he was one of the greatest and noblest figures in all history. He was called "Honest Abe" by those who knew him because always, even in little things, he wanted to see perfect justice done; and thus it was, when he came to things of large importance, that the man was only a boy grown tall, not only in stature but in the things that make for righteousness in a nation.

The Spanish-American War — 1898

The war with Spain was not of this country's seeking. The island of Cuba, whose distress had aroused the sympathy of the whole world, was our near neighbor, and to sit idly by and witness the inhuman treatment practised by the Spanish soldiery upon the helpless islanders would hardly be a part creditable to any people. It was not our intention at first to do other than to relieve the suffering and distress of Cuba, near at hand, and this we tried to do peaceably in the supplying of food and other necessities of life.

As the next step, the United States sent a remonstrance to Spain telling her she should send a more humane governor to the island. But as matters grew worse instead of better, even under a change of governors, the sympathy of the United States became daily more deeply enlisted in the freedom of the Cubans.

The battle ship Maine was sent to Havana Harbor to protect, if need be, the Americans and American interests in Cuba. On the night of February 15th, 1898, an explosion occurred, sinking the ship almost immediately.

With the destruction of the Maine — whether by accident or intent — with the appalling loss of two hundred and fifty-six men, including two officers, relations with Spain became more and more strained, until war seemed inevitable. On April 11, 1898, President McKinley in a special message to Congress, said: "In the name of humanity and civilization, the war in Cuba must stop."

War indeed was formally declared April 25th, and in the brief space of one hundred and fourteen days history had added to its annals: the blockading of Cuban ports whereby the Spanish fleet was trapped; the invasion and siege of the island by United States regulars, volunteers, and rough riders; the destruction of the Pacific Spanish fleet in Manila Bay by Admiral Dewey; and, finally, the destruction of the remainder of the Spanish fleet under command of Admiral Cervera, Sunday morning, July 3d. The final outcome of this war was the freedom of Cuba and the possession by the United States of Porto Rico, Guam, and the Philippine Islands.

Peace

There is no country in the world less warlike than ours, and no country in the world that more potently argues for universal peace. We have never departed from the spirit of our Declaration of Independence, "that all men are created equal; that they are endowed by their Creator with certain inalienable rights; that among these are life, liberty, and the pursuit of happiness." We put it into our Constitution when we said, "in order to form a more perfect union, establish justice, insure domestic tranquillity, provide for the common defence, promote the general welfare, and secure the blessings of liberty to ourselves and our posterity" we "do ordain and establish this Constitution for the United States of America." Such has been, then, and always must be, our programme — the chart and compass of all our ways.

The American Flag

"A star for every state and a state for every star."

The flag of one's country is its dearest possession — emblem of home, and country, and native land. This is what one thinks and feels when he sees the flag, and this is what it means. Our flag is the emblem of liberty — the emblem of hope — the emblem of peace and good-will toward men.

There is a story, quite generally believed, that the first flag was planned and made in 1776 by Betsy Ross, who kept an upholstery shop on Arch Street, Philadelphia, and that this, a year later, was adopted by Congress. The special committee appointed to design a national flag consisted of George Washington, Robert Morris, and Col. George Ross, uncle of the late husband of Betsy Ross. The star that the committee decided upon had six points, but Mrs. Ross advised the five-pointed star, which has ever since been used in the United States flag. The flag thus designed was colored by a local artist, and from this colored copy Betsy Ross made the first American flag.

When Washington was in command at Cambridge, in January, 1776, the flag used by him consisted of a banner of thirteen red and white stripes with the British Union Jack in the upper left-hand corner.

The Betsy Ross house has been purchased by the American Flag House and Betsy Ross Memorial Association, and is pointed out as one of the interesting historical places in Philadelphia.

The official history of our flag begins on June 14, 1777, when the American Congress adopted the following resolution proposed by John Adams:

Resolved: That the flag of the thirteen United States be thirteen stripes, alternate red and white: that the Union be thirteen stars, white on a blue field, representing a new constellation.

"We take," said Washington, "the star from Heaven, the red from our mother country, separating it by white stripes, thus showing that we have separated from her, and the white stripes shall go down to posterity representing liberty."

In designing the flag there was much discussion as to the arrangement of the stars in the field of blue. It was thought at one time that a new stripe as well as a new star should be added for each new state admitted to the Union. Indeed, in 1794, Congress passed an act to the effect that on and after May 1, 1795, "the flag of the United States be fifteen stripes, alternate red and white; and that the union be fifteen stars, white in a field of blue. These additional stars and stripes were for the states of Vermont and Kentucky.

The impracticability of adding a stripe for each state was apparent as other states began to be admitted. Moreover, the flag of fifteen stripes, it was thought, did not properly represent the Union; therefore, on April 14, 1818, after a period of twenty-one years in which the flag of fifteen stripes had been used, Congress passed an act which finally fixed the general flag of our country, which reads as follows:

An Act to Establish the Flag of the United States.

Sec. 1. Be it enacted, etc., That from and after the fourth day of July next, the flag of the United States be thirteen horizontal stripes, alternate red and white; that the union have twenty stars, white in a blue field.

Sec. 2. Be it further enacted, that, on the admission of every new state into the union, one star be added to the union of the flag; and that such addition shall take effect on the fourth day of July succeeding such admission.

Flag Day

June 14th, the anniversary of the adoption of the flag, is celebrated as flag day in many of our states.

In order to show proper respect for the flag, the following rules should be observed:

It should not be hoisted before sunrise nor allowed to remain up after sunset.

At "retreat," sunset, civilian spectators should stand at attention and give the military salute.

When the national colors are passing on parade or review, the spectators should, if walking, halt, and if sitting, rise and stand at attention and uncover.

When the flag is flown at half staff as a sign of mourning it should be hoisted to full staff at the conclusion of the funeral. In placing the flag at half mast, it should first be hoisted to the top of the staff and then lowered to position, and preliminary to lowering from half staff it should first be raised to top.

On Memorial Day, May 30th, the flag should fly at half mast from sunrise until noon, and full staff from noon to sunset.

(Taken from the "Sons of the Revolution," state of New York.)

The Scout's Pledge to the Flag

"I pledge allegiance to my flag and to the republic for which it stands; one nation indivisible, with liberty and justice for all."

Congress

The Congress of the United States is its law-making body, and is composed of the Senate and House of Representatives. Senators are elected for six years, two from each state; representatives for two years, each state being represented in proportion to its population. The Vice-president of the United States is the president of the Senate, and the presiding officer of the House of Representatives is chosen by the members from their number; he is called the speaker. The salary of the senators and representatives is $7,500 a year and 20 cents per mile is allowed for traveling to and from Washington. The speaker's salary is $12,000 a year.

The President

The President is elected for a term of four years. He lives during his term of office at the White House, where presidential receptions and social affairs of state are held. The President's offices are connected with the White House. Here he receives his callers and here the meetings of his Cabinet are held. The salary of the President is $75,000, a year.

The Cabinet

The members of the Cabinet are the officers and heads of the several departments of the administrative government.

They are appointed by the President with the advice and consent of the Senate. The members of the Cabinet are as follows: secretary of state, secretary of the treasury, secretary of war, attorney general, postmaster general, secretary of the navy, secretary of the interior, secretary of agriculture, secretary of commerce and labor. The members of the Cabinet are such men as the President believes are qualified to serve during his administration of office, and are usually members of the same political party as the President.

United States Courts

The Supreme Court of the United States is at Washington, D. C., but there are other courts of the United States held in the several states, called district courts.

Washington, D. C.

The capitol at Washington is the home of Congress, and the Supreme Court. The Library of Congress, the Treasury, Army and Navy, Pension, Post-office, and many other buildings of public character are located in Washington. These during certain hours are open to visitors.

The Army

The President, in accordance with the Constitution, is commander-in-chief of the army and navy of the United States and of the militia of the several states when called to the actual service of the United States. The law provides that the total strength of the army shall not exceed at any one time 100,000. As now organized (1910) the total strength of the staff and line is 76,911 not including the provisional force and the hospital corps. These figures include the Porto Rico Regiment of Infantry, the Service School Detachments, the Military Academy (officers, soldiers and cadets), the Indian Scouts, 52,000 native scouts in the Philippine Islands, 193 First Lieutenants of the Medical Reserve Corps on active duty, and 11,777 recruits, etc. They do not include the veterinary surgeons, the officers of the Medical Reserve Corps not on active duty, nor the retired officers and enlisted men of the army. The appropriation for the maintenance of the army for the year 1909–10 was $100,330,181.

Militia

The law of our country states that in time of war every able-bodied male citizen, between the ages of eighteen and forty-five, shall be counted a member of the state militia. The state militia is divided into two classes: one, the organized, known as the national guard; and the other the unorganized, known as the reserve militia.

The membership of the national guard is voluntary. One may join or not, as he chooses, except that in some states the law requires that students at the state university shall receive military training for at least a part of their university course, and during that time they are accounted a part of the national guard of the State. The governor of each state holds the same relationship to the state militia as the President to the army and navy: he is commander-in-chief.

Military Academy

The United States Military Academy is at West Point, N. Y., on the Hudson River. The number of students is limited to 533, and appointments to the academy are made in accordance with the rule which permits each United States senator and each congressman to have one representative, and also gives the President the right to make forty appointments at large. Candidates for appointment must be between the ages of seventeen and twenty-two; must pass the required physical examination; also an examination in English grammar, composition and literature, algebra and geometry, geography and history. The course of instruction is four years; the discipline very strict. Only one leave of absence is granted during the entire four years, and this comes at the close of the second year. The pay is $709.50 per year, and on graduation a cadet is commissioned a second lieutenant. To receive an appointment to West Point, one must apply to his United States senator or to a congressman in the state in which he lives, or to the President.

The Navy

The enlisted strength of the navy, as in the army, is limited. The law allows 47,500 men and apprenticed seamen. The number of officers and enlisted men at the present time is 46,898, and the annual expenditure for the support of the navy at this date (1911) is about $130,000,000.

Naval Enlistment

The enlistment of men in the United States navy, as in the army, is voluntary. The term is four years. To be eligible for enlistment one must be between the ages of eighteen and

twenty-two. He must be of good moral character, must pass
the physical examination, must be able to write English, and
take the oath of allegiance.

Naval Militia

In the District of Columbia and in twenty of the states we
have what is known as the naval militia.   The assistant secretary of the navy stands in a special relation to the naval
militia through the governor and the adjutant-general of the
several states.   The naval militia holds the same relationship to the navy that the national guard does to the United
States army.

Naval Academy

The United States Naval Academy is at Annapolis, Md.
The students are called midshipmen, and candidates for appointment must be between the ages of sixteen and twenty.
The appointment of candidates is made as at West Point —
through senators and congressmen and the President, the only
difference being in the number of appointments that may be
made: each senator and representative may be represented by
two midshipmen at Annapolis, while at West Point he is represented by but one cadet.   The President has the appointment of seven men to the Naval Academy — two from the
District of Columbia and five from the United States at large.
He may also appoint one from Porto Rico, who must be a native.
The midshipmen's course is six years — four at Annapolis,
and two at sea.   The pay is $600 per year.

Civil Service

In the administration of the government of the United States,
thousands of men and women are employed in the various offices
at Washington, and are sometimes termed the great "peace
army."

In one period of our country's history, it was believed that
each President, when he came into office, had the right to turn
out of office every person employed by the government in any
of its civil departments, should it please him to do so, and to
put into office his own friends or the friends of his party.   This
right was claimed on the ground that "to the victor belong the
spoils" — a theory of government administration that has
been severely dealt with and reformed through what is known
as the "Civil Service Act."   The Civil Service Act was passed

by Congress January 16, 1883, and by this act a civil service commission was brought into existence. The three members of this commission are appointed by the President with consent of the Senate, not more than two of whom may be members of the same party. Thus, by this civil service act, positions in the government service are now obtained for the most part through competitive examinations, and such positions are not affected in any way by the incoming of a new President or the appointment of a new head of a department.

In some states and in most of the large cities civil service appointments are now made through competitive examinations. Any one interested in learning what positions may be secured in the service of the government, may apply to the Civil Service Commission at Washington, D. C., or make inquiry at the local post-office.

Foreign Service

The foreign service of our government is carried on through the diplomatic corps and the consular service. In the diplomatic corps, we have ambassadors, envoys, ministers, diplomatic agents, and secretaries; in the consular service, consuls general, consuls, and consular agents.

Our diplomatic representatives abroad look after our interests as a nation in the family of nations. They represent us socially as well as politically in the great foreign capitals of the world. They are received as our representatives of state, and it is their duty to sustain and promote good-will and friendly feeling between us and other nations.

The consular service is more directly responsible for our trade relationships in the great centres of the world. Through our foreign service, also, Americans abroad, whether as tourists, or residents, are protected in person and in property interests. Appointments to the foreign service are made by the President with the advice of the Senate.

As we send our representatives abroad, so the countries to which our representatives go in turn send their representatives to us. In the city of Washington, one may see representatives of all the principal nations of the earth living there as ambassadors, for the purpose of promoting friendly commercial and political relationships. The secretary of state is the representative of our government through whose office the great work of the foreign service is directly carried on, and upon him devolves therefore the great affairs of state relationships with other countries. When our independence as a nation was declared in 1776, it was important to gain as quickly as possible from other nations a recognition of our independence and of our entrance into the family of nations. France was the first to give us recognition, and the first to enter into a treaty relationship. Some of the most thrilling and interesting stories of our national life are to be found in the adventurous determination of our representatives to gain the recognition of our independence as a nation from the great powers of the earth. The name of Benjamin Franklin, sent to the court of France, stands at the head of our diplomatic service; and we may read with interest of the first appearance of our diplomatic representative, John Adams, at the court of Great Britain. When we speak of court in this sense, we mean, of course, the king's court — the place of meeting — usually the throne room. In our country, foreign representatives are received by the President at the White House, or by the secretary of state in his office apartments. Some foreign countries have built for their representatives in Washington palatial and beautiful residences, over which floats the flag of the country to which the palace or residence belongs. Our own country has already begun to make this residential provision for her representatives abroad, and in time will undoubtedly own residences in all of the principal foreign capitals.

State Government

The states of the United States are not all alike either in constitution or government, although there is a likeness at many points. For instance, each state has about the same officers, — a governor, lieutenant-governor, secretary of state, treasurer, auditor, adjutant general, superintendent of schools, etc.

Each state has its own state legislature: a senate to which state senators are elected, and a house of representatives sometimes called the assembly, to which state representatives or assemblymen are elected. Each state legislature makes laws only for its own state; therefore not all state laws are alike. Indeed, there is a great deal of individuality to each state, and rightly so. As each person has his own individuality, and as each family has its own characteristics, so each state has an individuality and characteristics peculiar to itself. The history of each state reveals its character, so also the climate, the hills, the valleys, the mountains, the plains, the lakes, the rivers, the harbors, the schools, the colleges, the towns, the villages, and the cities within its borders, all help in forming the character of a state.

Towns, Villages, and Cities

The government of the town, or the village, or the city is called local government. It is government close at hand—home government. And out of the home government of each town, village, and city in a state must come, by the votes of the people at the ballot-box, the men whom they choose as their representatives, in the government of the state and the nation — for the people rule through representatives of their own choosing.

Politics

In every presidential election, the people, through the rule of the majority, as determined by the Constitution, elect their chief magistrate, the President, who becomes the "first citizen" of the nation and is entitled "Mr. President." The people of a state by the same rule elect their chief magistrate and entitle him "His Excellency, the Governor"; he is the state's chief or leading citizen. The people of the city by the same rule elect their chief magistrate and entitle him "His Honor, the Mayor," the city's leading citizen. The people of the town, in the New England States, elect their chief officers — three to five men — and entitle them the "Selectmen"; although in towns of the middle and western states, they are called "Supervisors."

So, likewise, the people in town, village, and city by the same "rule of the majority" elect aldermen, councilmen, state senators, representatives or assemblymen, and congressmen.

And the state legislatures in turn elect, according to the Constitution of the United States, the state's United States senators, two in number. Thus, by the rule of the majority, are all officers of town, village, and city, county and state elected, except such few as are appointed by law to offices by superior officers, heads of departments, bureaus, or districts of supervision or administration.

Property

The ownership of property, both real and personal, and the protection of that ownership, is made possible in the organization of society — termed the government — and in the power of that government to make and enforce its laws. Real property is the kind of property which pertains to land, the ownership of which is transferred from one person to another, either by a deed recorded in the office of the register of deeds in the county court house, or else transferred by descent, or by will through the administration of the county court, usually called the probate court. This latter proceeding is in the case of the owner's death when his property is divided by the court and distributed to the heirs — the family or other relatives according to his will; or in case no will is left the law provides for the manner of its distribution.

The Register of Deeds: County Court House

The record title, therefore, of all real property is to be found in the office of the register of deeds in the county court house. It makes no difference what kind of real property it is, acre property or city property, here the title of ownership is always to be found, the books of record being always open to the public. Thus when one buys a piece of real property, a home for instance, he should receive from the owner a deed and an abstract of title, which is a paper showing the title as it appears on the records, and this title when not vouched for as perfect by an abstract title company, should be passed upon by a lawyer in order that any flaw or defect therein may be made right before the deed is passed from one owner to another. In some states, however, the law does not require the owner to furnish an abstract. When the title is proved or pronounced good, the deed should at once be placed on record.

Personal Property

Personal property is that form of property which in general terms is stated as movable, such as animals, furniture, clothing, tools, implements, money, stocks, bonds, mortgages, etc., the transfer of which from one owner to another is not as a rule a matter of public record, although in the case of a bill of sale — sometimes made of some forms of personal property — the county record may give evidence thereof. Therefore it is, that in the matter of taxation, the tax record or assessment comes under two general heads — a tax on real property and a tax on personal property.

Property and Government

It is desirable to be a property owner so long as the government under which one lives protects one in his property ownership. The government must do two things: it must protect the person and his personal rights as a citizen, and it must also protect property and the rights of property ownership from enemies within, as from without. In order that this may be done and done in all fairness and justice, we elect some citizens to make laws and term them legislators. We elect others to enforce or administer the laws, and term them executives — the President, the governor, and the mayor coming under this head. We elect other citizens to enforce and interpret the laws, and we term them judges and officers of the court. In fact, it is a principle in our government that no man or set of men shall have authority in all departments of government, legislative, executive, and judicial. You will see that the Constitution of the United States is divided into these three departments of government, and the state constitutions and city charters are, as a rule, likewise divided.

You will understand that any property you may obtain will be valuable to you only in proportion as you are protected in your rights of ownership by the government, and that the government not only protects your property, it also protects your life and its interest as well as the life and interests of all other citizens.

The building and maintenance of schools and colleges, libraries, art and natural history museums, parks, playgrounds, hospitals, etc., are carried on at the expense of the government by means of taxation, inasmuch as these things are in the interests of mankind and for its upbuilding. In the city the protection of life and property is found in one or the other of these different departments: police, fire, health, street cleaning, parks, water supply, etc.; and every good citizen should lend his hand to help in every way possible the enforcement of law in each department.

Citizenship

In any form of government, problems are continually arising as to the rights of property and the rights of persons, and it is well for us to remember this distinction: that the end of society (and by that term we mean government) is not the protection of property, but rather the upbuilding of mankind. If we bear this in mind and act upon it as a principle in life, we shall find ourselves standing and voting on the right side of public questions. We shall also be able to mark the man in private or public life who shows by his talk or his actions that he thinks more of property rights than he does of the rights of individuals. Any business that does not benefit society, but on the other hand degrades it, whether run by an individual or individuals in a firm, company, or corporation, is a business that ought by the law to be put out of existence. This is why the business of gambling, for instance, is made unlawful; also why the government had the right to make lotteries unlawful; also why some states (for instance New York) have passed laws making book-making at race tracks unlawful. For all of these things degrade and do not upbuild mankind. It is for every one then, to apply this principle to the town, village or city in which he lives, and determine just what stand he will take as to endorsing and protecting such business interests in his community. One is likely to find in any community men who seem to care nothing for any interests other than their own. They stand for property rights because it is for their interest to do so; but for the rights of mankind, the rights of society, apparently they care nothing. Here is the distinction then between the good citizen, and the bad citizen, the desirable and "the undesirable" citizen.

Practical Citizenship

In nearly every town, village, and city of any size or importance, there is at least one individual, and usually groups of individuals, working for the "betterment of society." They are people who take an interest in the people about them and do what they can to improve the conditions of life in the community. If one were to take a survey of the whole country and make a study of the social workers —- the men and the women who give freely of their time and of their money to make the world a better and happier place to live in — he would come to see that such service is a kind of service that grows out of the heart, and is the fruit of the kindly spirit which prompts the "good turn daily."

In doing the "good turn daily," then, one has abundant opportunity to do his part toward the social betterment of the community in which he lives. There are so many ways that one hardly knows what to write down as the most important, because all are important. It is not alone in big things, but in the little things as well, that the really great work is done.

The community — the town, the village, or the city in which one lives — has many problems to solve. The streets in the community are always interesting and one can do much in the streets to help keep them clean, attractive, and pleasing, as well as safe for the people and horses passing through. In a city where there is a large population the lives of the people are in greater danger at all times than in the country, and that is the reason why the city has to be so organized in its government that it can make special laws, or ordinances as they are called, for its own special protection against the dangers of city life.   The policemen of a city, wherever stationed in the daytime or in the night time, are there to protect the lives and property of individuals, at street crossings, at public buildings, at theatres, in the parks, and on playgrounds; and it is the privilege as well as the duty of all citizens to help them in every way possible to do their work well.   In the "good turn daily," one may be able to help in more ways than one if he is on the lookout.

"A scout's honor is to be trusted" to obey the laws and to see that they are not disobeyed by others.   "A scout's duty is to be useful and to help others.   He must be prepared at any time to save life or to help injured persons."   There are often accidents in the streets — many avoidable ones -- due simply to carelessness.   For instance, some boys were careless and threw broken glass bottles into the street, and a passing automobile came to a standstill because of a punctured tire.   The man who owned the automobile and was driving it got out and called one of the boys on the street to come over to him.   He did not call this particular boy because he thought he had thrown the glass, but because he thought he was a boy who would appreciate what he wanted to say to him.   He told the boy that he had just had a new tire put on his machine and appealed to him as to whether or not he thought he had been treated right through the carelessness of the one who threw that glass into the street.   The boy said no, he didn't think he had been, and, after a little more talk, added that he would do all in his power in that neighborhood to see that such things were kept out of the street in the future.   That boy was in line for the making of a first-class scout, and the man to whom he had been talking, being a good scout commissioner, had won the boy, because instead of being angry, he had been kind, courteous, and friendly — all qualifications of a good scout.

"A scout is a friend to animals."   "Yes," said a stable keeper, "I have two good horses laid up, each injured by stepping on a nail in a board in the street.   You know people are awfully careless about such things."   There are some people who never go out of their way to do helpful things, just as some people never go out of their way to know people, and for that reason are often alone and lonesome. It is the little things that count, just such little things as picking up from the street a board with a nail in it, and putting it aside — even that is a good turn.

Lincoln once said in speaking of a man whom he thought lacking in sympathy: "He is so put up by nature that a lash upon his back would hurt him, but a lash upon anybody's else back does not hurt him." There are many people in the world who seem to be like that man — not so many who feel that way towards mankind, possibly, but many who thoughtlessly feel and act that way toward animals. The lash on the back of an animal — the horse, the cow, the dog — hurts, and the good scout always takes the animal's part. He is kind to animals.

In the city, people often become careless as to the necessary precautions against fire and for this reason many lives are lost. In all well-regulated school systems, each school building is properly provided with fire escapes and the children regularly disciplined in fire drills. Proper fire precautions are not yet generally required by law as they should be in great buildings, factories, or workshops where men and women are employed in large numbers. If a scout should be employed in such a place, he might make himself very serviceable in case of a fire, because having thought of it beforehand, he would know what to do — his motto being, "*Be Prepared.*"

One very important thing in city life is the protection of one's health: it is essential to have good food, pure water, plenty of good, fresh air — things not always easily obtainable, but always most necessary. The scout learns through the many activities of scouting something of the market places and sources of supply for food; he has some idea as to the cost of living in his own home, and should become a good marketer himself, making himself competent to judge of the quality and prices of food. If he is wide-awake and intelligent, he knows the products of his own county as well as those of the state. He knows what food products are shipped in and sometimes finds that it would be cheaper, and more profitable as well, to produce them in his own community. An industrious scout may often make his own pocket money in this way or provide funds towards his own education.

In the Constitution of the United States is written this law: "No title of nobility shall be granted by the United States." The purpose of this law is to defeat any attempt to elevate one citizen above another in rank of s cial or political preferment. Ours is a country free from the entanglements of social distinction such as mark one man or family from another by way of title or patent of nobility; and yet, in our country of uncrowned kings and unknighted men, we would not forget the real deeds of valor, the services rendered, or the victories won. For it was the purpose in the mind and in the heart of our fathers who framed the Constitution that each succeeding generation should rise to the duties and responsibilities of the State; that the virtues of the State should not descend or be lodged in one family, or any selected number of families. but rather should be in the keeping of all the families, in the care and keeping of all the people.

Thus do we remember our Washington and our Lincoln. They served the generation to which they belonged; they lived and passed out of their generation having served the State: and all the virtues, cares, and responsibilities of the State — the government that is — they left to the generations that should come after them. And, therefore, each generation as it comes and goes must rise or fall in proportion as it raises or lowers the citizenship standard, for each generation must prove its own worth as must each individual his own virtues.

Practical Citizenship

As set forth in a letter from Colonel Theodore Roosevelt, Honorary Vice-president, Boy Scouts of America:

THE OUTLOOK
287 Fourth Avenue,
New York

Office of
Theodore Roosevelt

July 20th, 1911.

MY DEAR SIR:

I quite agree with Judge Lindsey that the Boy Scout Movement is of peculiar importance to the whole country. It has already done much good, and it will do far more, for it is in its essence a practical scheme through which to impart a proper standard of ethical conduct, proper standards of fair play and consideration for others, and courage and decency, to boys who have never been reached and never will be reached by the ordinary type of preaching, lay or clerical. I have been particularly interested in that extract of a letter from a scout master in the Philippines, which runs as follows:

"It might interest you to know that at a recent fire in Manila which devastated acres of ground and rendered 3,000 people homeless, that two patrols of the Manila scouts reached the fire almost with the fire companies, reported to the proper authorities and worked for hours under very trying conditions

helping frightened natives into places of safety, removing
valuables and other articles from houses that apparently were
in the path of the flames, and performing cheerfully and effi-
ciently all the tasks given to them by the firemen and scout
master. They were complimented in the public press, and in
a kind editorial about their work.

"During the recent Carnival the services of the boys were
requested by the Carnival officers, and for a period of ten days
they were on duty performing all manner of service in the
Carnival grounds, directing strangers to hotels, and acting as
guides and helpers in a hundred ways."

What these boy scouts of the Philippines have just done,
I think our boy scouts in every town and country district should
train themselves to be able to do. The movement is one for
efficiency and patriotism. It does not try to make soldiers
of boy scouts, but to make boys who will turn out as men
to be fine citizens, and who will, if their country needs them,
make better soldiers for having been scouts. No one can be a
good American unless he is a good citizen, and every boy
ought to train himself so that as a man he will be able to do
his full duty to the community. I want to see the boy scouts
not merely utter fine sentiments, but act on them; not merely
sing, "My Country 'Tis of Thee," but act in a way that will give
them a country to be proud of. No man is a good citizen unless he so acts as to show that he actually uses the Ten Commandments, and translates the Golden Rule into his life conduct — and I don't mean by this in exceptional cases under
spectacular circumstances, but I mean applying the Ten Commandments and the Golden Rule in the ordinary affairs of
every-day life. I hope the boy scouts will practise truth and
square dealing, and courage and honesty, so that when as
young men they begin to take a part not only in earning their
own livelihood, but in governing the community, they may be
able to show in practical fashion their insistence upon the
great truth that the eighth and ninth commandments are
directly related to every-day life, not only between men
as such in their private relations, but between men and
the government of which they are part. Indeed the boys
even while only boys can have a very real effect upon
the conduct of the grown up members of the community,
for decency and square dealing are just as contagious as
vice and corruption.

Every healthy boy ought to feel and will feel that in order
to amount to anything, it is necessary to have a constructive,

and not merely a destructive, nature; and if he can keep this feeling as he grows up he has taken his first step toward good citizenship. The man who tears down and criticises and scolds may be a good citizen, but only in a negative sense; and if he never does anything else he is apt not to be a good citizen at all. The man who counts, and the boy who counts, are the man and boy who steadily endeavor to build up, to improve, to better living conditions everywhere and all about them.

But the boy can do an immense amount right in the present, entirely aside from training himself to be a good citizen in the future; and he can only do this if he associates himself with other boys. Let the boy scouts see to it that the best use is made of the parks and playgrounds in their villages and home towns. A gang of toughs may make a playground impossible; and if the boy scouts in the neighborhood of that particular playground are fit for their work, they will show that they won't permit any such gang of toughs to have its way. Moreover, let the boy scouts take the lead in seeing that the parks and playgrounds are turned to a really good account. I hope, by the way, that one of the prime teachings among the boy scouts will be the teaching against vandalism. Let it be a point of honor to protect birds, trees and flowers, and so to make our country more beautiful and not more ugly, because we have lived in it.

The same qualities that mean success or failure to the nation as a whole, mean success or failure in men and boys individually. The boy scouts must war against the same foes and vices that most hurt the nation; and they must try to develop the same virtues that the nation most needs. To be helpless, self-indulgent, or wasteful, will turn the boy into a mighty poor kind of a man, just as the indulgence in such vices by the men of a nation means the ruin of the nation. Let the boy stand stoutly against his enemies both from without and from within, let him show courage in confronting fearlessly one set of enemies, and in controlling and mastering the others. Any boy is worth nothing if he has not got courage, courage to stand up against the forces of evil, and courage to stand up in the right path. Let him be unselfish and gentle, as well as strong and brave. It should be a matter of pride to him that he is not afraid of anyone, and that he scorns not to be gentle and considerate to everyone, and especially to those who are weaker than he is. If he doesn't treat his mother and sisters well, then he is a poor creature no matter what else he does; just as a man who doesn't treat his wife well is a poor kind of citizen no matter what his other qualities may be. And, by the way, don't ever forget to let the boy know that courtesy, politeness, and good manners must not be neglected. They are not little things, because they are used at every turn in daily life. Let the boy remember also that in addition to courage, unselfishness, and fair dealing, he must have efficiency, he must have knowledge, he must cultivate a sound body and a good mind, and train himself so that he can act with quick decision in any crisis that may arise. Mind, eye, muscle, all must be trained so that the boy can master himself, and thereby learn to master his fate. I heartily wish all good luck to the movement.

Very sincerely yours,
THEODORE ROOSEVELT.

Mr. James E. West,
   Executive Secretary
     Boy Scouts of America,
     New York City.

America

MY country, 'tis of thee,
  Sweet land of liberty,
    Of thee I sing;
Land where my fathers died,
Land of the Pilgrims' pride,
From every mountain side
    Let freedom ring.

My native country, thee
Land of the noble free,
    Thy name I love;
I love thy rocks and rills,
Thy woods and templed hills;
My heart with rapture thrills
    Like that above.

Let music swell the breeze,
And ring from all the trees
    Sweet freedom's song;
Let mortal tongues awake,
Let all that breathe partake,
Let rocks their silence break,
    The sound prolong!

Our father's God, to Thee,
Author of liberty,
    To thee we sing:
Long may our land be bright
With freedom's holy light;
Protect us by Thy might,
    Great God, our King.
                    — *Samuel F. Smith,* 1832.

The Star-Spangled Banner

O SAY, can you see, by the dawn's early light,
  What so proudly we hail'd at the twilight's last gleaming?
Whose broad stripes and bright stars, thro' the perilous fight,
  O'er the ramparts we watched were so gallantly streaming;
And the rocket's red glare, the bombs bursting in air,
  Gave proof thro' the night that our flag was still there!
O say, does that star-spangled banner yet wave
  O'er the land of the free and the home of the brave?

On the shore, dimly seen thro' the mists of the deep,
  Where the foe's haughty host in dread silence reposes,
What is that which the breeze, o'er the towering steep,
  As it fitfully blows, half conceals, half discloses?
Now it catches the gleam of the morning's first beam,
  In full glory reflected, now shines on the stream —
'Tis the star-spangled banner. O long may it wave
  O'er the land of the free and the home of the brave.

And where is that band who so vauntingly swore,
  'Mid the havoc of war and the battle's confusion,
A home and a country they'd leave us no more?
  Their blood has washed out their foul footsteps' pollution.
No refuge could save the hireling and slave
  From the terror of flight, or the gloom of the grave —
And the star-spangled banner in triumph shall wave,
  O'er the land of the free and the home of the brave.

O thus be it ever when freemen shall stand
  Between their loved homes and foul war's desolation,
Blest with vict'ry and peace, may the heav'n-rescued land
  Praise the Power that hath made and preserved us a nation.
Then conquer we must, when our cause it is just,
  And this be our motto, "In God is our trust" —
And the star-spangled banner in triumph shall wave,
  While the land of the free is the home of the brave.
              — *Francis Scott Key*, 1814.

APPENDIX

BOY SCOUT EQUIPMENT

As stated in the chapter on "Scoutcraft," for the convenience of boys who wish to secure uniforms or other equipment, the National Council has made arrangements with certain manufacturers to furnish such parts of the equipment as are most needed by boys. A number of these manufacturers have taken advertising space in this book and it is desired that in case goods are ordered as a result of their advertisement they be informed of the fact. Some of them have made arrangements for the distribution of material through Mr. Sigmund Eisner, of Red Bank, New Jersey, who has the contract for making the official uniforms.

It should be remembered at all times that the sole purpose of the National Council in entering into any arrangement whatever with manufacturers is to secure a low price on the very best material possible. The manufacturers have agreed to sell all the material listed in this book at a uniform price in all parts of the country. In case local dealers or agents for the National Outfitter ask a price different from that given in the price list herewith, National Headquarters should be notified.

Every effort is made to have all parts of the uniform and equipment available to scouts through local dealers. If such arrangements have not been made in your community, the National Headquarters will be glad to help in making such an arrangement. Many scout masters prefer to order uniforms and other supplies direct from National Headquarters. In order to cover the expense involved in handling these supplies, the manufacturers in some cases have agreed to allow National Headquarters the same trade discount allowed to local dealers. Trade through National Headquarters, if sufficiently large, will help to meet a part of the current expenses of the National Organization.

In this suggested list of equipment all articles marked with a star (*) may be secured either through a local dealer or by ordering direct through National Headquarters in New York City.

Directions for Ordering

Important: When ordering supplies care should be taken to see that the exact amount of remittance is included with the order. If check is used add New York Exchange. Make checks and money orders payable to Boy Scouts of America. All orders received without the proper remittance will be shipped C. O. D., or held until remittance arrives.

* *Axe*: Any local hardware dealer can suggest quite a variety of good axes which may be used by the scout, but because of quality and price, the Boy Scout axe is suggested. Weight without handle, 12 oz. Made of one piece of solid steel — special temper, axe pattern hickory handle, missionized hand forged — non-rusting finish. Price 35 cents. Axe scabbard or shield, 25 cents extra.

Bandanna or Neckerchief: These are so common that every boy will recognize at once what is mean by a bandanna. The members of each patrol wear bandanas made in the colors of their patrol. These can be purchased at any local dry goods store at ten or fifteen cents each.

* *Belts:* Any good belt will meet the scout's needs. But for his convenience the belt illustrated herewith is suggested. Price 40 cents.

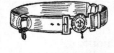

* *Breeches:* Standard material — belt guides — pockets —full pattern—legs laced below the knee, the lacing to be covered by stockings or leggings. Order by age according to following table:

Boys' sizes: Price $1.00.

Age-size	Waist	Seat	Inseam	Calf	Ankle
18	32	37	26	$13\frac{1}{2}$	$9\frac{1}{2}$
17	31	$36\frac{1}{2}$	$25\frac{1}{2}$	$13\frac{1}{4}$	9
16	30	35	25	13	9
15	29	34	$24\frac{1}{2}$	$12\frac{3}{4}$	$8\frac{3}{4}$
14	28	$32\frac{1}{2}$	24	$12\frac{1}{2}$	$8\frac{1}{2}$
13	27	31	23	$12\frac{1}{4}$	$8\frac{1}{4}$
12	$26\frac{1}{2}$	$30\frac{1}{2}$	22	12	$8\frac{1}{4}$

Appendix

Extra Sizes: Breeches above eighteen-year size will be made to order and will cost twenty-five cents more per garment.

	Waist	Seat	Inseam	Calf	Ankle
1	32	38	27	13½	9½
2	33	39	27	13¾	9¾
3	34	40	28	14	9¾
4	35	41	27	14½	9¾
5	36	42	28	15	10
6	37	43	27	15¼	10¼
7	38	44	28	15½	10½

Bugle: It is recommended that the standard bugle used in an army or drum corps be used. Each patrol should purchase these from a local music store.

Camp Knives, Forks and Spoons: Ordinary table-knives, forks and spoons may be used. An inexpensive knife, fork and spoon for use in camps, like set illustrated herewith, may be secured for about eight cents per dozen through almost any local hardware store.

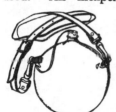

Canteen: A canteen of this design may be carried by each scout on hikes and long tramps. Many army supply houses carry these in stock, where they may be secured if desired.

* Coats: Standard material—four bellows pockets — standing collar — dull metal buttons with Boy Scout emblem. Order by age according to following table:

Boys' sizes: Price $1.35.

Age	Breast	Waist	Length	Sleeve	Collar
18	34	32	26	31	16
17	33	31	25	30½	15½
16	32	30½	24½	29½	15
15	31	30	24	28½	14½
14	30	29	23½	27½	14
13	29	28½	23	26	13½
12	28	27½	22	25	13

Extra Sizes: Coats above eighteen-year size will be made as extra size and will cost twenty-five cents more per garment than boys' sizes.

	Breast	Waist	Length	Sleeve Length	Collar Finish
1	35	32	27	32	$16\frac{1}{4}$
2	36	33	$27\frac{1}{2}$	32	$16\frac{1}{2}$
3	37	34	28	$32\frac{1}{2}$	$16\frac{3}{4}$
4	38	35	$28\frac{1}{2}$	$32\frac{1}{2}$	$17\frac{1}{4}$
5	39	36	29	33	$17\frac{1}{4}$
6	40	37	$29\frac{1}{2}$	33	18
7	42	38	30	$33\frac{1}{2}$	$18\frac{1}{2}$

Norfolk Coat for Scout Masters: Made of standard olive drab cotton cloth, two pleats, back and front, with belt. Price, $3.00.

Compass: Every scout should learn how to use his watch as a compass. However, should he desire to own a compass, he will find no difficulty in securing one at any local jeweler's.

Drinking Cup: A drinking cup for individual use is recommended. The folding cup shown in the illustration is made of brass and is nickel plated. Price 10 cents.

Drum: The selection of this is left to each local troop desiring this piece of equipment. Place your order with local music dealer.

First Aid Kit: This kit for the use of the individual scout can be secured through this office or the Red Cross Society in Washington, New York and San Francisco. Price 25 cents.

Hats: Four hats are suggested as follows:

1. *Boy Scout Hat.* Olive drab felt — standard quality — detachable ties. Price $1.15.

No. 1

No. 2

Nos. 3 and 4

2. *Boy Scout Summer Hat.* Olive drab drill, inside seams reinforced with leather, eyelets in crown for ventilation, detachable ties. Price 50 cents.

3. *Boy Scout Hat.* Extra fine, fur felt, made for hard service. Price $2.00.

4. *Scout Master's Hat.* Quality same as above, but larger dimensions. Price $2.50.

Be sure to indicate size desired when ordering.

* *Haversack:* Waterproof canvas, leather straps — buckles and separate pockets — scout emblem on flap. Price 60 cents.

Hospital Corps Pouch: This pouch has been made up specially by the American Red Cross Society and contains the following:

    1 Shears
    1 Tweezers
    1 Carbolized Vaseline
    1 Pkg. Safety Pins
    2 Wire Gauze Splints
    1 2-oz. Bottle Aromatic Spirits of Ammonia
    1 A.R.C. First Aid Outfit (cardboard)
    2 1-yd. packages Sterilized Gauze.
    3 1-inch Bandages.
    3 2½-inch Bandages
    2 Triangular Bandages (cartons)
    1 U. S. A. Tourniquet

Arrange with the American Red Cross Society for purchase of these. Price $3.00.

* *Knickerbockers:* Boy Scout olive drab drill, belt guides, pockets, knee buckles, full pattern. Price 75 cents.

Age-Size	Waist
19	32
17	31
16	30
15	29
14	28
13	27
12	26½

* *Knives:* No. 1, Price $1.00.

Stag handle, brass lining, german silver bolsters and shield. Large polished cutting blade, screw driver, can-opener and leather boring tool (U. S. Pat. 6-10-02.)

No. 1

No. 2

Number 2, Price 50 cents.

Genuine ebony handle, brass lining, german silver bolsters and shield. Large cutting blade can be opened without using the fingernail. Shackle for hanging to belt.

Lanyard: This piece of equipment is so simple in construction that every scout ought to make his own lanyard. These are used for carrying the scout whistle or knife.

* *Leggings:* (Puttees). The style of leggings is the same as United States Army puttee legging. Made of best waterproof army duck. Price 55 cents.

* *Mess Kits:* Number 1. Price 75 cents.

Coffee or tea can, cup, stew or fry pan, with cover, one broiler two handles.

Number 2. Price 50 cents.

No. 1

No. 2

Coffee or tea can, cup, stew or fry pan, one handle.

Patrol Flags: The patrol flags are made from a good quality muslin or wool bunting in the colors of the local patrol. Scouts make their own patrol flags. Material may be purchased at a local dry goods store. The size of the flag is 11 in. by 27 in. Emblems can be secured from National Headquarters.

27 N.Y.

Ponchos: A good poncho is almost an absolute necessity for the scout when on a march or in camp. Ponchos suitable for scout purposes can be secured from local dealers at prices from $2.50 upward.

Shelter Tents: Scouts should make their own tents. Directions for making tents are given in the text of this book.

* *Shirts:* Boy Scout shirt, standard material — two bellows pockets — open front, coat style — standard button same as coat. Order by size. Price $1.00

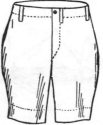

Summer Shirts: Same as above, light weight. Price 75 cents.

* *Shorts:* Standard ma-

terial — belt guides. Full running pant pattern — especially
desirable for summer use. Order according to age and waist
measurement. Price 50 cents.

* *Shoes:* Any good shoe that is made
up for the purpose of ease, and comfort
in tramping will serve the boy scout's
needs. The Boy Scout shoe is convenient,
inexpensive and especially designed for
scouting. Price $2.50.

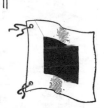

Signal Flags: These can be made from muslin or bunting
which may be secured at local stores. It is recommended that

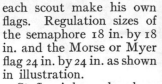

each scout make his own
flags. Regulation sizes of
the semaphore 18 in. by 18
in. and the Morse or Myer
flag 24 in. by 24 in. as shown
in illustration.

Staff: Ash or bamboo,
two metres, (6 ft. 6½ in.),
in length and about one
and one-half inches in diameter; marked off on one
side in centimetres up to
one-half metre, and the
balance in metres. On the
other side it should be
marked off in inches up to
one foot and the balance in feet. The staff
should have a blunt end. Scouts should make their own
staffs whenever it is possible for them to secure the lumber.

Hoe or rake handles make excellent staffs. These can be
procured through any local dealer at a nominal sum.

The Scout Staff and Its Uses

Many boys, upon taking up the Scout Movement, are dubious
about the value of the scout staff and many friends of the
movement ask "Why does a boy scout carry a staff?"

Experience has proven it to be one of the most helpful
articles of equipment. In order to show this we are reproducing,
through the courtesy of Lieut-Gen. Sir Robert S. S. Baden-

Powell, illustrations from printed matter used by the English boy scouts. These illustrations show a number of different ways in which the staff will prove a handy and valuable article; in fact, essential to the Scout outfit.

* *Stockings:* To match uniforms, made of heavy material and suitable for scouting. Price 30 cents in cotton, $1.25 in wool.

Sweaters: Any local clothing store will be able to secure for the scout the kind and quality of sweater needed.

* *Telegraph Instruments:* Beginners' telegraph instru-

ments, to be used in learning the Morse code, may be secured
through any electrical supply house. The instrument illustrated, five ohms, price, $1.30.

Tracking Irons: Excellent tracking
irons can be made of $\frac{7}{8}$-inch heavy band
iron, using the design presented here. Any
local blacksmith will gladly assist the boys
in making their irons.

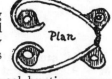

Troop Colors: Made of superior wool bunting upper

half, red; lower half,
white. Reproduction
of the official badge
super-imposed in green
and gold. Sufficient
space left for troop
number and name of
city. Size of flag, 22 in.
by 36 in. Letters to be
attached by the local troop. Price without letters $1.00.

Trousers: Full length for scout masters: Made of
Standard olive drab cotton cloth, belt loop. Price $2.00. If
breeches are preferred, they may be had at same
price. Better quality of boy
scout suits — made of U. S.
Army standard olive drab cloth.
Coat $2.50, breeches $2.00.

Watch: Every scout should
possess a good watch. No particular make of watch is recommended. The choice of this
article is left entirely with the boy
and may be bought through a
local jeweler.

Water Bottle: In some cases where the individual scout is
not furnished with a canteen, the patrol may desire to carry a
supply of water on the march. For this purpose
water bottles capable of carrying a large
quantity of water may be secured. These
should be purchased through some army
supply house.

Whistles: Scout standard whistle, for
use in signaling by whistle. Made of brass,
gun metal finish, ring at end to attach to
lanyard. Price 10 cents.

Suggestions for Measuring

Name...

Street...................City...........................

Coat Measure

L — All around at breast under coat ....

M — All around at waist under coat ....

Sleeve

C to D — From centre of collar seam to shoulder seam....
.... Then

E — To elbow...

F — To full length ....

Breeches

M — All around at waist under coat.....................

Leggings

G — Size of calf......................................

H — Size of instep....................................

COPYRIGHTED 1910

Hat

Size of hat...
Size of linen collar worn ....

Answer following questions plainly:

Age?...............Height?..........Weight?..........

BOOKS FOR REFERENCE

This list of reference books has been prepared for the use of scouts, to supplement information given in the handbook prepared for their use. It has been the aim to give as wide a selection as possible, in order that the boy scout might not fail to find in the local public library, some book on any subject in which he may have particular interest. The list includes literature directly or indirectly related to scouting, as well as some appropriate books of fiction.

For convenience the books have been listed in accordance with the subject headings of the various chapters of the Handbook. Some of the most experienced librarians of the country have submitted material which has aided in the preparation of this list. For this kindly coöperation, sincere thanks is given.

Many of the books have been carefully reviewed by someone connected with the boy scouts, and in many cases through the courtesy of the publishers copies of these books are available for reference purposes at the office of the National Headquarters. Suggestions for additions or improvements upon this list will be gladly received at any time. Communications should be addressed to the Executive Secretary, 200 Fifth Avenue, New York City.

Scoutcraft

Notes on Scouting and
  Reconnaissance......Jas. F. M. Livingston...London, Clowes
Pioneering and Map-
  making for Boy Scouts C. R. Enock..........London, Pearson
Scouting for Boys.... { Lieut.-Gen. Robert { C. Arthur Pearson, Ltd.
  { Baden-Powell ...... { Henrietta St., London.
Three Amateur Scouts..Jadberns..............Lippincott
The Boy Scouts.......Chipman..............Burt Co.
Yarns for Boy Scouts { Lieut.-Gen. Robert { C. Arthur Pearson, Ltd.
  { Baden-Powell ...... { Henrietta St., London.

Woodcraft

ANIMALS

American Natural His-
  tory................Hornaday.............
Animal Artisans.......C. J. Cornish ......Longmans, Green & Co.
Animals at Home .....Lillian Bartlett........American Book Co.

Squirrel and Other Fur
  Bearers............John Burroughs.......
Stories of Animal Life..C. F. Holder.........American Book Co.
Stories of Humble
  Friends ....Katharine Pyle........American Book Co.
Story of the Trapper...A. C. Laut ....
The Romance of Animal
  Arts and Crafts......H. Coupin and
                        John Lea Lippincott
The Romance of the
  Animal World.......Edmund Selous........Seeley & Co.
The Wolf Patrol .....John Finnemore ......
Trapper Jim ....Edwin Sandys.........
Ways of Wood Folk....W. J. Long...........
Wild Animals at Play...Seton................Doubleday Page & Co.
Wild Animals I Have
  Known ....Seton................Scribners
Wilderness Ways .....W. J. Long ....
Wild Life in the Rockies.Enos A. Mills........Houghton Mifflin Co.
Wild Life of Orchard
  and Field..........Ingersoll.............
Wolf, the Storm Leader Frank Caldwell.......Dodd, Mead & Co.
Wood Folk at School...W. J. Long ....Ginn & Co.

ASTRONOMY

A Field Book of the
  Stars..............W. F. Olcutt.........Putnam
Astronomy...........Julia McNair Wright...Penn Pub. Co.
Astronomy by Obser-
  vation.............Eliza A. Bowen ......American Book Co.
Astronomy for Every-
  body..............Simon Newcomb .....Doubleday, Page & Co.
Astronomy with an
  Opera Glass........G. P. Serviss.........
A Study of the Sky. ...H. A. Howe ....Scribners
Astronomy with the
  Naked Eye ....G. P. Serviss.........Harper Bros.
Children's Book of the
  Stars..............Milton...............Macmillan Co.
Earth and Sky Every
  Child Should Know..J. E. Rogers.........
How to Identify the
  Stars..............W. J. Milham........
How to Locate the Stars ....Hinds, Noble & Co.
Popular Astronomy....G. Flammarion........
Round the Year with
  the Stars ....G. P. Serviss..........
Starland.............Ball.................Ginn & Co.
Steele's Popular As-
  tronomy...........J. D. Steele..........American Book Co.
The Friendly Stars.....M. E. Martin........
The Romance of Mod-
  ern Astronomy ......McPherson...........Lippincott

BIRDS

Bird Guide — Part I
    Water Birds ....Chester A. Reed.......Doubleday, Page & Co.
Bird Guide — Part 2
    Land Birds..........Neltje Blanchan.......Doubleday, Page & Co.
Bird Homes...........A. E. Dugmore.......Doubleday, Page & Co.
Birds in their Relation
    to Men.............Weed & Beerborn.....Lippincott
Bird Life ....Frank Chapman......Appleton
Bird Neighbours.......Neltje Blanchan......Doubleday, Page & Co.
Bird Neighbors........John Burroughs.......Doubleday, Page & Co.
Birds of Eastern North
    America ....Chapman............Appleton
Birds that Every Child
    Should Know ....Neltje Blanchan......Doubleday, Page & Co.
Birds that Hunt and
    Are Hunted........Neltje Blanchan.......Doubleday, Page & Co.
Birds Through the Year.A. F. Gilmore.........American Book Co.
Citizen Bird ....M. O. Wright.........
Elo the Eagle and
    Other Stories........Floyd Brallian ....Pacific Pub. Co.
Everyday Birds .....Bradford Torrey.......
Field Book of Wild
    Birds and Their
    Music..............F. S. Mathews........Putnam's Sons
First Book of Birds ...H. M. Miller ....
Second Book of Birds..H. M. Miller ....
Flamingo Feather......Munroe...............
How to Attract the
    Birds..............Neltje Blanchan......Doubleday, Page & Co.
How to Attract the
    Birds..............Trafton..............
How to Know the Birds H. & E. Parkhurst.....Scribners
How to Know the Wild
    Birds of Ohio........Dietrich Lange.......
How to Study Birds...
In Birdland...........Leander S. Kyser......McClurg Co.
Land Birds East of the
    Rockies.............C. A. Reed...........
Lord of the Air.......C. G. D. Roberts.....
Nestlings of Forest and
    Marsh..............Irene G. Wheelock ....McClurg Co.
Our Birds and How to
    Know Them........J. B. Grant...........Scribners
Our Own Birds.......Wm. L. Baily........Lippincott
Tenants of the Trees ..C. Hawkes............
The Blue Goose Chase.H. K. Job ....
The Romance of Bird
    Life.................John Lea....... ....Lippincott
Short Stories of our
    Shy Neighbors......Mrs. M. A. B. Keely..American Book Co.
The Sport of Bird
    Study ....Job ....Outing Pub. Co.
Wild Birds of City
    Parks..............

Appendix

Lessons with Plants ...Bailey ....
Manual of Gardening..L. H. Bailey...........
Nature's Garden.......Neltje Blanchan ....Doubleday, Page & Co.
New England Ferns and
   Their Common Allies Helen Eastman ....
New Manual of Botany Asa Gray.............
New Manual of Botany
   of the Central Rocky
   Mountains..........John M. Coulter, re-
                      vised by Aven Nelson
Our Garden Flowers....Harriet Louise Keeler..
Plants and Their Chil-
   dren................ ......Wm. Starr Dana......American book Co.
Rocky Mountain Wild
   Flower Studies   ....Burton O. Longyear ...
Southern Wild Flowers
   and Trees...........Alice Lounsbery.......
The Fern Collector's
   Guide ....Willard Nelson Clute...
The Garden Yard......B. Hall..............
Young Folk's Nature
   Field Book..........J. Alden Loring.......Dana Estes Co.

FUNGI

Edible Fungi of New
   York ....Charles H. Peck.......N. Y. State Museum
Flowerless Plants: Ferns,
   Mushrooms, Mosses,
   Lichens and Seaweeds.E. H. Hale ....
Mushrooms ....Atkinson..............Holt & Co.
One Thousand Ameri-
   can Fungi ....McIllvain & Macadam Bobbs, Merrill & Co.
Studies of American
   Fungi ....Atkinson..............
The Mushroom.......M. E. Hard ....Ohio Library Co.
The Mushroom Book.. Nina L. Marshall.....Doubleday, Page & Co.

HANDICRAFT

Clay Modelling........Paul N. Hasluck......David McKay
Dynamos and Electric
   Motors..............   "   ....   "
Electric Bells..........   "   ....   "
Electro-Plating.........   "   ....   "
Glass Writing, Emboss-
   ing and Facia Work.   "   ....   "
How to Make Baskets. Mary White   ....Doubleday, Page & Co.
Leather Working ......Paul N. Hasluck......David McKay
Photography ....   "   ....   "
Photographic Cameras..   "   ....   "
   "   Chemistry   "   . .   "
   "   Studies...   "   ....
Upholstery ....   "   .....

INSECTS AND BUTTERFLIES

Ants, their Structure,
Development and Be-
havior ....W. M. Wheeler.......Columbia Univ. Press
Beehives and Appliances.Paul Hasluck..........David McKay
Directions for Collecting
and Preserving Insects Nathan Banks ....U. S. National Museum
Bulletin
Everyday Butterflies ...
How to Keep Bees ....Anna B. Comstock.....Doubleday, Page Co.
How to Know the
Butterflies ....J. H. and Mrs. Comstock D. Appleton & Co.
Insect Life............Comstock.............
Little Busy Bodies ....Marks Moody........Harper Bros.
Manual for the Study
of Insects...........J. H. and A. B. Comstock
Moths and Butterflies..Julia P. Ballard.......Putnam's Sons
Our Insect Friends and
Enemies ....J. B. Smith..........Lippincott
Our Insect Friends and
Foes................B. S. Cragin.........Putnam's Sons
The Butterfly Book....W. J. Holland ....Doubleday, Page & Co.
The House-Fly — Dis-
ease Carrier........L. O. Howard........Stokes Co.
The Moth Book.......W. J. Holland ....Doubleday, Page & Co.
The Romance of Insect
Life...............Edmund Selous.......Seeley & Co.
The Way of the Six-
Footed ....

ROCKS AND PEBBLES

About Pebbles ....Alpheus Hyatt ....D. C. Heath & Co.
Boy Mineral Collectors J. G. Kelley ....
Common Minerals and
Rocks ....Wm. O. Crosby.......D. C. Heath & Co.
Stories of Rocks and
Minerals ....H. W. Fairbanks. .....
The Boy Geologist at
School and in Camp..E. G. Houston ....
The Earth and Its
Story ....A. Heilprin ....
The Romance of
Modern Geology.....Grew ....Lippincott

REPTILES

Poisonous Snakes of
North America......Leonard Stejneger .....Gov. Printing Office
The Reptile Book .....Ditmar...............Doubleday, Page & Co.

SHELLS AND SHELLFISH

American Marine Shells.Bulletin No. 37 ......U. S. National Museum,
Washington

Mollusks of the Chi-
cago Area...........F. C. Baker ....Chicago Academy
The Little Water Folk. C. Hawkes............Crowell Co.
The Lymnaedæ of
North America ......F. C. Baker ....Chicago Academy of
Sciences
The Shell Book .....Julia E. Rogers........Doubleday, Page & Co.
West Coast Shells......Josiah Keep...........
Worms and Crustacea .Hyatt.................D. C. Heath & Co.

TREES AND SHRUBS

A Guide to the Trees..Alice Lounsbery.......
Familiar Trees and
Their Leaves ....Mathews..............
Field and Forest Handy
Book ....Dan C. Beard.........
First Book of Forestry.Roth..................
Forest Trees and Forest
Scenery.............Schwartz.............Grafton Pres
Handbook of Trees of
New England... .....Dame and Brooks......Ginn & Co.
Handbook of the Trees
of the Northern
United States and
Canada..............Hough................
How to Tell the Trees ....Hinds, Noble & Co.
How to Know Wild
Fruits.·.............Maude C. Peterson....
Manual of the Trees of
North America. .....Charles Sprague Sar-
gent.................
North American Trees..Britton...............
North American Forests
and Forestry........Bruncken..............Putnam
Our Native Trees .....Keeler...............Scribners
Our Northern Shrubs...Harriet L. Keeler......
Our Shrubs of the
United States. ......Apgar.................
Practical Forestry for
Beginners in Forestry J. C. Gifford..........
School of the Woods ...W. J. Long............
Studies of Trees in
Winter ....Huntington ....Sargent
Ten Common Trees ...Susan Stokes..........American Book Co.
The Forest............S. E. White...........
The Forester's Manual
or Forest Trees that
Every Scout Should
Know ....Seton.................Doubleday, Page & Co.
The Magic Forest......White ....Grosset & Dunlap
The Tree Book........Julia E. Rogers.......Doubleday, Page & Co.
The Way of the Woods.Breck.................Putnam's Sons
Trees of the Northern
United States.......Austin C. Apgar ......

The Trees of California . Jepson . . . .
The Woodsman's Hand-
    book . . . . United States Depart-
               ment of Agriculture
               Bulletin No. 36 . . . . . .
Trees That Every Child
    Should Know . . . . J. E. Rogers . . . .

MISCELLANEOUS — WOODCRAFT

Adventures in the Great
    Forests . . . . H. W. Hyrst . . . . Lippincott
Adventures of Buffalo
    Bill . . . . Cody . . . .
A d v e n t u r e s of Four-
    footed Folk . . . . Belle M. Brain . . . . . . Fleming H. Revell
A Journey to Nature . . J. P. Mowbray . . . . Grosset & Dunlap
American Boys' Handy
    Book. . . . . Beard . . . .
Amateur Taxidermist . . . Scorso . . . .
A W a t c h e r in the
    Woods . . . . D. L. Sharp . . . . Century Co.
Bent Iron Work . . . . . . Hasluck . . . . David McKay
Birch Bark Roll . . . . . . Seton . . . .
Boots and Saddles . . . . . Custer . . . .
Boy Craftsman . . . . A. W. Hall . . . .
Boy Pioneers . . . . Dan Beard . . . . Scribners
Boy's Book of Airships . . H. Delacomb . . . .
Boy's Workshop   . . . Craigin . . . .
Boy with the United
    States Foresters . . . . . Robert Wheeler . . . .
Box Furniture . . . . Louise Brigham . . . . Century Co.
Diomed . . . . Sargent . . . . Grosset & Dunlap
Chats on Photography . . Wallington . . . . Lippincott
Electricity . . . . Fowler . . . . Penn Pub. Co.
Electric Instrument
    Making for Amateurs . Bottome . . . .
Electricity for Boys . . . . Adams . . . .
Electricity for Every-
    body . . . . Atkinson . . . .
Electricity for Young
    People . . . . Jencks . . . .
Electricity Made Easy . E. J. Houston and A. E.
               Kennelly . . . .
Excursions . . . . Thoreau . . . . Houghton Mifflin Co.
Famous Indian Chiefs . Johnston . . . .
Field and Forest Handy
    Book . . . . Beard . . . . Scribners
Four Afoot . . . . Barbour . . . .
Frank, t h e Y o u n g
    Naturalist . . . . Castleman . . . . Hurst Co.
Frontiersman's Pocket-
    book . . . . Pocock . . . .
Harper's How to Under-
    stand Electricity . . . . . Onken and Baker . . . . .

The Complete Photo-
grapher..............Bailey................Doubleday, Page & Co.
The Mountains........S. E. White..........
The Open Window..........................Grosset & Dunlap
The Young Electrician.H. Hall..............Macmillan Co.
The Young Mechanic.....................Putnam's Sons
Things a Boy Should
Know about Elec-
tricity..............T. M. St. John........
Things a Boy Should
Know about Wireless.St. John..............
Trapper Jim ....Sandys ....
Two Little Savages....Seton ....
Vehicles of the Air.....Longheed ....Reilly & Britton Co.
Walden, or Life in the
Woods............Thoreau............Houghton Mifflin Co.
Ways of Nature.......Burroughs ....Houghton Mifflin Co.
Wilderness Homes......Kemp... ....Outing Pub. Co.
Wild Neighbors ....Ingersoll ....
Wireless Telegraphy ...A. F. Collins..........
Woodcraft ....Sears.................Century Co.
Woodmyth and Fable..Seton ....Century Co.
Wonders of Man and
Nature..............R. Whiting............
Woodcraft ....Nessmuk..............Forest & Stream
Woodworking for Be-
ginners ....Wheeler ....
Young Folk's Nature
Field Book..........J. A. Loring ....Dana Estes Co.

CAMPCRAFT

Around the Campfire...C. G. D. Roberts......
An Old Fashioned Sugar
Camp...............P. G. Huston ....Revell Co.
At Home in the Water.Corson ....Association Press
Billy in Camp ....Carr.................McClurg Co.
Boat Building and
Boating for Beginners.Dan Beard...........Scribners
Boat Sailing ....Kensaly ....Outing Co.
Building Model Boats..Hasluck ....David McKay
Camp and Trail.......Isabel Hornabrook....
Camp and Trail.......S. E. White..........Outing Pub. Co.
Camp and Trail
Methods...........Kephart ....
Camp Cookery........Horace Kephart. ......Outing Pub. Co.
Camp Fire and Wigwam.Ellis.................Winston Co.
Camp Fire Musings ...W. C. Gray..........Revell
Camping and Camp
Cooking ....Bates.................
Camping and Camp
Outfits.............G. O. Shields..........
Camping for Boys.....Gibson ....Association Press
Camping Out.........Stephens.............Hurst & Co.
Camp Kits and Camp
Life................Hanks................Scribners

TRACKS, TRAILING, AND SIGNALING

Northern Trails (Books 1
     and 2).............Wm. J. Long.........Ginn & Co.
Our Country's Flag....E. S. Holden.........
Phrenology............Olin.................Penn. Pub. Co.
Physiognomy.........Lomax............... "   "   "
Return to the Trails..C. G. D. Roberts ....
Sign Language.........Seton................Doubleday, Page & Co.
The Trail of the Badger.Hamp...............
The Trail to the Woods.Hawkes..............American Book Co.
Tracks and Tracking . Brunner ....Outing Pub. Co.
Trail of the Sand Hill
     Stag...............Seton................
Watchers of the Trails..C. G. D. Roberts......
Young Trailers........Altsheler.............

HEALTH AND ENDURANCE

Body and its Defences.Jewett...............
Confidential Talks with
     Young Men........Sperry..............Revell
Control of Body and
     Mind.............Jewett...............Ginn & Co.
Daily Training........Benson & Miles......
From Youth into Man-
     hood ....Hall................
Good Health.........Jewett...............Ginn & Co.
Health...............Walter C. Wood......Penn Pub. Co.
Health, Strength and
     Power............Sargent.............
Home Treatment and
     Care of the Sick....Lovering.............Otis Clapp & Son
How to Keep Well.....Wilson...............Crowell
Japanese Physical
     Training...........Hancock.............
My System.. ....Muller...............
Rural Hygiene........Brewer ....Lippincott

CHIVALRY

Adaptability..........Ellen E. Kenyon Warner.Hinds, Noble & Co.
Adventure Among Red
     Indians............Hyrst ....Lippincott
Age of Chivalry.......Bullfinch.............
An Iron Will.........Orison Swett Marden..Crowell
A Skilled Workman....W. A. Bodell ....Revell Co.
Aspiration and Achieve-
     ment...............Frederick A. Atkins ...Revell Co.
Aspirations and In-
     fluence.............H. Clay Trumbull.....Sunday School Times
Book of Famous Verse.Agnes Repplier........
Boy's King Arthur.....Lanier...............
Boy's Life of Captain
     John Smith.........Johnson ....
Careers of Danger and
     Daring   Cleveland Mofett......

Winning Their Way. . .Faris. . . . .
With Spurs of Gold. . . .F. W. Green and D. V
                          Kirk
Young Men Who Over-
    came. . . . . .Robert E. Speer. . . . . . .Revell C

FIRST AID TO THE INJURED

American Red Cross
    Abridged Text-book
    and First Aid. . . . . . .Major Chas. Lynch. . . .
Backwoods Surgery and
    Medicine. . . . . .Moody . . . .
Boys Coastwise. . . . . . . .Rideing . . . .
Emergencies. . . . . .C. V. Gulick. . . . .
Exercise in Education
    and Medicine . . . . . . .R. T. McKenzie. . .
Fighting a Fire. . . . . . . .C. T. Hill. . . . .
First Aid in Illness and
    Injury. . . . . .Pilcher . . . .
First Aid to the In-
    jured. . . . . .F. J. Warwick. . . . . .Penn Pub. Co.
Health, Strength and
    Power. . . . . .D. A. Sargent. . . . .
Heroes of the Life-boat
    and Rocket. . . . . .Ballantyne. . . . .
Heroes of the Storm. . .Douglas . . . .
Life Boat and Its Work.Lewis . . . .
Nursing. . . . . .S. Virginia Leves. . . . . .Penn Pub. Co.
Our Seacoast Heroes. . .Daunt. . . . .
Stories of the Life-boat .Mundell. . . . .
The Beach Patrol. . . . .Drysdale. . . . .
The Life-boat . . . . .Ballantyne. . . . .

GAMES

Book of Athletic and
    Out-door Sports. . . . .Bingham. . . . .
Book of College Sports.Walter Camp. . . . .
Boy's Book of Sports. .Fannie Thompson. . . . . .Century Co.
Boys' Drill Regulations
Games for Everybody. .May C. Hofman. . . . . . .Dodge Pub. Co.
Games for All Occa-
    sions . . . . .Mary E. Blain . . . . .Barse & Hopkins
Games and Songs of
    American Children. . .Newell. . . . . .Harper Bros.
Education by Play and
    Games. . . . . .G. E. Johnson. . . . . .Ginn & Co.
Money Making Enter-
    tainments. . . . . .Rook & Goodfellow. . . .Penn Pub. Co.
Play. . . . . .Emmett D. Angell. . . . .Little, Brown & Co
Practical Track and
    Field Athletics. . . . . . .Graham and Clark. . . . .Duffield Co.
Social Activities for Men
    and Boys . . . . .A. M. Chesley. . . . . .Association Press
Outdoor Games for All
    Seasons. . . . . .Beard. . . . . .Scribners

The Story of our Navy
for Young Americans.Abbott...............Dodd, Mead & Co.
The Story of our Great
Lakes ....E. Channing & M. F.
Lansing............Macmillan Co.
The Story of the
Thirteen Colonies....Guerber ;............American Book Co.
The Young Alaskans...Hough...............
The Young Citizen.....Dole ....Heath
Training for Citizenship.Smith...............Longmans, Green Co.
Uncle Sam's Business ..Marriott.............
U. S.................Townsend............Lothrop
Washington and His
Generals...........Headley ....Hurst & Co.
Washington's Farewell
Address..................................Duffield Co.
When America Became
a Nation ....Jenks................Crowell Co.
When America was New.Tudor Jenks..........Crowell Co.
When America Won
Liberty............Tudor Jenks..........Crowell Co.
Young Americans......Judson ....
Young Continentals at
Bunker Hill........McIntyre.............Penn Pub. Co.
Young Continentals at
Lexington...........McIntyre.............Penn Pub. Co.
Young People's History
of the War with Spain.Prescott Holmes.......Henry Altemus Co.

MISCELLANEOUS

A Guide to Biography.Burton E. Stevenson...Baker, Taylor Co.
American Indians......Yonge................
A Vagabond Journey
Around the World...Franck ....Century Co.
Book of Golden Deeds..Catlin................
Boy's Life of Captain
John Smith..........Eleanor Johnson.......Crowell Co.
"Boy Wanted" ....W. Waterman.........
Childhood of Jishib, the
Ojibwa ....Jenks.................
Choosing a Life Work..L. R. Fiske..........Eaton & Mains Co.
Choosing a Vocation...Parsons..............
Christopher Carson,
known as Kit Carson J. S. C. Abbott. ......
Courage ....Charles Wagner.......
David Crockett: His Life
and Adventures......J. S. C. Abbott.......
Dashing Paul Jones....Frank Sheridan.......David McKay
David Crockett, Scout..Allen. ....
Famous Indian Chiefs..O. W. Howard ....Century Co.
First Across the Con-
tinent ....N. Brooks............
Handy Parliamentary
Rules..............Craig................Hinds, Noble & Co.

STORIES FOR SCOUTS

Arizona Nights........S. E. White...........
Around the World with
the Battleships......Miller.................McClurg Co.
Backwoodsmen........D. Roberts ....
Black Rock. ....Gordon (Ralph Connor,
pseud)..............
Bob Burton..........Horatio Alger, Jr.......Winston Co.
Bar B. Boys or the
Young Cow Punchers.Edwin S. Sabin........Crowell Co.
Battling for Atlanta....Byron A. Dunn........McClurg Co.
Boys of Other Coun-
tries................Taylor................Putnam's Sons
Boy Trappers.........Harry Castleman.......Hurst & Co.
Camping on the St.
Lawrence............E. T. Tomlinson .....
Cattle Brands.........A. Adams.............
Cattle Ranch to College.Russell Doubleday.....
Chilhowee Boys.......Morrison.............Crowell Co.
Chilhowee Boys in
Harness.............Sarah E. Morrison.....Crowell Co.
Chilhowee Boys in War
Times ....Sarah E. Morrison.....Crowell Co.
Cast up by the Sea....Sir Samuel W. Baker. .Hurst & Co.
Cruise of the Canoe
Club ....W. L. Alden..........
Cruise of the Ghost....   "   ....
Dale and Fraser, Sheep-
men................S. F. Hamp   ....
Dashing Paul Jones....Sheridan.............David McKay
Dare Boys of 1776.....Stephen Angus Co......A. L. Chatterton Co.
Dorymates...........C. R. Monroe.........
Forest Runners........Altsheler.............
For Freedom's Cause...T. C. Harbauch.......David McKay
Fox Hunting.........C. A. Stephens........Hurst & Co.
Frank in the Woods...Castleman ....Hurst & Co.
Freckles ....Porter...............Grosset & Dunlap.
From Atlanta to the
Sea.................Byron A. Dunn........A. C. McClurg Co.
Frontier Boys on the
Overland Trail.......Wyn. Roosevelt.......Chatterton Co.
General Nelson's Scout.Byron A. Dunn........A. C. McClurg
Huckleberry Finn......Twain. ....
Hans Brinker of the
Silver Skates........Mary Mapes Dodge....Grosset & Dunlap
In the Clouds for Uncle
Sam................Ashton Lamar........Reilly & Britton
Ivanhoe ....Scott. ....
Jack Among the Indians.G. B. Grinnell.........
Kim..................Kipling. ....
Kidnapped............Stevenson.............
Knights Who Fought
the Dragon.........Edwin Leslie.........Sunday School Times Co.
Larry Deeter's Great
Search..............Howard R. Garis......Grosset & Dunlap
Little Metacomet......Hezekiah Butterworth..Crowell Co.

Little Smoke..........W. O. Stoddard.......
Log of a Cowboy......A. Adams.............
Luke Walton..........Horatio Alger, Jr......Winston Co.
Marching Against the
   Iroquois ....Everett T. Tomlinson..
Marion and His Men..John De Morgan .....David McKay
Master of the Strong
   Hearts..............E. S. Brooks.........
Off the Rocks.........Grenfell...............S. S. Times
On the Indian Trail....Egerton R. Young......Revell Co.
On the Old Kearsarge..Cyrus Townsend Brady.Scribners
On General Thomas's
   Staff ....Byron A. Dunn.......McClurg
Paul Revere ....John De Morgan.....David McKay
Peggy Owen ....Lucy Foster Madison..Penn Pub. Co.
Raiding with Morgan...Byron A. Dunn.......McClurg
Range and Trail or the
   Bar B's Great Drive.Edwin L. Sabin........T. Y. Crowell Co.
Rip Van Winkle.......Washington Irving.....Burse & Hopkins
Robinson Crusoe......Defoe ....Houghton Mifflin Co.
Silent Places..........S. E. White..........
Stories of the Good
   Green Wood.........C. Hawkes...........Crowell Co.
Story of Sonny Sahib ..S. J. Duncan..........
Sheridan's Troopers on
   the Borders.........De B. Randolph Keim.David McKay
Sir Raul.............James M. Ludlow.....Revell Co.
Stories from Life......Orison Swett Marden..American Book Co.
Struggling Upward.....Alger, Jr. ....Winsted Co.
Swiss Family Robinson.J. D. Wyss...........
Talking Leaves........W. O. Stoddard. .....
Tan and Freckles......C. L. Bryson ....Revell Co.
Ten Years Before the
   Mast. ....Dana, Jr. . ...Houghton Mifflin Co
The Air Ship Boys.....Sayler................Reilly & Britton
The Boy Aviators in
   Nicaragua..........Wilbur Lawton........Hurst & Co.
The Boy Aviators in
   Africa ....Wilbur Lawton ....Hurst & Co.
The Boy Aviators' Polar
   Dash..............Wilbur Lawton........Hurst & Co.
The Boy Aviators in
   Record Flight. ......Wilbur Lawton.......Hurst & Co.
The Boy Aviators in
   Secret Service.......Wilbur Lawton.......Hurst & Co.
The Boy Aviators'
   Treasure Quest......Wilbur Lawton.......Hurst & Co.
The Boy Fortune
   Hunters in Alaska...F. Akes ....Reilly & Britton
The Boy Fortune
   Hunters in Panama..F. Akes ....Reilly & Britton
The Hill..............Horace A. Vachell ....Dodd, Mead & Co.
The Pilot.............Cooper...............
The Pioneers.......... " ....
The Spy... .... " ....

INDEX

INDEX

THE COUNTRY LIFE PRESS. GARDEN CITY, N. Y.

Do You Know This Manual From Cover to Cover?

Well, here is another rule for you to memorize:

"Whenever Hungry Eat Peter's Chocolate"

Alpine climbers, hunters, campers, and woodsmen of all descriptions consider Peter's Chocolate the regulation food for camp or trail.

It is absolutely the most sustaining; has the most delicious taste that always makes you want more, and does not create thirst.

Don't you go camping this summer without a liberal supply. You can get the nut chocolate or the plain chocolate as you prefer, but be sure to ask for *Peter's*, the Original Milk Chocolate.

Peter's comes in several varieties:

Peter's Milk Chocolate
Peter's Milk Chocolate Croquettes
Peter's Almond Milk Chocolate
Peter's Milk Chocolate with Roasted Hazelnuts
Peter's Bon-Bons

A FEW PAGES FROM

OUR BOY SCOUT BOOK

FULLY DESCRIBING THE
BOY SCOUTS OF AMERICA

PUBLISHED WITH THE APPROVAL OF
THE BOY SCOUTS OF AMERICA

WRITTEN BY
JOHN L. ALEXANDER.

ILLUSTRATED BY
GORDON GRANT.

56 PAGES
ILLUSTRATED IN COLORS

SENT ANYWHERE FOR 10¢ (STAMPS OR COIN) BY
MINUTE TAPIOCA Co ORANGE, MASS.

In conjunction with the BOY SCOUTS OF AMERICA we have published a book called "Boy Scouts." The text of the book is written by Mr. J. L. Alexander and the illustrations are by Gordon Grant. It is the only illustrated book of the Boy Scouts. We have made arrangements with the National Headquarters of the Boy Scouts of America to allow a commission of two cents to any patrol on each book sold for ten cents by the members of that patrol. We will send, express collect, to the Scoutmaster any number of these books which he thinks can be disposed of within thirty days by the boys under him. At the end of that time he is to send us eight cents for each book sold and return the remaining books.

If a local organization is in need of funds to purchase pictures, furniture, uniforms or anything else needful for its rooms or activities, this affords an excellent opportunity for the boys to earn part or all of the necessary amount.

This book, "Boy Scouts," will be sent anywhere for ten cents in stamps or coin by

Minute Tapioca Co., Orange, Mass.

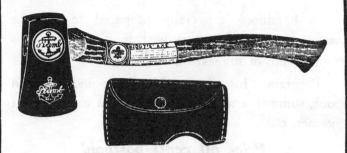

Boy Scouts and Scout Masters

The Hill & Loper Co., Danbury, Conn., are making a special hat for *you* — a hat that's *built for scouting* — one that will *hold its shape and color* and all the snap and dash that are put into it, in spite of "wind and weather." It's made to supply the increasing demand for a *better* Boy Scout Hat. It's made from Fine Fur Felt — from the same stock and by the same skilled workmen that produce the Hill & Loper Co.'s famous "HI-LO" Felt Hats which are sold to the most particular trade all over the country. It's *"Scout"* style, through and through, and built on the thorough, thoroughly honest principles that your great organization stands for. It is approved by your National Council, and *you'll* approve it as soon as you see it and try it on. You can get one of these Boy Scout or Scout Master Hats from your local dealer or from National Headquarters, Boy Scouts of America. Be sure to look for the Scout Seal, stamped on the Sweat Leather. None genuine without this seal. If there is no dealer in your locality send your size and the regular price — $2.00 for "Boy Scout" or $2.50 for "Scout Master" Hat, direct to

National Outfitter
SIGMUND EISNER

Red Bank   **New Jersey**

BOY SCOUT SHOES

OFFICIAL SEAL

BOTTOM STAMP

HERMAN'S
U.S
ARMY
SHOE

FOR BOY SCOUTS OF AMERICA

T E O'DONNELL
INSPECTOR

Price
$2.50

Joseph M. Herman & Co., of Boston, the world famous manufacturers of Herman's **U. S. Army Shoes,** the kind the soldiers, sailors, marines and militia wear, have created the **most comfortable** and **best wearing shoe for boys that ever was known.** It is made on the **sensible orthopedic last designed by army surgeons.** The regular army stamp is on these shoes and so is the official Boy Scout seal. Look for these marks when buying. The genuine

U. S. Army — Boy Scout Shoe

is made of **Shrewsbury leather** with **double sole of solid oak leather reinforced** so that it **cannot break away.** The upper has a **cool lining** and is **soft** and **pliable.** This is not only the **best shoe for wear** that a boy can put on but is **handsome and snappy** — one that **any boy will be proud to show to his friends.** Be sure to **mention your size** when ordering.

Knives Recommended by Committee on Equipment of Boy Scouts of America

Ask your hardware dealer for these knives

Price 50c

Made to cut and stay sharp

Two Blades, Ebony Handle, "Easy Opener," Brass Lined, and German Silver Bolsters

Made to cut and stay sharp

Stag Handle, Large Blade, Screwdriver, Leather Punch, Can Opener, Brass Lining, German Silver Bolsters

Price $1.00

New York Knife Co. 225 Fifth Ave., New York Works . . . Walden, N. Y.

"It's time
you owned
a Waltham"

The Watch for the Boy Scout as well as for the veteran. The boy of today doesn't want a clock watch bought in a notion store at the price of a toy. He wants an accurate watch bought from a jeweler—one he can take pride in and one that teaches him to respect time. An accurate time-piece, like scouting, cultivates habits of precision and punctuality.

WALTHAM

Watches are noted time-keepers in every grade. There are moderate priced Waltham watches that keep perfect time. Even low priced Walthams maintain wonderful records for accuracy. The pride of owning a watch of the world-wide reputation of Waltham, adds immensely to any boy's happiness.

Send for Descriptive Booklet of Waltham Movements
or Ask Your Jeweler.

WALTHAM WATCH CO.   -   -   Waltham, Mass.

MADE WITH A BROWNIE CAMERA.

The Camera for Field Service:

BROWNIE

Easy to carry on the march; simple to operate. Loads in daylight with Kodak Film Cartridges. Ideal for the equipment of every detachment of Boy Scouts. Negatives can be easily developed in the field—No dark-room required.

Write for the Book of the Brownies.

EASTMAN KODAK CO., Rochester, N. Y.

"Be Prepared"

When you get your camp supplies don't forget to buy a box of

"STEERO" Bouillon Cubes

Reg. U. S. Pat. Off.

Made by American Kitchen Products Co., New York

Add them to the list of supplies on page 152 of your Handbook. A box of 100 Steero Cubes is the right size for six boys for a week.

Steero Cubes will save a lot of cooking in camp. All you have to do is to put a Steero Cube in a cup and pour boiling water on it. You can make dandy soup for dinner, supper, or any time you're hungry. You can't help getting it just right every time, and there isn't any waste because

"A Cube Makes a Cup"

<u>Send for Free Samples</u> and try them at home, so you'll know just what they are.

If the grocer, druggist or sporting goods dealer doesn't have Steero Cubes, send 35c for a box of 12 Cubes, prepaid, enough to make 12 cups. We also put them up in boxes of 50 and 100 Cubes—they are cheaper this way.

Distributed and Guaranteed by
Schieffelin & Co., 215 William St., New York
Under Pure Food Law, Serial No. 1

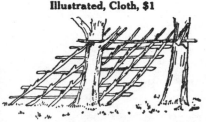

More Ponies for Boys

Two Blooded Shetlands, each with Cart and Harness made especially to fit the pony, will be given *each month* to boys who sell

The Saturday Evening Post

COUNTRY AND CITY BOYS

No matter whether your town is a large one or a small one, you have as good a chance to earn a Pony Outfit as has a boy in any other town or city. The ways of scoring equalize the opportunities of country and city boys. Thus, Harry Royster, Yazoo City, Mississippi, earned our last Pony Outfit by selling only 555 copies within two months.

Start Now To Earn Your Pony

Your pony, guaranteed to be well-broken and safe for you to drive, will yet be full of life and a good traveler. The complete outfit is worth $150.00. (You can have cash if you prefer.) If you want a pony, write at once for details and for copies of the weekly. These you can sell at five cents each. Full information will be sent you with the weekly. Write today. Gold watches and other premiums for boys who do good work.

The Curtis Publishing Company, 405 Arch St., Philadelphia, Pa.